BEHAVIORAL PRINCIPLES IN THE PRACTICE OF MANAGEMENT

WILEY SERIES IN MANAGEMENT

BEHAVIORAL PRINCIPLES IN THE PRACTICE OF MANAGEMENT

W. E. SCOTT, JR.
Indiana University

P. M. PODSAKOFF
Indiana University

John Wiley & Sons
New York   Chichester   Brisbane   Toronto   Singapore

Library of Congress Cataloging in Publication Data

Scott, W. E. (William Edgar), 1929–
  Behavioral principles in the practice of management.

  Bibliography: p.
  Includes indexes.
  1. Organizational behavior. 2. Management.
I. Podsakoff, Philip M. II. Title.
HD58.7.S36 1985   158.7   84-15181
ISBN 0-471-06248-0 (pbk.)

Printed in the United States of America

10 9 8 7 6 5 4 3 2 1

To the Memory of my father W. E. Scott, Sr., and to my mother, Inez

W. E. Scott

To my parents, Mike and Jane Podsakoff

P. M. Podsakoff

PREFACE

Our world is replete with fascinating phenomena, but the most fascinating of all is behavior, our own and that of others. It is also the principal concern of management practitioners and, no doubt, the most perplexing. Seasoned managers everywhere are eager to tell us of their need to cope more effectively with problems that are behavioral in nature. So, too, are our graduates who write to inform their professors of their regret in having slighted their behavioral courses or to complain that their educational program was deficient in its treatment of behavior.

Such expressions do not surprise us, and not merely because they are "old hat." The simple fact is that *the whole of management practice is behavior.* It is the behavior of organizational leaders as they monitor and analyze the changes occurring in the external environment, as they formulate strategy and develop technology, and especially as they direct the behavior of others. It is this latter responsibility that has given rise to pleas for a more fruitful account of behavior, but the practitioner will also find that knowledge gained from a scientific analysis can be applied to oneself as well as to others. In other words, the more we know about the behavior of others, the better we understand ourselves.

It may seem a bit presumptuous to state that we have written this book in response to demands for an account of human behavior that would enable practitioners to deal with it more effectively. As everyone knows, human behavior is complex. A few might argue that its complexity places it beyond our ken, but all the evidence is to the contrary. Although it cannot be denied that human behavior is among the most complex phenomena ever submitted to scientific scrutiny and that much remains to be learned, it is clear to us that the scientific analysis of behavior has progressed to the point that an effective behavioral technology is within the grasp of practitioners knowledgeable regarding the behavioral principles that have evolved. It will not be perfect, but it will be far more effective than the present rules of thumb, and we can expect it to become even more effective as behavioral scientists and practitioners work to develop it. Thus, though our enterprise may seem presumptuous, we began and completed it confident that the account of behavior provided herein will indeed enable the practitioner to cope with behavior more effectively.

This book is intended as a primary text for advanced undergraduate and graduate courses in organizational behavior. However, we believe it can serve equally well when used in conjunction with other texts for such courses as organizational psychology, organizational theory, organizational development, and human resource management, whether they are a part of a graduate curriculum or an executive development program.

We cannot properly recognize the many individuals whose advice, love, comfort, and intellectual stimulation were so important to us during the completion of the book. Perhaps they will forgive us if we simply state that we are deeply indebted to our wives, Jean and Vernie; to all our doctoral students, past and present; and to our colleagues around the United States and here at Indiana University.

W. E. Scott, Jr.

P. M. Podsakoff

CONTENTS

SIX
THINKING, PROBLEM SOLVING, AND DECISION MAKING

SEVEN
THE BEHAVIOR OF INDIVIDUALS IN GROUPS

EIGHT
ORGANIZATIONAL LEADERSHIP

ONE
INTRODUCTION

Of all the phenomena with which managers must cope, human behavior surely heads the list in terms of importance and complexity. It is only natural, therefore, that students of management would turn to the behavioral sciences for whatever help they might offer.

It is obvious that they have indeed sought help from the behavioral sciences. "People problems" arise almost daily in the life and times of management practitioners, and many seem difficult, if not impossible, to resolve. However, management interest in the behavioral sciences has not always been deep or abiding—and possibly for good reasons. Quite frankly, earlier scientific conceptions of human behavior, not far removed from prescientific notions, did not seem to produce much that was useful to the practitioner. But we have come to expect progress from a flourishing science, and it is clear that we have not been disappointed in this case. Important advancements in our understanding of human behavior have been achieved over the past 25 years, and especially noteworthy, we maintain, are the contributions of a group of scientists who have come to be known as behaviorists. Proceeding on the basic assumption that behavior shows some order that can be discovered through firsthand observation, they have conducted literally thousands of studies in which the relations between behavior and various classes of environmental events have been analyzed and described. The principles that have emerged from this effort make it possible to explain behavior and to predict it more accurately. Most important, these principles can serve as useful guides for purposes of modifying behavior and sustaining behavior currently in progress.

The relevance of these principles in the practice of management becomes all the more obvious when we delve into the manager's role. An examination of that role reveals, among other things, that one of the ongoing responsibilities of practitioners is the identification of those classes of human behavior that are essential to organizational effectiveness. We also find that practitioners must ensure that functional behavior, once identified, is developed and sustained at a reasonable rate. And in achieving that end, we find that practitioners inevitably turn to the environment. In other words, they have no

1

recourse but to behave so as to produce changes in the organizational environment in their attempts to develop, evoke, and sustain human behavior there. It, therefore, follows that there are practical benefits to be gained from a perusal of those principles that describe lawful relations between behavior and alterable features of the environment.

The benefits of a behavioral or reinforcement analysis are not yet widely recognized in managerial circles. That may be due, in part, to the fact that an extensive treatment of the concepts and principles has not been readily available to students of management. But other roadblocks have been noted. It has been said, for example, that because behaviorists have worked primarily with infrahuman organisms in highly controlled settings, they have nothing important to tell us about human behavior in complex settings. Moreover, the complaint has been heard that behaviorists ignore feelings and complex "cognitive" processes even when they become interested in human behavior.

Misunderstanding is also evident in the assertion that what the behaviorist has told us about behavior is either trivial or nothing more than common sense. Such impressions may have been encouraged in the field of organizational behavior by the packaging of simplistic versions of reinforcement principles in the form of "B-MOD" programs. When those programs fail, and some have, then it is to be expected that practitioners will come to dismiss a reinforcement analysis as trivial, invalid, or both.

That management practitioners should cultivate and maintain a healthy skepticism is beyond question. "Movements" have appeared before in the practice of management, and most have been found wanting. But to ignore or reject a scientific paradigm[1] before it is fully comprehended could prove to be a grave mistake. Those who have examined the reinforcement paradigm have found that behaviorists are basically interested in *human* behavior. To be sure, they began with rats and other infrahuman subjects whose genetic and conditioning histories could be controlled. However, the experimental analysis of behavior was extended to the human species more than 40 years ago. Thus, in applying reinforcement principles in human affairs, it is no longer a matter of extrapolating from the rat to the human being without test.

It is also true that early behaviorists tended to ignore feelings and the more complex behavioral processes usually described as problem solving, decision making, and thinking. Quite possibly, they did so out of the necessity of beginning with the simple before proceeding to the more complex. But whatever the reasons, it can no longer be said that such processes are neglected in an experimental analysis. Studies conducted by behaviorists have consistently shown that a reinforcing stimulus has two basic effects. When it follows after or is made contingent on a certain class of responses called operants, the probability that such behavior will occur in the future is modified. Secondly, a reinforcing stimulus will always *elicit* responses that are called re-

[1]Kuhn (1970) has characterized a scientific paradigm as a disciplinary matrix comprised of a set of basic premises, an explanatory network including both principles and theory, and observational strategies judged to be appropriate by the community of scholars responsible for the development of the paradigm.

spondents or reflexes. Respondent behavior, typically the focus of concern in most discussions of feelings and emotions, is obviously important. It presents difficult problems for the scientist, for though certain types of respondents occur at the periphery of the body, others occur beneath the skin and are not easily observed for that reason. However, behaviorists and physiologists using behaviorists' methods have learned a great deal about the properties of respondent behavior and the manner in which it is related to environmental events.

Problem solving, thinking, and other forms of self-control have likewise been taken up. In fact, a reinforcement analysis of such processes was initiated over 25 years ago. The analysis is far from complete, for we are dealing with exceedingly complex behavior that is often fleeting as well as covert. But significant advances have been made as a consequence of recognizing that thinking, problem solving, and other so-called cognitive processes are not mysterious inner causes of behavior, but rather comprise more behavior to be explained. As we learn more about the properties of this class of operant behavior and the environmental events of which it is a function, an interesting corollary arises: It should be possible, eventually if not now, to teach individuals to think, solve problems, and otherwise control their own behavior more effectively.

There remains the question of generalizing from our observations of behavior in carefully controlled environments to behavior in natural settings. If it were possible to comprehend a subject matter as complex as human behavior by studying it in situ, then its mysteries would have been cleared up long ago. However, experience has taught us that natural phenomena can only rarely come to be understood in that way. In the case of human behavior, scientists first had to analyze the relationships between behavior and environmental events when all other variables were held constant or otherwise controlled. Then, by a process of systematic replication, those relationships were examined under an ever-widening set of conditions. In this manner, the effects of combinations of variables, approaching the complexity of those found in organizations, have been analyzed.

It is true, of course, that not every conceivable arrangement of variables has been investigated. However, it is not necessary to wait on a science to complete its work before its contributions can be applied for practical purposes. In short, it can be stated with utmost confidence that a reasonable grasp of established behavioral principles can be of considerable help in coping with human behavior in organizations. And in that regard, management practitioners need all the help they can get.

AN OVERVIEW OF THIS BOOK

The primary objective in writing this book was to set forth the principles of behavior that have emerged from an experimental analysis. Toward that end, the principles of *respondent* behavior, sometimes referred to as reflexes, are discussed in Chapter 2. Respondent behavior refers to a broad class of responses that, to put it roughly, are inherited. As a consequence of our genetic history, we come into our world equipped with a set of physiological mechanisms capable of being activated by certain stimuli or properties of stimuli that comprise that world. There has been a tendency to relegate respondent behavior to a position of minor importance in human affairs. But for many reasons, detailed in Chapter 2 and elsewhere, we do not take that position.

We shall use the symbol r to designate respondent behavior, whatever its form or topography. There are many types of r's, ranging from the familiar salivation response and other autonomic responses (changes in heart rate, respiratory rate, and sweat gland activity) to "psychoneural" responses that have been found to occur in several of the neural structures comprising the central nervous system. Also included are certain rather complex skeletal responses commonly referred to as "species-typical" approach and consummatory responses on the one hand and avoidance and defensive reactions on the other.

A wide variety of stimulus events have been found to produce respondents on their first presentation to the organism. Some quickly lose their power to produce or *elicit* the typical respondent pattern after a few presentations. Others maintain this capability over a longer period of time and after many presentations though they, too, eventually show this *habituation* effect.

When a neutral stimulus that does not elicit a respondent pattern is paired with one that does (a *UCS* or unconditioned stimulus), the neutral stimulus will come to elicit all or some portion of the respondent pattern elicited by the *UCS*. The neutral stimulus becomes a conditioned stimulus (*CS*) and the respondent it elicits the conditioned respondent (*Cr*). The methods by which respondents are brought under the control of new stimuli are called the classical conditioning procedures, the details of which are discussed in Chapter 2.

Chapter 3 is devoted to an extensive discussion of the principles of *operant* behavior, designated by the symbol R. Operant behavior is defined as a class of behavior that operates on the environment to produce changes in it (Skinner, 1953, p. 65). Operant behavior is also sensitive to its stimulus consequences.

The concept of a reinforcement contingency will be encountered many times in Chapter 3. In its most general form, the concept refers to the relations between operant behavior and the environmental events of which that class of behavior is a function. A reinforcement contingency always refers to three things: (1) the stimulus setting (*Ss*) in which the operant occurs, (2) the operant itself (*R*), and (3) the reinforcing consequences (*Sc*). One example of a reinforcement contingency is described in the form of the *positive* reinforcement principle. It is stated as follows: If an operant of a given topography (*Rx*) is followed by a positive reinforcing stimulus (*Sc+*) in a given setting (*Ss*), then the probability that the operant will be emitted again in that setting is increased. The basic principle signifies that operant behavior is sensitive to its stimulus consequences and is shaped and maintained by them. What this principle does not emphasize is that some feature or combination of features, present in a setting in which an operant is reinforced, will acquire control over the operant. We should be quite clear about the matter. Stimuli that come before or set the occasion on which an operant is reinforced do, in fact, come to control that operant. The controlling stimulus is called a discriminative stimulus (or S_D). It does not automatically produce the operant in the same way that a loud noise will *elicit* the startle reflex, so we cannot say that given an S_D, the Rx is always guaranteed. However, the probability of Rx given an S_D may, depending on the prior reinforcement history, approach if not equal 1.00. We use the term *evoke* to describe the control exercised by an S_D over an operant response.

In Chapter 4, we present the various theoretical explanations of reinforcement that have been proposed. It is possible to remain strictly empirical and not worry about why a reinforcing event changes the probability of an operant on which the event is made contingent. However, if we can determine how and why reinforcing events work, we may be in a better position to identify effective reinforcers before we have tried them out. Moreover, we may be able to learn more about the conditions under which they are most effective. Of the several explanations that have been proposed, the most logical to us is the "arousal" interpretation of reinforcement. It appears that all stimulus events that have reinforcing properties have one thing in common, namely, their ability to elicit moderate activity in that portion of the central nervous system known as the reticular activating system. This explanation seems to encompass most of the known facts about reinforcing events, and, in addition, has helped us to identify stimulus events that we have not ordinarily considered as having reinforcing properties.

Because it seems to be the case that any stimulus event that is effective in sustaining or shaping operant behavior will also elicit respondent behavior of some form, we have an added reason for understanding respondent behavior. We are also required to expand our three-term contingency discussed in Chapter 3 to a *four-term* reinforcement contingency. In symbolic form, it is depicted as follows:

$$S_D : Rx \equiv Sc + \rightarrow r$$

where S_D = a discriminative stimulus that
: = sets the occasion for or evokes
R_x = an operant of a given topography that
$\equiv$ = is followed by
$Sc+$ = a positive reinforcing stimulus that
$\rightarrow$ = elicits
r = a respondent pattern of a given form

We conclude Chapter 4 with a discussion of the ramifications of a four-term reinforcement contingency. Among other things, we must consider the fact that when a reinforcing event is made contingent on an operant, it is also classifically paired with some feature or features of the setting. If we remove the :, the Rx, and the $\equiv$ from our four-term contingency, it becomes obvious that the S_D, a stimulus event, can be classically conditioned to the $Sc +$. We can see, then, that the S_D not only sets the occasion for an operant, but that it is also paired with a stimulus event serving as an unconditioned stimulus. The S_D can therefore be expected to *elicit* some components of the respondent behavior elicited by the $Sc+$ as well as to evoke the operant. We should be careful *not* to conclude, however, that the S_D first elicits respondents that, in turn, cause the operant because the respondent pattern may occur during or after the operant as well as before it appears. On the other hand, it is necessary to consider the possibility of interaction effects. That is to say, the respondent behavior may compete with or disrupt the operant, or it may facilitate it.

With the foundation of principles and theory laid down, we go on to examine verbal behavior in Chapter 5. We do so for a number of quite important reasons. First, most human beings acquire an extensive verbal repertoire, which is developed and maintained by the operation of the principles described in Chapters 2 and 3. Secondly, verbal stimuli produced by others are very important features of the environment of the human being. A wide variety of human operant responses can be controlled by verbal stimuli in the form of instructions, advice, commands and so on, particularly when we can assume, as we often can, that both speaker and listener have a similar verbal reinforcement history. Furthermore, verbal stimuli signifying acceptance, approval, criticism, or censure will frequently serve as powerful reinforcers of operant behavior as well as elicitors of emotional responses. Both the manner in which such stimuli come to have these effects as well as the circumstances under which they are likely to be most effective must be considered in an analysis of human behavior. Finally, we must consider the ramifications of self-instruction. Individuals who have become accomplished speakers as well as listeners may respond verbally—and often covertly—before they behave otherwise in novel or problematic situations. Thus, an analysis of verbal behavior is necessary for an understanding of individuals as self-determining organisms.

The organization is, of course, a natural setting in which many controlling variables may be found. Therefore, in Chapter 6 we endeavor to analyze the effects of some of the more complex arrangements of reinforcement contingencies that may prevail there. For example, an operant performance will produce multiple reinforcing consequences when practitioners alternately, though possibly inadvertently, apply both positive and negative reinforcing events. On the dark side, we should be alert to the fact that respondent and operant behavior roughly described as anxiety, frustration, conflict, and aggression can be produced by a combination of contingencies that, when analyzed, are revealed as quite normal and orderly.

Because prior exposure to settings in which the contingenies are unstable or obscure often proves aversive, human beings may "stop and think" before behaving otherwise in those and similar settings. Thus, we take up an analysis of operant problem solving in Chapter 6. A problem-solving operant is defined as any behavior that, if successful, produces discriminative stimuli evoking operant behavior that satisfies the prevailing contingencies. A simple, though quite basic, example of a problem-solving operant is the behavior of asking a "significant other" to tell us what to do. Their verbal response serves as an S_D evoking a solution operant providing their description of the contingencies (including the behavior) is accurate. Other more complex forms of problem-solving behavior, usually described as thinking and decision making, are also analyzed in Chapter 6.

In Chapter 7 we take up the behavior of individuals in groups. Organizations are typically comprised of many individuals whose presence and behavior are important features of the controlling environment of each member. That fact becomes obvious when we examine those factors responsible for the behavior and success of that entity with which practitioners are vitally concerned—the work group.

Individuals are often found behaving in close proximity though we cannot say that they are behaving as members of a common group. Nevertheless, certain behavioral processes may, on occasion, be observed among a collection of individuals that can also be found to occur in groups. Good examples are the processes of social facilitation and imitation, which are examined first.

When the reinforcement contingencies are such that each individual can produce more in the form of reinforcing consequences by behaving in concert with others or "cooperantly," a group will evolve and be sustained so long as those contingencies prevail. When it does, we are likely to observe social facilitation, imitative behavior, and a number of other important behavioral processes, including leadership.

Our analysis of leadership, begun in Chapter 7, is more fully explored in Chapter 8. In that analysis, we make explicit something that has been implied throughout the preceding chapters, namely, that the behavior of a given individual may serve as, or mediate, stimuli that elicit, set the occasion for, or reinforce the behavior of others. In our analysis, organizational leadership remains what it has always been—operant behavior that "makes a difference in the performance and satisfaction of followers" (Bowers and Seashore, 1966). It is necessary, therefore, to explore the topography of effective leadership behavior and to examine the variables of which those operants are a function. Here we find that among the variables controlling the leader's behavior is the behavior of those who are led, but there are other controlling variables that must be considered.

An underlying premise of this book is that effective management practitioners must be, among other things, effective behavioral technologists. As such, the practitioner must be able to identify and respond differentially to very specific classes of subordinate operant behavior that have been shown or are otherwise judged to be important to the success of the organization. Organizational leaders are also faced with the problem of identifying stimulus events that prove to be effective reinforcers for the individuals with whom they interact. They must further design schedules or programs for the delivery of reinforcers to ensure that behavior of a specific form is not only brought under the control of appropriate stimuli in the work setting but is also sustained at some reasonable rate. These and other practical details are taken up in Chapter 8. Our treatment of practical details should prove to be a useful beginning, but it cannot, of course, be regarded as comprehensive or as the final word.

The emphasis upon behavioral principles and theory in this book is not accidental. If our view of the management practitioner as a behavioral technologist is correct—and we are convinced that it is—then it is of fundamental importance that the practitioner *not* be divorced from the scientific discipline on which an effective technology is based. In the first place, not all the reinforcement contingencies that must surely prevail in organizations have been subjected to an experimental analysis. Therefore, the design and administration of behavioral control systems are in many ways like designing an experiment. Some extrapolation is necessary, and, like all extrapolations, some may prove to be incorrect. When that is the case, the treatments or procedures can then be selectively modified, noting all the while the behavioral consequences. In this manner, behavioral technologists may fine-tune their applications until they begin to work for the benefit of all members of the organization. It seems apparent that practitioners who are familiar with principles are more likely to be effective at every stage of this endeavor and certainly more effective than scientists familiar with principles but lacking in practical knowledge.

Secondly, it is certain that the experimental analysis of organizational behavior will, now that it has begun, proceed at an increasing pace. We can thus be assured that additional and quite useful knowledge about organizational reinforcement contingencies will be produced in the years to come. The management practitioner, like all effective technologists, will wish to keep abreast of these developments, a feat that would be next to impossible unless one has acquired a foundation of basic principles.

Thirdly, there is no reason why practitioners cannot contribute to the science on which their technology rests, and there are many excellent reasons why they should. A familiarity with basic principles makes possible this intricate and very fruitful exchange between scientist and technologist. A description of an interaction between a behavioral scientist and a practitioner (Ferster, 1967) illustrates the point nicely. After watching an especially effective therapist modify the behavior of a small autistic child, Dr. Ferster commented that although he saw applications of every behavioral principle he knew, he could not have designed her treatments. Moreover, as Dr. Ferster observed the complex interaction between the technologist and the child, a number of interesting theoretical and empirical issues arose that could fruitfully be taken back to the experimental laboratory for resolution. That the interaction was *mutually* beneficial was reflected in the subsequent behavior of the therapist. Although she was already effective, she was better able to observe and explain the numerous and quite subtle steps she took in modifying the child's behavior after Dr. Ferster had provided her with a simple and concise language (in the form of behavioral principles). She was also able to analyze more clearly those facets of her own activities that were most effective and to refine her treatment accordingly.

Finally, it has been repeatedly demonstrated that the behavioral control procedures discussed in this book are quite powerful. Teenagers, parents, teachers, and organizational leaders alike have been taught to apply them effectively. But because they are powerful, it is strongly recommended that management practitioners implement them only after a reasonable grasp of the basic principles has been achieved. We do not wish to discourage the management practitioner. Behavior of considerable complexity can be produced and sustained through the application of principles that, once understood, are not so complex. However, nothing is more hazardous—and possibly more irresponsible—than jumping into a deliberate behavioral control program without the fullest possible comprehension of the ramifications of one's efforts.

A discussion of behavioral control is likely to evoke concern, if not anxiety and other emotional responses. The student of management may, therefore, prefer one of the more traditional models in which human behavior is postulated to be a function of internal events—cognitions, expectancies, needs, and so on—that are assumed to be relatively independent of environmental events. Such models seem to be more palatable because they do not appear to raise the issue of behavior control. However, when the practices that have evolved from such models are more closely examined, they are revealed as procedures for controlling behavior. Such practices are often weak or ineffective, but not all of them can be characterized in that manner. And when they are ultimately revealed as effective controlling practices in the face of denials that behavior can be controlled, such practices are likely to be viewed as insidious forms of exploitation.

The facts of behavioral control cannot be made to disappear by a process of wishful thinking. Nor can we guard against abuses by continuing to deny that human behavior can be controlled. In rejecting traditional models, we obviously have not treated the human being as a nonthinking automaton incapable of controlling his or her own behavior. Nor is the importance of such concepts as freedom and democracy thereby denied. But we *are* led to a careful examination of controlling practices and to the possibility of reducing exploitative practices by making effective countercontrol procedures more probable.

Management practitioners *should* be concerned about behavioral control. The possibilities of misuse are very real in formal organizations, where practitioners are likely to be powerfully reinforced for conserving resources. Only by a careful examination of the controlling features of their behavior and of the short- and long-term consequences of their practices can they avoid exploitative practices.

In summary, the view emphasized here is that management practitioners are behavioral technologists. The more effective among them are leaders in the best sense of the word. They control the behavior of others and promote the development of self-control, but they do not weaken individuals by despotic practices. On the contrary, they constantly seek ways to strengthen the group, for, after all, leaders are only as effective as the groups they lead. We are confident that a perusal of the principles of reinforcement will contribute to the development of leadership in this sense.

TWO
PRINCIPLES OF RESPONDENT BEHAVIOR

As we have noted in Chapter 1, human behavior falls into two broad classes: respondent behavior and operant behavior. The first class to be discussed in this book is *respondent* or phylogenic behavior, which is designated by a small *r.*

At birth, the human organism comes with a "ready-made" physiology, which is particularly sensitive to certain classes of stimuli. When these stimuli are presented or when the organism otherwise comes into contact with them, they produce or *elicit* particular types of behavior called *respondents* in a rather exacting manner. Shortly after birth, for example, stimulation of an infant's fingers elicits a "grasping" response. Similarly, stimulation of an infant's feet will often produce an extension of the big toe and a fanning motion of the small toes (which is called the Babinski reflex). A loud noise will produce a "startle" response. Exposure to cold air or water on the skin produces "goose pimples," and tactile stimulation around a child's mouth will elicit a "sucking" response and salivation.

The effects that environmental stimuli have on respondent behavior are, of course, not completely automatic, and the intensity of the response will vary with the intensity of the stimulus. To be effective in eliciting respondent behaviors, stimuli must exceed a minimum intensity level or *threshold*. Stimulus events that are presented at intensity levels below this threshold will not elicit respondent activity or will elicit only some fractional components of a full-blown response. As the intensity level increases beyond the threshold, the magnitude and speed of the response will also generally increase. An individual's threshold is affected by several factors, including his or her sensory sensitivities, fatigue, and age. The threshold is also affected by how frequently a stimulus is presented to the individual. With repeated presentations of the same stimulus, an individual's responsiveness to that stimulus may diminish or *habituate*. In most instances, however, the eliciting properties of the stimulus will be reinstated after it has been withdrawn and is then presented again after some period of time has elapsed.

Other stimuli that have no obvious effect on the behaving organism acquire eliciting properties when they are consistently paired with those that do. The process by which one stimulus acquires the eliciting properties of another was initially called *stimulus substitution*. It is now more commonly referred to as *respondent* or *classical conditioning*. The term *stimulus substitution* is not meant to imply that a stimulus that initially possesses eliciting properties loses these properties to another stimulus in the classical conditioning process. Rather, it means that, through conditioning, other stimuli also acquire some control over respondent behaviors.

In much of the early research conducted on classical conditioning, scientists frequently chose to examine responses that could be readily measured and did not pay much attention to the total respondent pattern. More recent research, however, has indicated that respondent behavior may be divided into three components. The *autonomic* component is comprised of activity produced in the autonomic nervous system, including salivation, vasodilation, vasoconstriction, increases and decreases in heart and respiratory rates, skin resistance, and other internal bodily changes associated with our emotions. *Species-typical approach and consummatory responses* on the one hand and *avoidance, withdrawal, and defensive* reactions on the other hand comprise a second component of respondent behavior. All members of a species respond in the same general manner when confronted with primary positive and negative reinforcers—thus the classification as species typical. Examples of approach and consummatory responses are the visual tracking and sucking responses of infants. An example of a species-typical avoidance or withdrawal respondent is the "startle" pattern elicited by a loud noise. The third component of the respondent pattern is not readily observed without proper instrumentation. This component is comprised of neurophysiological activity in various structures of the central nervous system. For lack of a better term, we shall refer to this component of the respondent pattern as *psychoneural* respondents. This class of respondents figures importantly in the "feelings" we express. Respondent activity in the reticular arousal system, for example, may be described by the human adult as a feeling of alertness when a moderate level has been elicited, as boredom when occurring at a low level, and as a feeling of tension or anxiety if environmental events have elicited a high level of arousal. Respondent activity elicited in certain portions of the hypothalamus may sometimes be described as "pleasant" or as a "feeling of satisfaction" whereas activity in other portions of the hypothalamus is sometimes described as "unpleasant" or "painful." Needless to say, psychoneural respondents figure importantly in any discussion of emotions such as joy, elation, satisfaction, frustration, anger, and rage. As we shall see later in Chapter 4, they also figure prominently in the analysis of the properties of reinforcing events.

THE IMPORTANCE OF RESPONDENT
BEHAVIOR IN HUMAN AFFAIRS

The significance assigned to respondent behaviors in human affairs has been quite varied. Some scientists have tended to overlook, if not belittle, the importance of respondent behavior in human activities. Perhaps this is the result of the fact that most of the early research on classical conditioning was conducted with animals or because the "automatic" nature of elicited responses did not appear to explain complex learning and behavioral processes.

On the other hand, other social scientists, particularly those in the field or organizational behavior, have often overplayed the importance of respondent activity by giving primary causal status to affective responses such as satisfaction in their explanations of human behavior. For example, some theories of human motivation, including Herzberg's (1966, 1976) motivation-hygiene theory, make the assumption that, in order to increase employee productivity, a manager must increase employee satisfaction, thus identifying satisfaction as a primary cause of human performance.

We believe that both of these positions are too radical and that there is a need for a more balanced perspective on the significance of respondent behaviors. Such an approach would not overstate the importance of respondents by endowing them with causal status. However, a more balanced approach would acknowledge several reasons why an understanding of respondent behavior is important. First, respondent behavior is with us all the time. It is part of an individual's behavioral repertoire as long as he or she is alive. Of course, respondent activity waxes and wanes as the individual encounters different environmental events and as the result of the habituation process. Nevertheless, it is an integral part of our behavior, and any comprehensive understanding of human affairs requires its analysis.

Respondent behavior is important for reasons other than the fact that it is a part of our behavioral repertoire, however. For, as noted recently by several behavioral scientists (Gray, 1975; Henton and Iverson, 1978; Rescorla, 1977; Rescorla and Solomon, 1967; Scott and Podsakoff, 1982), contained in every operant conditioning procedure is the potential for classical conditioning to take place. By this we mean that events that are known as reinforcers also control respondent behavior. And any situation in which reinforcement occurs may elicit respondent behavior after, concomitant with, or before the operant response occurs. A substantial amount of evidence exists that indicates that these collateral respondents may in some circumstances facilitate the rate or frequency of operant behaviors whereas in other situations they may disrupt or even displace them. In addition, more obvious kinds of respondent activity called emotional or affective behavior cause some of the greatest problems for managers. As an example, respondent or emotional behavior elicited when people are not reinforced or when they are punished, may preclude the occurrence of more functional forms of operant responding resulting in positive reinforcement. And, as we shall see later, when managers are classically paired with positive or negative reinforcers, their mere presence will come to elicit respondent behavior in their subordinates that may either impair or improve their operant responding. An analysis of the factors that affect operant behavior will, therefore, require an understanding of respondent behavior and of the environmental events that affect it.

The classical conditioning of respondents is also important because it serves as the basis for establishing conditioned, secondary, or generalized reinforcers. Most of the reinforcing events administered by management practitioners in organizational settings, (e.g., pay and other forms of compensation, praise, compliments, social approval, and so on) have acquired their reinforcing properties by being paired with other reinforcing stimuli through the classical conditioning process. If managers are expected to identify, administer, and schedule reinforcing events effectively, understanding the nature of these events, the manner in which they acquire their reinforcing properties, and the conditions under which they are likely to be effective should prove invaluable.

Finally, another reason for examining respondent behavior is that it may serve as the raw material from which operant behavior develops or evolves. Understanding the origins of operant behavior has been of interest to behavioral scientists for decades. Recent evidence reviewed by Segal (1972) suggests that certain components of the respondent pattern elicited by a given environmental stimulus are susceptible to operant shaping and thus serve as progenitors of operant behavior. As additional evidence is provided regarding the role that elicited responses play in the development of operant repertoires, understanding respondent behavior and the factors that influence it increases in importance.

In this chapter, we will examine the role that classical conditioning plays in the behavior of individuals in organizations. We will begin our analysis by briefly reviewing the history of the study of respondent conditioning and by identifying the factors that affect this conditioning process. Then we examine the manner in which relatively new or novel stimuli acquire conditioned or generalized reinforcing properties through the classical conditioning process. Next we will discuss the role that respondent conditioning has in the acquisition of an individual's emotional responses and affective feelings. Although classical conditioning is not the only process by which affective responses may be acquired, it will become quite evident that the conditioning of respondent behavior has a prominent role in the way people feel about and evaluate their jobs, fellow workers, supervisors, and other stimuli in their work settings. We will then conclude the chapter with a discussion of the role that respondent behavior has in the development of an operant repertoire. This discussion will be brief because research in this area is relatively recent. The analysis of the potential facilitating or disruptive effects or both that respondent behaviors may have on operant responses will be taken up in Chapter 4.

THE STUDY OF RESPONDENT CONDITIONING

Descartes' Theory of Reflected Behavior

It is difficult to identify precisely the moment in history that the study of respondent conditioning began. René Descartes (1596–1650), a seventeenth-century French philosopher and mathematician, is often credited with being one of the first individuals to recognize the potential importance of reflexive behavior in human affairs. Descartes' observations of the mechanical figures in the gardens at the Versailles palace led him to develop an explanation of bodily movements based on mechanical rather than supernatural causes. The figures in the royal gardens operated on the principles of fluid mechanics. When tiles in the garden were stepped on or pushed down, water was pumped through hidden tubes that caused the figures to move and make sounds. Descartes thought that the human body, like these figures, might also be a kind of complex machine that possessed a fluid that was responsive to external environmental stimuli. According to Descartes, these stimuli produced excitation in receptor nerves that was transferred to the brain and then *reflected back* through the nerves to produce movements in the muscles of the body.

Whytt's Analysis of Reflex Action

Descartes' suggestion that some bodily activities could be accounted for by external environmental events was a significant step in the direction of identifying the causes of respondent behavior. But the suggestion was not immediately taken very seriously. Indeed, it was almost a century after Descartes' discussion of "reflected" actions that Robert Whytt (1714–1766), a Scottish physiologist, again focused attention on the important role of external stimuli in producing or eliciting respondent behaviors. From his numerous experiments and observations of the effects that a sharp needle, acrid solutions, and other irritants had on the contractions of the leg, stomach, and heart muscles of various animals, Whytt was able to isolate and identify the relationship between an environmental stimulus and particular bodily responses as the defining properties of reflexive (respondent) behaviors. Following Whytt's discovery, the study of reflexive behavior intensified to the point that, by the end of the nineteenth century, literally hundreds of bodily reflexes had been identified, and the lawful relationships between various properties of stimulus events (e.g., their intensity, frequency, etc.) and the latency, magnitude, and duration of associated respondents were quite well known.

The advances in our understanding of the number and types of bodily reflexes that resulted from the research of Whytt and his followers were substantial. However, the findings of this line of research left those interested in a scientific account of behavior with two disturbing facts. First, bodily reflexes accounted for only a portion of the behavior displayed by higher animals and human beings. Second, the irritants (stimuli) used in the physiology laboratory to elicit these responses were not very representative of the large number of environmental events that were observed to influence human behavior in natural settings. Before the importance of respondent behavior in human affairs could be established, it had to be demonstrated that stimulus events other than those used in the physiology laboratory could *acquire* control over these types of responses.

Pavlov's Study of Respondent Conditioning

Ivan Petrovich Pavlov (1849–1936), a Russian physiologist at the turn of the century, was among the first to study systematically the process by which relatively neutral stimulus events acquire control over respondent behaviors. While performing research on the salivary secretions of the digestive system in dogs, Pavlov became interested in the fact that his subjects would begin to salivate *prior* to the delivery of food. Not only would the dogs salivate when meat powder (the unconditioned stimulus or *UCS*) was placed into their mouths, but also when other (conditioned) stimuli that had been associated with the powder were presented. This initial finding led Pavlov to the discovery that "any visual stumulus, any desired sound, any odour, and the stimulation of any part of the skin, either by mechanical means or by application of heat or cold, have never failed in our hands to stimulate the salivary glands, although before they were all ineffective for that purpose" (Pavlov, 1928, p. 86).

CLASSICAL CONDITIONING PROCEDURES

The procedures used by Pavlov to produce respondent conditioning are illustrated in Figure 2.1. As indicated by this figure, respondent conditioning results from the association of two stimulus events. The first stimulus is called the neutral or to-be-conditioned stimulus (*NS*). Neutral stimuli are environmental events that may produce orienting reflexes on the part of an animal (e.g., the turning of the head toward the stimulus, the focusing of the eyes on the stimulus, etc.), when first introduced, but otherwise seem to have little effect on the behaving organism. In many of Pavlov's experiments, a metronome or a bell served as the neutral stimulus. The second stimulus is called an unconditioned stimulus, or *UCS*. Unconditioned stimuli are environmental events that *elicit* or automatically produce unconditioned respondents (*UCr*'s). In Pavlov's research, meat powder was frequently used as the unconditioned stimulus because it elicits a prominent salivation response. During the conditioning process, the neutral stimulus (tone of the bell) was paired temporally with the presentation of the meat powder. As a result of repeatedly sounding the bell and then presenting the meat, the bell eventually also came to elicit salivation on the part of the dog. Through the process of pairing the bell with the presentation of food, the bell became a conditioned stimulus

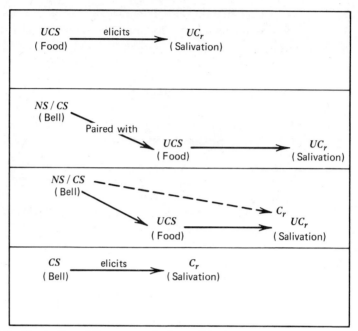

Figure 2.1   Illustration of the respondent conditioning procedure.

(CS), which then elicited a conditioned response (Cr) similar in topography to the original unconditioned response. Thus, Pavlov had demonstrated that new stimuli could acquire control over respondent behaviors when they were paired with other stimuli that already possessed some measure of control over these respondents.

In classical conditioning, when the presentation of the conditioned stimulus is followed by the unconditioned stimulus, the conditioned stimulus is said to be *reinforced*. Repeated pairings of the CS with the UCS are generally essential to the establishment of the conditioned response (Cr). If, during the acquisition of a conditioned response, the unconditioned stimulus is presented following only a proportion of the CS presentations or on an intermittent basis, the conditioned stimulus is said to be partially reinforced. Under partial reinforcement, little or no classical conditioning is likely to occur (MacKintosh, 1974). Only when the CS is followed by the UCS on a fairly continuous basis is the conditioned response generally established.

The establishment of a conditioned response to a conditioned stimulus does not, of course, mean the Cr will be elicited by the CS indefinitely. Even after the conditioned response has been established, repeated presentations of the conditioned stimulus in the absence of the unconditioned stimulus will gradually cause the Cr to diminish in intensity. The repeated presentation of the CS without the unconditioned stimulus is called *extinction*. In some instances, the effects of extinction are so complete that the conditioned stimulus will no longer elicit the conditioned response.

After a conditioned response is established to a conditioned stimulus, other stimuli that are similar to the *CS* may elicit the *Cr* even though they have never been paired with the *UCS*. The process by which stimuli other than the one that has been followed by the presentation of the unconditioned stimulus elicit the conditioned response is called *stimulus generalization* or *induction*. Pavlov, in describing results obtained from his laboratory research, provides several examples of classical stimulus generalization.

> If a tone of 1000 d.v. is established as a conditioned stimulus, many other tones spontaneously acquire similar properties, such properties diminishing proportionately to the intervals of these tones from the one of 1000 d.v. Similarly, if a tactile stimulation of a definite circumscribed area of skin is made into a conditioned stimulus, tactile stimulation of other skin areas will also elicit some conditioned reaction, the effect diminishing with increasing distance of these areas from the one for which the conditioned reflex was originally established [Pavlov, 1927, p. 113].

As Pavlov's examples suggest, the greater the similarity between the auditory stimulus and the original *CS* or the closer in proximity the tactile stimulus was to it, the more the generalization that occurred.

The counterpart of stimulus generalization is *stimulus discrimination*. Stimulus discrimination is said to occur when an individual responds to one stimulus but does not respond or responds differently to other stimuli that are similar to it. Discrimination is achieved by pairing the presentation of a *UCS* with the occurrence of one stimulus but not with the occurrence of other stimuli. Often the result of this process is that the individual comes to respond to rather subtle properties of the *CS* while not responding at all to other similar stimuli.

The reader may have noticed that discriminations are established as a result of combining reinforcement and extinction procedures. Conditioned stimuli that are reinforced (i.e., followed by the presentation of the *UCS*) come to elicit the conditioned response. To other stimuli, on the other hand, that continue to be presented in the absence of the *UCS,* the conditioned response subsides and eventually may not be elicited at all.

Factors That Affect the Strength of Respondent Conditioning

The dotted line in Figure 2.1 represents the fact that a number of pairings between a neutral and unconditioned stimulus must generally occur before the conditioned stimulus will elicit a *Cr*. Though some evidence suggests that rather complete conditioning may take place in as few as one pairing between the neutral and unconditioned stimulus, this is probably the exception rather than the rule. Research subsequently undertaken since Pavlov's original findings has established that the actual number of pairings necessary to

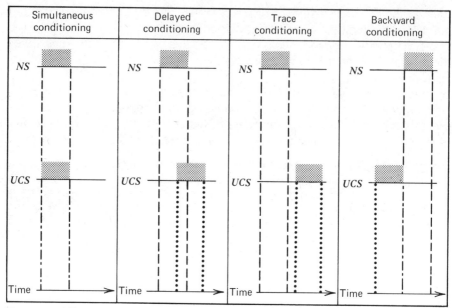

Figure 2.2 Types of *CS–UCS* temporal relationships.

transfer the eliciting properties from one stimulus to another depends on several variables (MacKintosh, 1974).

One of these is the magnitude of the unconditioned stimulus. Most research suggests that, up to a point, the greater the intensity, size, and magnitude of the *UCS*, the greater the speed and strength of conditioning that results. Thus, we would expect stronger conditioning to result from a situation in which a subject received greater amounts of food (or higher levels of shock in the case of the aversive conditioning) than we would with lesser amounts of food (or shock).

The interval of time between the occurrence of the neutral stimulus and the occurrence of the unconditioned stimulus has also been shown to be an important variable in determining the resultant strength of respondent conditioning. There are four temporal relationships that may result from the pairing of a neutral and unconditioned stimulus. These are illustrated in Figure 2.2. The vertical rises and drops in the neutral and unconditioned stimulus lines in this figure represent the presentation (onset) and withdrawal (termination) of the *NS* and *UCS*, respectively. Thus, the vertical rise in the *NS* line indicates when the neutral stimulus was presented to the subject or turned on whereas the vertical drop indicates when it was withdrawn or turned off. The same pattern holds for the unconditioned stimulus (*UCS*).

In a *simultaneous* conditioning procedure, the presentation and withdrawal of the neutral and unconditioned stimuli occur simultaneously; that is, the onset and termination of both the *NS* and *UCS* occur at the same time. In the *delayed* conditioning procedure, the presentation of the unconditioned stimulus occurs after the presentation of the neutral stimulus, but before the neutral stimulus is withdrawn. In a *trace* conditioning procedure, the presentation of the unconditioned stimulus occurs after the neutral stimulus has already been removed. Finally, in a *backward* conditioning procedure, the unconditioned stimulus precedes the presentation of the neutral stimulus. In this case, the onset of the neutral stimulus may occur either during the period that the unconditioned stimulus is still present or on its termination.

The significance of the temporal relationships between the neutral and unconditioned stimulus in respondent conditioning is found in the ability of the neutral stimulus to acquire the eliciting properties of the unconditioned stimulus. Of the four procedures, delay conditioning has generally been shown to be the most effective way of conditioning respondent behavior. Although the research conducted thus far does not provide unequivocal results, it generally does suggest that, up to a point, the shorter the delay between the neutral and unconditioned stimulus, the faster and stronger the conditioning that results. Following the delay conditioning procedure, in order of the effects they have on the strength of conditioning are the trace, simultaneous, and backward conditioning procedures. Few studies have actually been conducted that show the simultaneous presentation of the neutral and unconditioned stimulus to be an effective conditioning procedure. Even less research has demonstrated that the backward conditioning procedure is effective in producing respondent conditioning. It would, therefore, appear that for optimal results to occur, the neutral stimulus must precede the unconditioned stimulus in order to acquire its eliciting properties. Of course, the longer the interval between the *NS* and *UCS,* the less likely the neutral stimulus is to acquire the eliciting properties of the *UCS.*

The Range of Respondent Conditioning

The effects of respondent conditioning go well beyond Pavlov's conditioning of salivation in dogs. Contemporary research has demonstrated that a wide variety of subjects, unconditioned stimuli, and respondent behavior categories are susceptible to this conditioning procedure. Subjects employed in this research include animals such as cats, dogs, rats, rabbits, monkeys, and several different species of fish and birds. In addition, the behavior of human neonates, infants, and adults has also been shown to be successfully conditioned by using respondent conditioning procedures. Unconditioned stimuli used in this line of research have included appetitive stimuli, such as food, water, and sweet liquids, and aversive stimuli, such as electric shock, acidic solutions, drugs, and loud noises. The range of respondents affected by this type of conditioning has also been shown to be quite extensive. As noted earlier, autonomic, species-typical and psychoneural responses have all been shown to be influenced by the classical conditioning procedure. The wide variety and range of organisms and stimuli employed in the research conducted to date thus indicate that classical conditioning is not as limited a phenomenon as some scientists have suggested in the past.

CLASSICAL CONDITIONING AND CONDITIONED REINFORCEMENT

Within the framework of the basic principles we have elaborated on so far, we now turn our attention to the important role of classical conditioning in human affairs. First, we will focus on the function of classical conditioning in the establishment of conditioned reinforcers. Next we will examine the manner in which affective and emotional responses are acquired or, more properly, brought under the control of new stimuli through the respondent conditioning process. Then we will discuss the role of respondent behaviors in the development of operant responses.

Many of the events that influence adult human behavior do not initially affect the behavior of infants. The behavior of adult humans in organizations, for example, is influenced by both monetary and social stimuli, which may initially not prove reinforcing to a young child.[1] On the positive side, these events may include social reinforcers such as praise, commendations, attention, acknowledgment of good work, and gestures that indicate approval, as well as more traditional organizational rewards such as pay raises, promotions, and a better position in the company. On the negative side, they may include reprimands, ridicule, demotions, being assigned to low-level jobs, or being terminated. The former are called *conditioned positive reinforcers,* and the latter are called *conditioned negative reinforcers.* In view of the fact that the behavior of individuals in organizations is influenced by these events, or reinforcers, it is imperative that managers understand how they acquire their reinforcing properties and how they may be effectively administered.

Among the first to discuss the basic principles underlying the development of conditioned reinforcers was Pavlov (1927) when he described the results of an experiment conducted by his colleague, G. P. Frolov. Like Pavlov, Frolov was interested in examining how the salivatory responses in dogs were conditioned. Following the procedures of many of Pavlov's early experiments, Frolov first classically conditioned a dog to salivate to the sound of a metronome by pairing it with the presentation of food powder. Once a dog reliably salivated to the sound of the metronome, Frolov placed a black box in the dog's line of vision. The first time this occurred, the dog did not salivate. Following this test, the black box was "held in front of the dog for ten seconds, and after an interval of 15 seconds the metronome [was] sounded for 30 seconds" (Pavlov, 1927, p. 34). Even though no food was presented following these trials, by the tenth pairing of the box with the metronome, the black box also elicited salivation when it was presented by itself. The results of this

---

[1]It is, for example, frequently observed that children must "learn the value of money" or "the meaning of success" or "rejection."

study indicated that, in addition to acquiring the eliciting properties of food by being paired with its presentation, the metronome had also acquired the ability to sustain responses of other stimuli paired with it. Frolov's findings thus suggested that an initially neutral stimulus (in this case, a metronome) could, by being paired with an already reinforcing event, acquire conditioned or secondary reinforcing properties.

Additional evidence that conditioned reinforcers may be established by pairing a neutral stimulus with an already reinforcing event has also been provided in a series of early experiments conducted by John Wolfe (1936) and John Cowles (1937) at the Yale Laboratory of Primate Biology. Both Wolfe and Cowles were interested in examining how tokens acquire their reinforcing properties for chimpanzees. In his experiments, Wolfe (1936) utilized small disks that were similar to poker chips as tokens for his subjects. Initially, the chimpanzees displayed indifference to these tokens. The preliminary training phase of the experiment began by orienting the chimpanzees to their new environment and by having the experimenter insert the tokens into a mechanical vending machine, which then delivered a grape to the subjects. Once this initial step was completed, the chimps were then trained to pick the tokens up by themselves and deposit them into the vendor to receive grapes. Thus, during the initial phases of the experiment, poker chips (neutral stimuli) were paired with grapes (which, as anyone who has been to the zoo knows, are potent reinforcers for most chimpanzees).

Following these preliminary stages, the chimpanzees were then trained to perform simple tasks to obtain tokens. The majority of these tasks required the chimps to lift various weights, for which they received tokens that could later be exchanged for food. The results of Wolfe's (1936) experiments were quite revealing. He reported that, after the preliminary pairing of tokens with grapes, chimpanzees would readily learn to utilize the tokens to obtain food from the vendor, discriminate between tokens that had food value and those that didn't and also perform the weight-lifting task in order to obtain tokens. In addition, Wolfe found that when pairs of chimpanzees were placed in the same cage and given the opportunity to obtain and exchange tokens for food, "begging" and "stealing" behaviors occurred among some of the pairs. This latter finding is particularly interesting because it suggests that, like human beings, chimpanzees will often "beg, borrow, or steal" in order to obtain tokens (or, in the human case, money), which can be exchanged for other reinforcing events. In addition, the findings of this study indicate that, like primary reinforcers, conditioned reinforcers may sustain a wide variety of behaviors.

Similar results have been reported from a series of closely related experiments conducted by Cowles (1937). He found that, after preliminary training, his subjects could be taught to perform rather complex behavioral activities, as well as both size and color discriminations, in order to obtain tokens that had previously been paired with food.

More recent research by Kelleher (1958) utilizing chimpanzees as subjects provides additional evidence of the potent reinforcing effect that can be achieved by tokens that have been associated with food. Kelleher found that chimps would often continue to perform tasks in order to obtain tokens, even when 50 tokens had to be accumulated before they could be exchanged for food rewards.

The findings of the research conducted by Wolfe (1936), Cowles (1937), and Kelleher (1958) provide evidence that, for chimpanzees, conditioned reinforcers often acquire their properties by being paired with other reinforcing events. Subsequent research on conditioned reinforcement (cf. Gollub, 1977; Hendry, 1969; Kelleher, 1966; Kelleher and Gollub, 1962; Myers, 1958) has demonstrated the important role played by these events in the behavior of a wide variety of other animals as well. In the case of human behavior, there also appears to be a substantial amount of evidence that conditioned reinforcers acquire their properties by being paired with other reinforcing events (cf., Ayllon and Azrin, 1968; Statts, 1975). For example, good grades at school become conditioned reinforcers for many children because they are associated with the praise, attention, or social approval of teachers and parents alike. Similarly, evidence of "good performance" on a job, if it is followed by supervisory praise or approval, a raise in pay, a promotion to a better job, or respect from one's peers, may become a conditioned positive reinforcer. Particular individuals, situations, or places may also acquire reinforcing properties when they are paired with other reinforcing events. For instance, a particular teacher may become a conditioned reinforcer because he or she is instrumental to receiving a good grade or passing on to a higher class. And a particular restaurant may become a conditioned reinforcer because we frequently have a good meal or find good companionship there.

In the same manner, events, situations, verbal expressions, and particular people or places may also become conditioned aversive stimuli by being paired with other aversive events. A particular teacher, for example, may become a conditioned aversive stimulus to a student because the teacher gives boring lectures, administers poor grades to the student, or fails her. Likewise, a supervisor who continually reprimands a subordinate or gives him a poor performance evaluation may become an aversive stimulus that the subordinate avoids. Tasks on which we fail may also become aversive stimuli if such failure is accompanied by being "put down" or ridiculed by others. And running, jogging, playing baseball, or participating in other strenuous physical activities may become aversive and be avoided by people as they become older if these activities cannot be performed without experiencing pain or discomfort.

Of course, not all conditioned reinforcers maintain their reinforcing properties. Conditioned reinforcers, like all CS's, will lose their eliciting properties and, therefore, their reinforcing properties if they are not at least occasionally paired with other reinforcers. Some aspects of the Cowles (1937) and Wolfe (1936) studies cited earlier demonstrate this. Both of these researchers found that conditioned reinforcers (tokens) that were not at least occasionally paired with other reinforcers would eventually lose their ability to sustain the chimpanzee's behavior.

In an analogous manner, the restaurant we once enjoyed for its good food may lose its reinforcing properties because of the fact that it has hired a new chef and he does not cook as well as the previous one. And tasks that initially are aversive to us may lose their aversive properties because we become more skilled and experienced in performing them. However, some stimulus events are particulary potent reinforcers because they are paired with a large number of other reinforcing events. Such reinforcers are called *generalized reinforcers*. Because of their association with other reinforcing events, generalized reinforcers are likely to serve as effective rewards for many individuals in almost any situation. Money, social approval, attention, affection, and praise are good examples of generalized positive reinforcers for most individuals. Money, for example, is an effective reinforcer for most individuals because it can be exchanged for a variety of other reinforcing events including food, shelter, clothing, travel to exotic or interesting places, and expensive cars, and it is thus classically paired with those events. Disapproval, reprimands, and criticism are examples of stimuli that frequently serve as generalized negative reinforcers because they are often accompanied by other negative consequences for the individual such as rejection or the withdrawal of social support.

Perhaps it is because of the prominent role generalized reinforcers play in human affairs or because of the fact that they function effectively as rewards under most conditions or that they often influence human behavior even when the primary reinforcers on which they are based are only paired with them infrequently, that some people have suggested that these events reflect basic innate human needs. Such a proposition is plausible, but unlikely. For, as noted by Skinner, it neglects the complexity of the phylogenetic conditioning necessary to produce such an effect.

It is easy to forget the origins of the generalized reinforcers and to regard them as reinforcing in their own right. We speak of the "need for attention, approval, or affection," "the need to dominate," and "the love of money" as if they were primary conditions of deprivation. But a capacity to be reinforced in this way could scarcely have evolved in the short time during which the required conditions have prevailed. Attention, affection, approval, and submission have presumably existed in human society for only a very brief period, as the process of evolution goes. Moreover, they do not represent fixed forms of stimulation, since they depend upon the idiosyncrasies of particular groups. Insofar as affection is mainly sexual, it may be related to a condition of primary deprivation which is to some extent independent of the personal history of the individual, but the "signs of affection" which become reinforcing because of their association with sexual contact or with other reinforcers can scarcely be reinforcing for genetic reasons. Tokens are of even more recent advent, and it is not often seriously suggested that the need for them is inherited. We can usually watch the process through which a child comes to be reinforced by money. Yet the "love of money" often seems to be autonomous as the "need for approval," and if we confined ourselves to the observed effectiveness of these generalized reinforcers, we should have as much reason for assuming an inherited need for money as for attention, approval, affection, or domination [Skinner, 1953, pp. 80–81].

In addition, such a proposition ignores the fact that even though money, praise, approval, disapproval, and criticism may function as reinforcing events for many people in many different situations, such events do not function as reinforcers for *all* people in *all* situations.

Of course, the fact that generalized reinforcers do not reflect innate needs does not make them any less interesting or important. Such reinforcers have potent effects on human behavior, and managers who are able to identify and administer these stimuli properly are more likely to be effective than those managers who do not. Thus, understanding the process by which these events acquire their effects is important, and our analysis of this process should prove valuable to managers who wish to use these events effectively.

Our analysis of conditioned and generalized reinforcers is, however, far from complete. We have not, for example, clearly specified the nature of the respondents that are classically conditioned as a stimulus acquires its conditioned reinforcing properties. Recent evidence has provided a potential resolution to this problem. This evidence suggests that the property common to all reinforcing events may be that they produce psychoneural respondent activity in certain structures that comprise the central nervous system (cf. Berlyne, 1967; Glickman and Schiff, 1967; Scott, 1966; Scott and Erskine, 1980). Because of the important function reinforcing events have in human affairs, we will return to a discussion of these respondents in Chapter 4.

THE CLASSICAL CONDITIONING OF AFFECTIVE RESPONSES

Early Research on the Acquisition of Emotional Responses

John B. Watson was among the first to suggest that an individual's emotions and feelings are, in part, reflexive behaviors that are affected by respondent conditioning processes (Watson and Morgan, 1917). In a classic experiment, Watson and his assistant Rosalie Rayner (Watson and Rayner, 1920) set out to demonstrate how neutral stimuli could come to acquire control over "emotional" respondents. They chose for the subject of their study an eleven-month-old boy named Albert B. Albert was apparently a well-adjusted, happy child who was known for his lack of fear. Only one condition was found to produce an emotional "startle" or "fright" response consistently on the part of Albert. This was a loud noise produced by the striking of a piece of metal with a hammer. To other aspects of his environment, Albert was what may be called inquisitive. When presented with various objects (e.g., building blocks) or animals such as a rabbit, dog, white rat, or monkey, for example, Albert would generally approach, touch, and play with them.

For their experiment, Watson and Rayner used a white rat, to which Albert had previously demonstrated no fear, as the to-be-conditioned stimulus. Striking a bar of metal with a hammer was used to produce the unconditioned aversive stimulus of a loud sound. In the first experimental session, when Albert was initially presented with the white rat, he reached for it. As soon as he touched it, however, Watson or his colleague would strike the piece of metal with the hammer.[2] The loud noise which resulted caused Albert to "startle," bury his face, and eventually to cry. After two pairings of the loud noise with the presentation of the rat the first session was discontinued.

Seven days later, Albert was again presented the white rat. Although he did not immediately cry or startle, Albert generally avoided any contact with the rat. Later in this session, presentation of the rat was paired on five consecutive trails with the loud noise. These pairings had a rather dramatic effect on Albert's behavior. For, as observed by Watson and his colleague

> The instant the rat was shown the baby began to cry. Almost instantly he turned sharply to the left, fell over on left side, raised himself on all fours and began to crawl away so rapidly that he was caught with difficulty before reaching the edge of the table[3] [Watson and Rayner, 1920, p. 5].

When presented to Albert five days later, the white rat produced immediate crying and avoidance responses on Albert's part. Moreover, similar emotional and avoidance responses were found to generalize to other animated objects that were furry, such as a rabbit or a dog, as well as several inanimate furry objects, which included a sealskin coat and cotton wool. Truly, "furry" stimuli had acquired emotional properties for Albert by being paired with an unconditioned aversive stimulus (*UCS*). Thus, Watson and Rayner had demonstrated that emotional responses such as fear could be classically conditioned to stimuli that originally did not elicit them and that these emotional responses would generalize to other similar stimuli.

Contemporary Research on the Classical Conditioning of Attitudes

The results of Watson and Rayner's (1920) study were quite provocative. They suggested that human emotional responding was, in part, influenced by the respondent conditioning process. Moreover, the findings of this research suggested the possibility that human attitudes and evaluative responses, both of

---

[2]Though it has not always been recognized, the procedures utilized by Watson and Rayner not only contained elements of classical conditioning, but also of operant conditioning as well. Because the presentation of the loud noise was made only after Albert first reached for the white rat, a punishment procedure (see p. 41 of Chapter 3) was also being administered. Thus, in this study, like most situations in natural settings, classical and operant conditioning were intertwined.

[3]It is instructive to point out that all three classes of respondent behavior were observed or can be inferred from Watson and Rayner's description of Albert's responses to the rat. His immediate response of turning, raising up on all fours, and crawling away, for example, is indicative of species-typical "startle" and escape behaviors. Albert's crying and general discomfort further indicate emotional behavior that accompanies psychoneural activity described as "fear." And, no doubt, the above responses were accompanied by several changes in Albert's autonomic nervous system, including a quickening of his heartbeat and breathing patterns and an increase in adrenal activity and activity in his sweat glands.

which are believed to include an "emotional" component, may also be acquired by this conditioning process. One might expect that such an intriguing possibility would have generated a considerable amount of interest and additional research. However, this was not the case. It was several decades following Watson and Rayner's findings before systematic research into the role played by respondent conditioning in the acquisition of attitudes was undertaken.

It is probably not too difficult to identify the reason for the delay between Waston and Rayner's (1920) study and research on attitude acquisition. There are obvious problems in using human beings, infants or otherwise, to study the conditioning of emotional behavior. The intentional conditioning of a fear response in an eleven-month-old child is undoubtedly difficult for most of us to justify, even in the name of science. This ethical issue did not go unrecognized by Watson and his colleague, who noted that:

> At first there was considerable hesitation upon our part in making the attempt to set up fear responses experimentally. A certain responsibility attaches to such a procedure. We decided finally to make the attempt, comforting ourselves by the reflection that such attachments would arise anyway as soon as the child left the sheltered environment of the nursery for the rough and tumble of the home [Watson and Rayner, 1920, p. 3].

Nevertheless, it was perhaps in part because of Watson's choice of subjects and the emotional response conditioned (fear) that it wasn't until the early 1960s that research into the conditionability of attitudes was again studied. As one might expect, this contemporary line of research was much more systematic than that conducted by Watson and Rayner. Even so, it supports their findings and indicates that respondent conditioning is responsible for our affective feelings toward the tasks we perform, toward those people present when we are reinforced, and toward those who administer reinforcing events to us.

The Conditioning of Attitudes Toward Tasks and Work Activities. Several studies have demonstrated that the satisfaction or attraction an individual expresses toward features of his or her task setting, including components of the task itself, are affected by the respondent conditioning process. In this research, tasks that originally elicited neutral attitudinal responses were subsequently described as more attractive or satisfying as a result of the subjects' success on the task or because the individual received verbal reinforcement (praise) for their performance. On the other hand, initially neutral tasks on which a subject failed or received verbal punishment or reprimands were subsequently evaluated as less attractive or satisfying (Cartwright, 1942; Gebhard, 1948, 1949; Gewirtz, 1959; Leventhal, 1964; Leventhal and Brehm, 1962; Locke, 1965, 1966, 1967; Nowlis, 1941). The most comprehensive of these studies was a series of nine experiments conducted by Locke (1965, 1966, 1967). In his research, Locke employed a variety of tasks, including a word-unscrambling task, a task involving the listing of objects, a task involving the use of objects, and a pursuit rotor (tracking) task. The results of all nine of Locke's experiments showed that subjects' liking, attraction or satisfaction or a combination of these for the tasks they performed was a function of the degree of success achieved on the task or of the number of rewards received for performing it.

More recently, several studies have indicated that monetary rewards associated with the performance of a task also affect the satisfaction or attraction subjects express toward that task. Cherrington, Reitz, and Scott (1971), for example, found that subjects who received a bonus for their performance reported their tasks as significantly more attractive than subjects who did not receive a bonus. Similar results were obtained in a related study conducted by Scott and Erskine (1980). These researchers found that subjects who received monetary rewards for performing on a task evaluated the task as more attractive than subjects who did not receive rewards. Finally, Wimperis and Farr (1979) reported that subjects who received pay for their performance were more satisfied with their tasks than subjects who did not receive pay. The results of the preceding studies indicate that an individual's evaluation of the task or job he or she performs is affected by the reinforcing events associated with that task or job.

The Conditioning of Attitudes Toward People Associated with Rewards. Individuals in organizational settings rarely receive reinforcing or punitive events in isolation. More typically, other people are present when individuals are praised, commended, reprimanded, told what a good (or poor) job they are doing, or receive other forms of evaluation reinforcement. As in the case of our attitudes toward tasks that are associated with reinforcing events, we would expect that attitudes toward people present when an individual receives rewards should also be affected by the respondent conditioning process. Three lines of evidence provide support for this expectation. One of these lines of research indicates that our attraction to individuals we have never previously interacted with (or have seen, for that matter) is affected by the reinforcing events associated with them. Griffitt (1968), for example, manipulated the number of bonus points received for participating in an experiment in which subjects were asked to rate (evaluate) an anonymous, same-sex stranger. Some subjects received five bonus points for their participation whereas others received only one. Griffitt found that subjects expressed significantly greater interpersonal attraction toward the stranger associated with five bonus points than the stranger associated with only one bonus point, even though subjects never were permitted actually to observe the stranger under any condition. A follow-up study conducted by Griffitt and Guay (1969) produced similar results.

The second line of evidence indicates that an individual's attraction toward others who are simply *present* when he or she receives rewards is affected by the respondent conditioning process. In this line of research, subjects who receive positive or negative reinforcement in the presence of others who are not responsible for the reinforcement are shown to evaluate the others in a positive or negative affective fashion, respectively. Lott and Lott (1960), for example, had school children play in a three-person "rocket-ship" game. Successful players received toys as rewards whereas unsuccessful subjects received nothing. Lott and Lott found that rewarded subjects liked and were more attracted to members of their play groups than unrewarded subjects. These results were replicated in a series of related studies reported by James and Lott (1964), Lott and Lott (1968), and by Stotland (1959). In addition to these findings, a study by Lott, Lott, and Matthews (1969) has shown that even children who provide help or assistance to successful others, but receive no direct rewards themselves, respond as if they themselves had been rewarded. Lott, Lott, and Matthews (1969) manipulated the rewards children received for playing a game of Bingo. Twenty 6-subject groups were exposed to one of several different types of reward conditions. Each subject who played the game had a "helper" (assistant) who watched but wasn't allowed to win any rewards. "Helpers" of winners were found to respond as winners did and developed more liking toward other members in their group than either losers or their "helpers" did.

The third related line of evidence indicates that an individual's attitude toward groups in which he or she experiences success, shares rewards, or receives rewards from fellow group members is affected by the respondent conditioning process. Berkowitz and Levy (1956) reported that members of favorably evaluated (reinforced) groups expressed significantly more attraction to the other members of their group than individuals in groups that were not reinforced. Similar results have been reported by Frye (1966) and Blanchard, Adelman, and Cook (1975).

In an interesting test of the effects of luck on the interpersonal attraction of group members, Rabbie and Horowitz (1969) determined which groups in their experiment would receive rewards (radios for each group member) by the flip of a coin. These researchers found that subjects in groups who won a radio were significantly more attracted to their groups than control group subjects who did not receive the radios, even though winning was determined solely on the basis of chance. More recently, the effects of receiving rewards from one's fellow group members has been reported by Jacobs, Jacobs, Feldman, and Cavior (1973). These researchers had groups of subjects participate in a series of tasks. Following the tasks, each group member was provided with positive or negative feedback regarding his or her behavior by each of the other group members. Jacobs et al. (1973) found that individuals in groups that were allowed to receive only positive feedback (reinforcement) from their fellow members reported more interpersonal attraction than members of those groups only allowed to receive negative feedback.

The Conditioning of Attitudes Toward Individuals Who Administer Reinforcers. The results of the Jacobs et al. (1973) study indicate that an individual's attraction toward a group is affected by the reinforcing events he or she receives from the group's members. But groups of people are not the only ones who mediate or administer reinforcing events to us. In many instances, specific individuals (e.g., our parents, teachers, friends, or supervisors) mediate the reinforcers for our behavior. It should not be too surprising, therefore, that an individual's attraction toward another individual is affected by the reinforcers administered by the second individual.

Numerous laboratory studies have demonstrated that our attitudes toward specific individuals are influenced by the reinforcing events administered to us by those individuals. These studies show that the attraction expressed by subjects toward an individual who administers reinforcement to them (cf. Byrne and Ervin, 1969; Byrne and Rhamey, 1965; Garza and Lipton, 1978; Griffitt and Guay, 1969; Kaplan and Olczak, 1970; Keisler, 1961; Landy and Aronson, 1968; McDonald, 1962) or is responsible for reducing the threat of a potentially humiliating experience (Kleiner, 1960) is greater than the attraction expressed by subjects to individuals who don't administer rewards or reduce a threat.

Several field studies have also been reported on the relationship between individuals' liking or satisfaction for another person who administers rewards or punishments to them. A large number of these studies have focused on the relationship between leader reward-and-punishment behaviors and subordinate satisfaction. Reitz (1971), for example, found that leader behaviors such as praise, recommendations for pay increases, or special recognition were positively related to subordinates' satisfaction with their supervisor whereas leader behaviors such as reprimands and blaming subordinates for their poor performance were not related to satisfaction. Similar results have also been reported by Sims and Szilagyi (1975), Greene (1976), Hunt and Schuler (1976), Keller and Szilagyi (1976); Podsakoff, Todor, and Skov (1982); and Podsakoff, Todor, Grover, and Huber (1984). In addition, all these studies indicate a positive relationship between leader contingent reward behaviors and satisfaction with work or satisfaction with co-workers but no relationship or a negative relationship between leaders' punitive behaviors and these facets of subordinate satisfaction.

The majority of the field studies reported above have been cross-sectional, correlational studies, in which self-report measures of both leader behavior and satisfaction were obtained from subordinates. Studies of this type lack the precision and control that is afforded by laboratory research and are susceptible to problems because of the nature of self-report data. An interesting variation on the field studies conducted to date, which attempted to minimize the problems associated with self-reports, has been reported recently by Furman and Masters (1980). These researchers observed over 18,000 interactions between children in two social settings and classified their behavior as reinforcing, punishing, or neutral. They also observed and classified the children's affective reactions to these behaviors as positive, negative, or neutral. Their analysis indicated that positive affective reactions tended to follow reinforcing behaviors and negative affective reactions followed punishing behaviors. The observational nature of this study makes it less susceptible to the criticisms of the self-report studies. The results are, nevertheless, consistent with both the earlier laboratory and self-report field research and provide additional support for the suggestion that our attitudes toward those who administer rewards are influenced by the classical conditioning process.

RESPONDENT BEHAVIORS AS THE PROGENITORS OF OPERANT BEHAVIORS

Respondents are reflexive, "involuntary" behaviors that are elicited or automatically produced by particular environmental events or stimuli. As such, they may appear to bear little resemblance to, or have little impact on, the "voluntary," nonreflexive, or operant behaviors that are of prominent significance in organizations. But two recent lines of evidence suggest that, in this case, appearances are deceiving. One of these lines of research indicates that respondents interact with large segments of operant behavior. In some instances, respondents may be compatible with and, therefore, facilitate operant behaviors. In other cases, however, respondents may be incompatible with and impair, preclude, or otherwise interfere with operant responses. As noted earlier, we will discuss the effects of the interaction between respondent and operant behaviors in Chapter 4. The second line of research, which is not totally unrelated to the first, suggests that a more intimate relationship between respondents and operants exists. This line of research implies that certain classes of respondent behavior may be the raw material from which "voluntary" operant behaviors develop.

Perhaps we should not be surprised to find that respondent and operant behaviors are closely related. It has long been recognized, for example, that there are similarities between the effects that classical and operant conditioning procedures have on respondent and operant behaviors, respectively. Operants are frequently evoked by stimuli that share properties that are similar to those events an individual has been differentially reinforced to respond to. The process is called *stimulus generalization*. Respondents also generalize to stimuli that possess characteristics that resemble the conditioned stimulus (CS). The greater the resemblance or similarity, the more likely it is that the generalization will occur. Of course, the process of generalization can be reversed in the case of both operant and classical conditioning through *discrimination training*. As noted earlier, rather subtle discriminations can be obtained in classical conditioning when the presentation of the unconditioned stimulus (UCS) occurs only in the presence of very specific properties of the neutral or to-be-conditioned stimulus. Similarly, rather subtle properties of a stimulus can come to control operant behavior if an individual's responses are reinforced when these stimulus properties are present but not reinforced in their absence. Thus, we can "narrow" the range of stimulus properties that control a respondent just as we can "narrow" the range of stimulus properties that come to control a discriminated operant. Conditioned respondent and operant behaviors are also similar in that both are subject to the process of *extinction.* In the case of operant responding, extinction occurs when the positive reinforcer that is sustaining the operant no longer follows the behavior's occurrence. In such instances, the rate or frequency of the operant will generally diminish. In the case of the respondent behavior, the repeated presentation of the conditioned stimulus in the absence of the unconditioned stimulus will also produce extinction of the conditioned response. Because the conditioned stimulus is no longer paired with the unconditioned stimulus, it eventually loses its eliciting properties. Finally, operant and classical conditioning are similar in that both are limited or constrained by the biological makeup of the organism being conditioned (cf. Breland and Breland, 1961; Hinde and Stevenson-Hinde, 1973; Seligman and Hager, 1972). Thus, we cannot expect either process to work in instances where the individual being conditioned is not biologically or physically equipped to perform a particular response.

In addition to these similarities, more explicit propositions regarding the relationship between (involuntary) respondents and (voluntary) operant behaviors have also been made. For example, almost a century ago, William James (1890) noted that "voluntary movements must be secondary, not primary functions of our organism. . . . Reflex, instinctive and emotional movements are all primary performances . . . no creature not endowed with divinatory power can perform an act voluntarily for the first time" (James, 1890, pp. 486–487). More recently, similar suggestions have been made by several other behavioral scientists including Kimble and Perlmuter (1970), Segal (1972), and Skinner (1969).

It is, however, only recently that empirical evidence has been provided in support of the proposition that certain components of the respondent pattern elicited by a given unconditioned stimulus may serve as the raw material from which operants develop. At present, this evidence suggests that the relatively diffuse, undifferentiated skeletal responses that result from the presentation of a *UCS* are most susceptible to operant shaping and thus are the most likely progenitors of operant behavior. Much of the research on the relationship between respondent and operant behaviors has been conducted with animals (see, for example, Segal, 1972). However Piaget's (1963) analysis of the origins of intellect in children provides numerous instances of the development of operant responding from genetically based reflexes. Included among Piaget's examples are his observations of how the prehensile (grasping) responses of children become refined.

For the first few months following birth, a child's grasping responses appear to be purely reflexive and are affected primarily by the stimulation or touching of the child's palm. The movements of the child's hand during this stage of development appear to be random, and the child's grasp seldom lasts for a prolonged period of time.

Following this initial stage, a period begins in which the child acquires several simple movements, including opening and closing the hands, scratching various parts of the body, moving the fingers independently, and grasping objects and letting them go. At first, these movements are quite impulsive and uncoordinated. With repetition, however, they become more refined and are performed for longer durations of time without interruption. The primary reinforcement for much of the repetition of these activities appears to be the tactile and kinesthetic feedback received from the movement of the hands and fingers. However, as noted by Piaget (1963), as the sucking responses of the child also develop, the reinforcing properties of grasping objects and placing them into the mouth also become quite apparent.

In the final stages of development, children come to coordinate their grasping responses with their vision. During these stages the response becomes even more refined, and children readily reach and acquire objects within their range of movement (much to many mothers' dismay). As in the preceding stage of development, the reinforcement received by the child from the ability to grasp and play with or place the object obtained in his or her mouth is quite evident and performs an obvious function in the refinement of the behavior.

Although Piaget's (1963) explanation of the preceding events is quite different from our own, his extensive observations of the development of sensorimotor behavior in children is quite instructive. For consistent with the evidence reported by Segal (1972), and our analysis of the development of verbal behavior in Chapter 5, his observations suggest that as the diffuse, reflexive activity of the child is followed by reinforcement, the topography of these responses gradually changes (is shaped) and becomes more refined. Although additional details of the process need to be examined in more controlled settings, the evidence provided by Segal (1972) and Piaget (1963) does suggest that the reinforcement of undifferentiated respondent behavior plays an important role in the development of operant behaviors.

SUMMARY

Although respondent behaviors have been neglected or relegated to a role of minor importance by some social scientists, they have been venerated as primary causal variables by others. A more balanced perspective on the significance of respondent activities has been presented in this chapter. Such an approach does not assign primary causal status to respondents. It does, however, acknowledge the importance of respondent behavior and the classical conditioning process in several areas of human affairs. First, classical conditioning plays an important role in the development of conditioned reinforcers. Most of the reinforcing events administered by supervisors in organizational settings acquire their properties by being paired with other reinforcers through the classical conditioning process. Knowledge of this process, therefore, should prove invaluable to those individuals interested in understanding and influencing human behavior.

The classical conditioning of respondents also plays a prominent role in the acquisition of the affective feelings and attitudes individuals express toward their peers, jobs, supervisors, and other stimuli in their work settings. Leaders who understand how employee attitudes are acquired should be in a better position to influence and change them.

Recent research also suggests that certain components of the respondent pattern elicited by a given stimulus are susceptible to reinforcement contingencies and thus serve as the raw material from which operants develop. At present, the respondent components that appear to serve as the most likely progenitors of operant behavior are the rather diffuse, undifferentiated reactions that are most readily conditioned to neutral stimuli having little configural similarity to the unconditioned stimulus. Although all of the intricacies of the development of operants from respondent behaviors are not yet known, we expect that as the details become specified, the importance assigned to respondent behavior in human affairs will increase.

THREE
PRINCIPLES OF OPERANT BEHAVIOR

Most of the behavior we consider important in organizational settings produces an effect or is followed by changes in the environment in which it occurs. These behaviors may be relatively simple—such as pushing a button in order to start or stop a machine, "flipping" a light switch to illuminate a dark room, or pulling the drawer of a file cabinet open. However, the more complex behavior of the computer operator, the maintenance mechanic, and the electrical engineer also falls into this category.

Because of its prominence in human affairs, the behavior of individuals that produces changes in their environments has, of course, always been of concern to social scientists. As a result, a great amount of behavioral research has been directed toward the discovery of those relations between the behavior of various organisms (including human beings) and features of the environment in which the behavior is observed. The purpose of this chapter, therefore, is to describe the principles of operant behavior and to illustrate their significance in organizational settings.

A BASIC NOTATIONAL SYSTEM

The presentation of the principles of operant behavior is often facilitated by the use of a notational system that allows us to describe events and relations between events as succinctly as possible. The symbols and definitions of the notational system that is used throughout this chapter are as follows.

Behavioral Notation

Ss = stimulus situation; ambient setting

S_D = discriminative stimulus

$S_{D_{PR}}$ = a discriminative stimulus that sets the occasion for a response that is followed by positive reinforcement

$S_{D_{NR}}$ = a discriminative stimulus that sets the occasion for a response that is followed by negative reinforcement

$S_{D_{EXT}}$ = a discriminative stimulus that sets the occasion for a response that is followed by extinction

$S_{D_{PUN}}$ = a discriminative stimulus that sets the occasion for a response that is followed by punishment

R = operant response (behavior)

Rx = operant response that is in some sense organizationally desirable

Ry = operant response that is in some sense organizationally undesirable

Sc = stimulus consequence

$Sc+$ = positive reinforcer (appetitive stimulus)

$Sc-$ = negative reinforcer (aversive stimulus)

$\overline{Sc}+$ = removal of positive reinforcer

$\overline{Sc}-$ = removal of aversive stimulus

$\equiv$ = is followed by, leads to, or produces

$\rightarrow$ = elicits

THE LAW OF EFFECT AND OPERANT BEHAVIOR

Edward Lee Thorndike (1879–1949) was among the first to point out that an analysis of the environmental events or consequences that are produced by or follow behavior could prove to be crucial to our understanding of that behavior. Thorndike was dissatisfied with accounts of animal behavior such as Romanes' (1886), which stressed "reasoning" as a fundamental determinant for animal learning. He felt that such accounts suffered from a number of faults, among them being the human tendency to endow animals with strange and mysterious qualities presumably responsible for their behavior rather than to examine those features of the environment that might prove to be the important determinants.

Thorndike also felt that many of the "facts" about animal intelligence had been obtained or deduced more from anecdotal accounts of pet owners and psychologists searching for "intelligence" in animals than from carefully controlled studies of behavior.

Human folk are as a matter of fact eager to find intelligence in animals. They like to. And when the animal observed is a pet belonging to them or their friends, or when the story is one that has been told as a story to entertain, further complications are introduced. Nor is this all. Besides commonly misstating what facts they report, they report only such facts as show the animal at his best. Dogs get lost hundreds of times and no one ever notices it or sends an account of it to a scientific magazine. But let one find his way from Brooklyn to Yonkers and the fact immediately becomes a circulating anecdote. Thousands of cats on thousands of occasions sit helplessly yowling, and no one takes thought of it or writes to his friend, the professor; but let one cat claw at a knob of a door supposedly as a signal to be let out, and straightaway this cat becomes the representative of the cat-mind in all the books. The unconscious distortion of the facts is almost harmless compared to the unconscious neglect of an animal's mental life until it verges on the unusual and marvelous. It is as if some denizen of a planet where communication was by thought-transference, who was surveying humankind and reporting their psychology, should be oblivious to all our intercommunication save such as the psychical research society noted. If he should further misinterpret the cases of mere coincidence of thoughts as facts comparable to telepathic communication, he would not be more wrong than some of the animal psychologists. In short, anecdotes give really the abnormal or supernormal psychology of animals [Thorndike, 1911, pp. 24–25].

One final problem that Thorndike identified with much of the research that attempted to establish the "reasoning" abilities of animals was that the methodologies utilized in such research were often faulty. Such efforts, he maintained, were inadequate because frequently only one subject was tested under each experimental manipulation, and because the history of the subjects utilized in many of the experiments was not known or controlled. As a result, unknown or unaccounted for intervening or extraneous variables or both may have influenced the findings in any number of ways. Generalizability of research findings in such situations, Thorndike held, was limited to telling us what one animal does under certain conditions but would not inform us about what a species of animal would do. For this, experiments with more than one animal whose prior conditioning history was known or controlled for and who was freed from the influence of the observer were necessary.

Thorndike supported his convictions by substituting anecdotes and casual observations with controlled experiments and by showing that certain types of animal learning could be accounted for simply in terms of those environmental events that were produced by or followed the behavior that was emitted. For his now famous experiments, Thorndike used variations on an apparatus called a "puzzle box" (Fig. 3.1), as an enclosure in which a hungry cat, dog, or other animal was confined. For the sake of brevity, we will concentrate primarily on his research with cats. The escape from any particular box could be achieved when the hungry cat pulled a cord, pressed a lever, or stepped on a platform in such a way as to release a latch that held the door closed. Such behavior was reinforced with a small amount of food. Thorndike took special care in watching the specific behavior the cats exhibited on successful escapes from the box as well as in recording the time necessary for escape on each of the successive trials. He observed that when the cats were first confined in the puzzle boxes, most of them acted similarly. Each would exhibit numerous responses including biting, clawing, striking out with its paws, and trying to squeeze through openings in the box until one or a series of these behaviors would manipulate the latch on the door in such a way that it would open. However, once a successful escape had been accomplished, the behavior of the cats on succeeding trials in the box became less and less variable. On these repeated trials, the cats emitted less behavior that was unsuccessful in producing an escape and more of the successful responses.

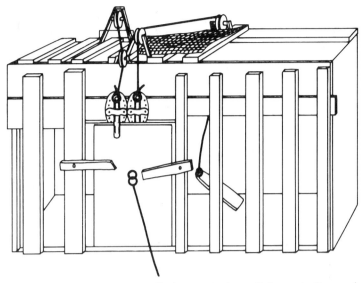

Figure 3.1 An illustration of Thorndike's puzzle box. Cats and other animals enclosed in this box learned that various actions on their part would permit escape. *Source:* E. L. Thorndike, "Animal Intelligence," June 1898.

In other words, the probability of successful escape behaviors had increased while other forms of behavior decreased.

That successful behavior increased in probability or frequency is indicated in Figure 3.2, which shows that less time was required to get out of the puzzle box on repeated trials. Thorndike concluded that much of an animal's behavior exhibited in response to present circumstances occurs because of the effects or consequences that the behavior produced in similar situations in the past. In the case of the cats in the puzzle box, for example, the behavior that produced the consequences of escape and food attainment increased in probability on future trials. He called the effect that the consequences of a response had on the subsequent probability of that response the *law of effect*.

Thorndike's notion that the consequences of behavior may have subsequent effects on the probability of behavior that was previously successful drew attention to the nature of various types of consequential events. The analysis of the effects that consequential environmental events have on the probability, or rate, of behavior falls under the rubric of *operant conditioning*.

Operant Behavior Defined

Operant behavior may be defined as that behavior that is sensitive to its consequences or outcomes (Bijou, 1976). It is behavior whose rate is susceptible or readily affected by environmental changes that are produced by, or follow, it. As indicated earlier, much of the behavior of interest to us in organizational settings is operant behavior. In fact, any behavior, including walking,

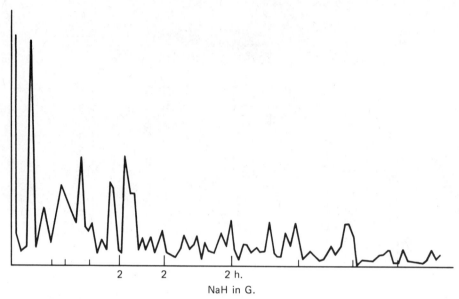

2 2 2 h.

NaH in G.

Figure 3.2 An illustration of the "learning curve" attained by a cat when placed in a puzzle box on repeated trials.
Source: E. L. Thorndike, "Animal Intelligence," June 1898.

turning, grasping, calculating, talking (either overtly or covertly), loading, inspecting, and so on, that is modified or maintained by environmental events that follow it is a form of operant behavior. In general, an operant is considered a class of responses that is affected by similar consequences rather than a single response instance. An operant is operationally defined, therefore, by its sensitivity to stimuli that come after it or that are a consequence of its occurrence.

REINFORCEMENT CONTINGENCIES

The relationships between behavior and various features of the surrounding environment are called *contingencies of reinforcement*. The statement that describes those relations is an "if—then" statement. It states that something is dependent or conditional on the occurrence of something else. In our particular case, it states that an environmental event with certain characteristics is dependent on the occurrence of a particular operant. In the language of probability theory, a contingency may be said to exist between an environmental event (Sc) and a response (R) when the probability (Sc/R) > probability ($Sc/\bar{R}$). That is, a contingency exists between an operant, R and a stimulus, Sc, as long as the probability of Sc is greater when R is emitted than when it is not emitted. In its simplest form (where there is no special significance attached to the antecedent stimulus situation), a contingency of reinforcement may be represented thus.

$$Ss : R \equiv Sc$$

where Ss = *ambient stimulus setting* to which no special significance has been attached
: = sets the occasion for or evokes
R = an *operant response*
$\equiv$ = *is followed by* or *produces*
Sc = *consequent stimulus*

The actual effect of a contingent stimulus on the probability of behavior is determined by the nature of that stimulus and whether or not the stimulus is presented or withdrawn after the response is emitted. In order to make the effects that environmental events may have on operant behavior more fully understandable, we will examine the four basic contingencies—which specify the relationships among an ambient stimulus setting, responses of a particular operant class, and consequent stimuli—in the context of those principles or procedures of behavioral change with which they are associated.

Principle of Positive Reinforcement.   *If, in a given setting, an operant of a given topography is followed by a stimulus consequence identified as a positive reinforcer, there will be an increase in the probability that operants of that topography will occur again in that setting.*

The reinforcement contingency may be depicted symbolically as follows.

$$Ss : Rx \equiv Sc+$$

where Ss = the ambient stimulus setting
: = sets the occasion for
Rx = the designated operant
$\equiv$ = is followed by or produces
$Sc+$ = a positive reinforcing stimulus (or "reward")

Examples of the use of the principle of positive reinforcement abound in organizational settings. Let us assume that, for a particular individual, a supervisor's praise serves as a positive reinforcer (or $Sc+$). When praise follows the occurrence of effective task operants and increases the probability of such behavior in the future, we have an instance of positive reinforcement. Other examples of the use of positive reinforcement may include recognition or approval for a job well done, promotions or advancement for "creative" or "innovative" behaviors that result in more efficient manufacture of a product, or increasing the privileges for dependable role performance on the part of an employee. Of course, we do not mean to imply that recognition, praise, promotions, or increased privileges serve as effective reinforcers for all organizational participants. What may prove to be a positive reinforcer for one individual is not always effective in modifying or sustaining the behavior of another. But neither is it true that each individual is idiosyncratic in terms of those events that prove reinforcing to him or her. As a result of the fact that many individuals in our society share similar conditioning histories, praise and the recognition by one's supervisor, as well as promotions and opportunities for advancement in the organization, often serve as effective forms of positive reinforcers.

Principle of Extinction. *If, in a given setting, an Ry of a given topography is followed by a reduction in, the withdrawal of, or the absence of a positive reinforcer, there will be a decrease in the probability that Ry's of that topography will occur again in that setting.*

Symbolically

$$Ss : Ry \equiv \overline{Sc} +$$

where the only new term, $\overline{Sc} +$ = a reduction in, withdrawal of, or absence of a positive reinforcer

Extinction refers to a procedure in which an operant that was previously reinforced no longer produces or is followed by reinforcement. Perhaps the most widely used form of the extinction procedure is ignoring behavior that has previously been reinforced with attention (Kazdin, 1975). This procedure will have desirable effects if the behavior ignored is dysfunctional or unwanted. However, functional or desirable organizational behaviors are also susceptible to the extinction process. Thus, managers who ignore or pay little attention to operant behaviors that are necessary for organizational effectiveness will unfortunately also reduce the frequency of these responses.

Behavior usually does not extinguish rapidly. Rather, decreasing the rate of a response by removing or withholding the reinforcing events previously associated with it is a gradual process requiring time and patience on the part of the management practitioner or behavioral change agent. Often the initial effect of the extinction procedure is a momentary increase in the rate, vigor, or magnitude of the behavior to be eliminated. This increase in the strength of the response may also be accompanied by displays of emotional behavior on the part of the individual whose behavior is being extinguished. Because of this unexpected increase—rather than decrease—in undesirable behaviors, a common mistake made by a naive manager is to abandon the treatment. Unfortunately, the effect of such a practice is that the behavior will not only continue to be emitted but may occur in even greater strength. If the manager is patient, however, the initial "outburst" of behavior and emotion will eventually subside, and the response will begin to decrease in frequency.

The actual speed with which behavior is extinguished after its initial increase in frequency has subsided is determined by a number of variables. Each of these variables affects the number of responses emitted during the extinction process or, put more technically, the response's *resistance to ex-*

tinction. According to Reynolds (1968, pp. 33–34), among the most important variables that have been found to determine resistance to extinction are these.

1. The *schedule* on which the response was reinforced prior to extinction. In general, responses that are intermittently or only occasionally followed by reinforcement are more resistant to extinction than responses that have been continuously reinforced. Because of their importance to the maintenance of operant behavior, we will return later in this chapter to a discussion of reinforcement schedules.

2. The *magnitude* of the reinforcer and the number of reinforcements received by the response prior to the imposition of the extinction procedure will affect a response's resistance to extinction. In general, the greater the magnitude of the reinforcer or the greater the number of responses that have been reinforced or both, the more difficult it will be to extinguish the behavior.

3. The *number of times* a response has been extinguished previously also affects an operant's resistance to extinction. The greater the number of times an operant has undergone extinction, the less resistant to extinction it becomes.

Owing to the fact that the reduction in the rate of a response that results from the use of the extinction procedure may be rather slow, behavior that may cause injury or prove dangerous to a worker or behavior that is extremely disruptive may necessitate the application of other behavioral techniques. These may include the use of punishment.

Principle of Punishment. *If, in a given setting, an Ry of a given topography is followed by a stimulus consequence identified as a negative reinforcer, there will be a decrease in the probability that Ry's of that topography will occur in that setting.*

Symbolically,

$Ss : Ry \equiv Sc-$

where $Sc- $ = a negative reinforcer (a "punitive" or aversive stimulus)

A negative reinforcer or aversive stimulus may be defined as an environmental event that, when presented following a response, decreases the frequency or rate of that response in the future. An example of such a stimulus might be criticism by an individual's supervisor for the production of a defective product. If the behavior resulting in defective output is followed by criticism and the probability of that behavior decreases as a result, the punishment procedure may be said to be in effect.

In most instances, the severest form of punishment at a manager's disposal is the "firing" of a worker. However, such an action on the manager's part is likely to prove more complex than a simple punishment procedure because a number of positive reinforcers are also withdrawn from the subordinate's

milieu, making it at the very least a combination of the punishment and extinction procedures. Being hit, shoved, burned, shocked, or kicked are readily
recognizable forms of punishment for most people (with the possible exception of a masochist). Because of sanctions against such behavior by managers, however, verbal reprimands, disapproval, or requiring a subordinate to
perform an undesirable job serve as more familiar forms of punishment in
organizational settings. Being caught in a "lie"; having to accept the blame for
a poorly finished product or a slumping sales record; or having to tell a peer,
subordinate, or supervisor something we find disagreeable may also serve as
more subtle forms of punishment. Perhaps that is why few people can "bring
themselves" to tell a peer or subordinate that his or her performance or "personality" is lacking and needs improvement.

Few of us enjoy being punished, and for that reason the efficacy and use of
punishment by practicing managers become rather controversial issues,
which we will examine in some detail in Chapter 8.

Principle of Negative Reinforcement. *If, in a given setting, an Rx of a given
topography is followed by a reduction in, the withdrawal of, or the absence of
a negative reinforcer, there will be an increase in the probability that Rx's of
that topography will occur again in that setting.*

Symbolically,

$$Ss : Rx \equiv \overline{Sc} -$$

where $\overline{Sc} -$ = a reduction in, the withdrawal, or the absence of a negative reinforcer

Although the presentation of an aversive stimulus will decrease the rate of
the behavior on which it is made contingent, the withdrawal of such a stimulus
following a response will increase its rate. Let us assume, for example, that
disapproval by one's supervisor serves as an aversive stimulus. If acceptable
task performance on the part of an individual worker is followed by the withdrawal of the supervisor's disapproval and the subordinate's performance
increases in probability, the negative reinforcement procedure is said to be in
effect.

Behavior that terminates an already present aversive stimulus is called
escape behavior. We are all familiar with forms of escape behavior. A little
boy may escape a "bully" by running away from him or hiding behind his
mother. We turn on an air conditioner to escape hot, humid weather or a heater
to escape cold weather. We may leave a room in which an argument is in
progress. People take vacations to "get away from it all." A sunbather retreats
to the shade or jumps into the pool when the sun gets too hot. Organizational
examples of escape behavior include "shutting down" a boiler that has
reached the danger level, turning on an exhaust fan to remove noxious odors
from a paint room, walking away from a fellow worker who is "talking too
much," switching off a machine that is making unusual noises, and performing

Effects on the Frequency of Behavior

	Increase (↑)	Decrease (↓)
Present Stimulus (→)	Positive Reinforcement Procedure	Punishment
Withdraw Stimulus (←)	Negative Reinforcement Procedure	Extinction Procedure

Manipulation of Consequent Stimulus

Figure 3.3 Summary of the four basic behavioral change procedures.

tasks properly in the supervisor's presence in order to stop the supervisor from "bitching" at us. It would appear, then, that escape behaviors occur in abundance in natural settings. Most individuals readily learn to behave in a manner that allows them to eliminate or reduce the potency of aversive stimuli with which they come into contact.

Reinforcement Contingencies—A Short Review

We have been discussing the four basic contingencies of reinforcement or procedures for behavior change. Though we have not exhausted the contingencies that do exist, it may prove wise to review the procedures so far examined. Two of the procedures, the positive and negative reinforcement procedures, increase the probability of operant responses that they follow. The other two, the extinction and punishment procedures, decrease the probability of the operant responses on which they are made contingent. Figure 3.3 further clarifies the procedures involved in our discussion of behavioral principles. As suggested by this figure, a consequent stimulus may be manipulated either by presenting (→) or withdrawing (←) it following a particular response. The effects of such manipulations can be either an increase (↑) or decrease (↓) in the probability of the behavior in question. If a stimulus follows or is produced by a response and that response increases in probability in the future, positive reinforcement is indicated. If a stimulus is presented contingently and the response decreases in probability, punishment is indicated. On the other hand, if we withdraw or remove a stimulus after a response and the response decreases in probability, the extinction procedure is in effect. And, finally, if a stimulus is withdrawn and the response increases in probability in the future, we have a case of negative reinforcement.

PRIMARY AND SECONDARY REINFORCERS

We may conclude on the basis of our prior discussion that operant behavior is influenced primarily by its stimulus consequences. These consequences are generally grouped into two subclasses, primary or unconditioned reinforcers and secondary or conditioned reinforcers.

Primary Reinforcers

Some environmental events, called *primary reinforcers*, have reasonably similar effects on all members of the human race because we all share common phylogenic origins. Food, water, and the removal of painful stimuli are readily identifiable members of this category. The presentation of food to a hungry individual who requests it or the withdrawal of a powerful aversive stimulus contingent on a plea for mercy, for example, will more than likely increase the probability of such requests and pleas, respectively, in similar situations.

Other stimuli that appear to fit into the category of primary reinforcers are those features of the environment which change when we manipulate them. Skinner (1953) was among the first to suggest that control over one's environment may prove reinforcing.

> It is possible that some of the reinforcing effects of "sensory feedback" are unconditioned. A baby appears to be reinforced by stimulation from the environment which has not been followed by primary reinforcement. The baby's rattle is an example. The capacity to be reinforced in this way could have arisen in the evolutionary process, and it may have a parallel in the reinforcement we receive from simply "making the world behave." Any organism which is reinforced by its success in manipulating nature, regardless of the momentary consequences, will be in a favored position when important consequences follow [Skinner, 1953, p. 78].

More recently, discussions by Bijou (1976) on "ecological reinforcers," Kish (1966) on "sensory stimuli," and Scott and Erskine (1980) on various types of "response-produced stimuli" would seem to suggest that certain stimuli that result from our behavior and produce changes in neural activity may also prove to be primarily reinforcing. Because of the apparent importance of these neural changes to the process of reinforcement in general, we will discuss them in Chapter 4 when we examine various theories of reinforcement.

Secondary Reinforcers

Aside from primary reinforcers, any of a wide variety of environmental events called *secondary* or *conditioned reinforcers* come to serve as powerful reinforcing events for most human beings. Most of those stimulus events that are identified as reinforcing in business situations are ones that may be said to have *acquired* reinforcing properties or have become conditioned reinforcers. Acquisition of such properties is achieved when stimuli having no obvious effects on the behaving organism are paired or associated with other stimulus events that already possess reinforcing properties.

> Conditioned reinforcers are stimuli that possess reinforcing properties because they have been associated with previously demonstrated reinforcing stimuli (either a primary reinforcer or a powerful secondary reinforcer) [Williams, 1973, pp. 565–566].

As we noted in Chapter 2, when a neutral stimulus (*NS*) has been paired with an unconditioned primary reinforcer (*UCS+*), the neutral stimulus takes on many of the properties of the *UCS+* and, like the *UCS+*, will serve as a positive reinforcer. However, stronger conditioning effects are achieved when a neutral stimulus is paired with a large number of unconditioned primary reinforcers or conditioned secondary reinforcers. In this case, the neutral stimulus becomes a *generalized* positive reinforcer.

Money is perhaps the best example of a generalized positive reinforcer. Skinner (1953) has suggested a number of reasons for this. First, money can be exchanged for a great variety of primary (as well as other secondary) reinforcers, and, therefore, its effects are relatively independent of an individual's momentary deprivation levels. Secondly, because of its well-defined physical dimensions, rather precise contingencies between money and the behavior to be modified can be established. And, finally, because the exchange value of money is often more clearly specified than other reinforcers, its effects on behavior are, in most instances, more easily conditionable. Of course, praise, attention, approval, and other evaluative responses provided by one's supervisor or peers also frequently serve as effective generalized positive reinforcers for most organizational participants because, as in the case of money, these events tend to serve as cues to the relative availability of other reinforcing events (Hill, 1968).

ORGANIZATIONAL REINFORCERS

In organizational settings, a large number and variety of environmental events often prove to be reinforcing. Reinforcers that are considered among the most important in these settings may be divided into those that are intrinsic and those that are extrinsic.

Intrinsic Reinforcers

Intrinsic reinforcers are those that result from an individual's interaction or contact with the physical, nonsocial environment in the accomplishment of his or her work. The sensory consequences of locomotor behavior or other forms of physical action, as well as the response-produced stimulus consequences that we experience in interacting with or manipulating the physical environment in the performance of a job, are but a few examples. In general, tasks that allow for movement within, or control over, our physical environment are reinforcing and would be reported by most individuals to be more enjoyable and interesting than tasks that do not produce such consequences. Of course, this does not imply that jobs that produce such reinforcing effects will be performed more effectively or more efficiently. Even when intrinsic reinforcers do result from the completion of a job, they may not be effective for any number of reasons (Miller, 1975). First, it is possible that the intrinsic reinforcers do not follow the desired behavior *quickly* enough. For reinforcing events of any type to be effective in establishing and maintaining task performance, they should follow the desired behavior as quickly as possible. The evidence suggests that reinforcing events are still effective after considerable delays in the human case. Nevertheless, delays in reinforcement typically (1) reduce the rate of acquisition of a desired response, (2) decrease the rate of a desired response and (3) reinforce and, therefore, increase less desirable behaviors that occur in the interval between the desirable response and the delayed reinforcer. In general, then, the longer the delay between a response and a reinforcing stimulus, the less the behavior will be controlled by that reinforcer.

Second, the consequences may not be large or sizable enough to effect the desired behavior. Reinforcers must be of sufficient *magnitude* if they are to be used to modify human performance. In most situations, the efficacy of the reinforcer will increase as its size or magnitude increases. The magnitude of a reinforcer is, of course, a relative rather than an absolute concept. For an individual who has received reinforcers that are low in magnitude in the recent past, a reinforcer of moderate size will be more effective than if that same reinforcer follows behavior after a period when the individual had just received large amounts of reinforcement.

Third, intrinsic reinforcers may be unrelated to primary role behavior. Reinforcers should follow *only* those behaviors that are desirable. All too frequently, individuals in organizations receive reinforcement for behaviors that do not meet the criterion for desirable responses. If the only time an individual receives reinforcers resulting from movement within his or her environment is when he or she is on a "break," at lunch or from behavior irrelevant to task completion, it is unlikely that high performance levels will result. For reinforcers to be effective, then, they should follow that behavior that is considered functional to the organization.

Finally, intrinsic reinforcers may prove ineffective in bringing about and sustaining task behavior because of "habituation" effects. As we will note in Chapter 4, the more frequently a reinforcer occurs, the less effective it generally becomes (Miller, 1975). Thus, intrinsic reinforcers may lose their effectiveness in modifying or sustaining behavior if they occur at a high rate.

Extrinsic Reinforcers

Aside from intrinsic or task-mediated reinforcers, managers have at their disposal more traditional forms of organizational reinforcing events that we will call *extrinsic reinforcers*. Extrinsic reinforcers require either the mediation or presence of another person in order to be effective. In organizations, the "other person" is often the manager or supervisor. Included in this category of reinforcers are the familiar verbal evaluative forms (praise, compliments, approval, recognition, acceptance, and other types of acknowledgments of "good work"), as well as the more conventional organizational reinforcers such as increases in salary, bonuses, and promotions.

As in the case of intrinsic reinforcers, extrinsic reinforcers should be administered with minimum delays, be of sufficient magnitude, be contingent on desirable behavior, and be administered in such a manner that habituation effects do not set in. However, further difficulties may arise in the application of such reinforcing events because they are mediated by another individual. Skinner (1953), for example, has noted that there are a number of reasons why "behavior reinforced through the mediation of other people will differ in many ways from behavior reinforced by the mechanical environment" (Skinner, 1953, p. 299). First, social contingencies are more variable across situations and may change more over time than those that are task-mediated. The human mediator, for example, may reinforce an individual for a particular response one day while punishing that behavior or ignoring it the next day. Or behavior followed by socially mediated reinforcers in one situation or context may be punished in another situation. Second, social contingencies are often administered inconsistently. One manager may reinforce the behavior of a subordinate whereas another one punishes it. Moreover, socially mediated reinforcers have a greater likelihood of being applied inappropriately than do those mediated by the mechanical environment. As a result, desirable behaviors may go unreinforced, and undesirable behaviors may be followed by reinforcing events. This may happen when the management practitioner inadvertently reinforces an employee's "silly" or "joking" behaviors without recognizing that this might increase such behavior at the cost of a reduction in functional organizational responses. Finally, because it is difficult for a mediator to observe someone else's behavior constantly, social reinforcement contingencies are often administered on intermittent schedules. In general, therefore, the application of socially mediated consequences is more complex than that of task-mediated consequences.

These differences in the administration of socially mediated reinforcers have a number of effects on the behavior controlled by them (Skinner, 1953). First, since socially mediated contingencies are often more variable than those that are not mediated by another person, the behavioral repertoire of individuals in social situations is often found to be more changeable or more flexible than behavior controlled purely by the mechanical environment. Because operant behavior is controlled by environmental events, one would expect that the more these environmental events change, the more the behavior is likely to change. Unstable and often deviant or unproductive forms of behavior are thus more likely to occur in settings where socially mediated contingencies prevail. Behavior reinforced by socially mediated contingencies is also likely to be more resistant to extinction as a result of the intermittent schedules of reinforcement that prevail with such contingencies.

Implications derived from the analysis of extrinsic (socially mediated) reinforcers are important, for they suggest that (1) management practitioners should be taught to identify and administer extrinsic rewards correctly in order to bring about and maintain functional or desirable organizational behavior on the part of their subordinates and (2) that functional operant behavior, as well as the conditions under which it is to occur, should be specified so that extrinsic reinforcers are more effectively applied.

THE "SHAPING" OF DESIRABLE TASK BEHAVIORS

The effects that reinforcing events have on human behavior are often quite powerful. Managers who are knowledgeable in the use of these reinforcers can increase the rate or frequency of desirable organizational behaviors. However, in certain instances, the behavior a manager identifies as functional to the organization is not part of a subordinate's behavioral repertoire, making the behavior impossible to reinforce because it does not occur at all. The question then becomes how such behavior can be developed. One procedure by which we can add new behaviors to an individual's repertoire is called "shaping." Behavioral shaping is familiar to us in everyday life. By means of this process children learn to walk, stand erect, throw baseballs and footballs, talk, and acquire other motor and verbal operant skills. Shaping is accomplished by differentially reinforcing successive approximations of a "target" response. This allows us to change an individual's initial repertoire, through successive stages, to a more complex form.

An organizational example of the use of behavioral shaping is provided in Figure 3.4. In this example, a manager has chosen as a "target" task behavior

<u>Step 5</u>	$Ss\ (Rx_5 \equiv \underline{Sc}+)$ reinforce Rx_5 (target behavior)
	$Ss\ (Rx_4 \equiv \overline{Sc}+)$ withdraw reinforcement from Rx_4
<u>Step 4</u>	$Ss\ (Rx_4 \equiv \underline{Sc}+)$ reinforce Rx_4 (a closer approximation of Rx_5 than Rx_3)
	$Ss\ (Rx_3 \equiv \overline{Sc}+)$ withdraw reinforcement from Rx_3
<u>Step 3</u>	$Ss\ (Rx_3 \equiv \underline{Sc}+)$ reinforce Rx_3 (a closer approximation of Rx_5 than Rx_2)
	$Ss\ (Rx_2 \equiv \overline{Sc}+)$ withdraw reinforcement of Rx_2
<u>Step 2</u>	$Ss\ (Rx_2 \equiv \underline{Sc}+)$ reinforce Rx_2 (a closer approximation of Rx_5 than Rx_1)
	$Ss\ (Rx_1 \equiv \overline{Sc}+)$ withdraw reinforcement of Rx_1
<u>Step 1</u>	$Ss\ (Rx_1 \equiv Sc+)$ reinforce the first rough approximation (R_1) of the desired "target" behavior (Rx_5)
	$Ss\ (R_O \equiv \overline{Sc}+)$ withdraw reinforcement of other responses (R_O) that do not approximate Rx_5

Figure 3.4 Shaping of a "target" response via differential reinforcement of successive approximations.

the skill necessary for a new worker to use a spray gun properly to paint a car. The target behavior (Rx_5), which includes holding the gun correctly, pressing and releasing the trigger at appropriate times, moving the arm and wrist to and fro properly, and so on, must be specified by the manager prior to the shaping procedure. When an individual first operates the gun, the initial responses are not likely to be effective in producing the desired effect. In this initial stage, the manager positively reinforces any behavior Rx_1 (i.e., moving wrist to and fro while enacting the gun's trigger), which even roughly approximates the "target" response while extinguishing (removing the reinforcement from) all other behaviors (R_O) that do not approximate the "target." As the shaping process continues, the requirements of the behavior necessary to produce reinforcement by the manager are increased to Rx_2 (moving wrist and arm to and fro smoothly while enacting the gun's trigger). At the same time, the reinforcement for the earlier approximation (Rx_1) is withdrawn (extinction procedure). Through this process of differentially reinforcing successive approximations, the worker will progress from a rough behavioral approximation (Rx_1) to the acquisition of the "fine-grained" behavior we associate with the use of a spray gun (Rx_5). In essence, the shaping of skills in industry may be accomplished when the manager

- Specifies, in behavioral terms, the desired "target" task behavior to be performed by the worker.
- Identifies which events are reinforcing to the worker whose behavior is to be "shaped."
- Identifies, from an examination of the worker's initial repertoire, which behaviors most closely approximate the target behavior.
- Applies differential reinforcement to successive approximations of the target response until performance mastery is reached.

In line with our discussion, Sidman (1962) has pointed out a number of important rules to ensure success when one is employing shaping procedures.

1. *Reinforce the behavior immediately.* If the reinforcement is delayed, it is likely to be preceded by some behavior other than that which the experimenter (manager[1]) intended to reinforce.
2. *Do not give too many reinforcements for an approximation of the desired final response.* Behavior that is initially reinforced must ultimately be extinguished as we move closer to the end point. If we reinforce intermediate forms of behavior too much, these once-reinforced but now-to-be-extinguished responses will continue to intrude and will unduly prolong the shaping process.
3. *Do not give too few reinforcements for an approximation of the desired final response.* This is the most common difficulty in shaping behavior; the experimenter (manager) moves too fast. He abandons a response before

---

[1]Words in parentheses were added by authors.

he has reinforced it enough and, as a consequence, both the response and the variations which stem from it extinguish before he can mold the next closer approximation to the final behavior. The subordinate may then return to his original behavior, as if he had never gone through a shaping process at all.

When this happens, the experimenter (manager) may be tempted to evade his responsibility by calling the subject stupid. What he must do is to start again and move the subject once more through the successive steps of the shaping process, taking care this time not to move too rapidly. If the experimenter (manager) is patient and willing to learn, he will usually find the subject equally willing.

4. *Carefully specify the response to be reinforced in each successive step.* Before abandoning one response and reinforcing the next approximation to the final behavior, the experimenter must watch the subject closely to determine what behavior is available for reinforcement. He should then specify that behavior as quantitatively as possible and adhere rigorously to the specification he has established. Otherwise, he may inadvertently reinforce a slightly different but highly undesirable form of response and unnecessarily prolong the shaping process.[2]

When used properly in controlled settings, shaping has been found to be effective in producing greater learning capacities in retarded children (Baer, Peterson, and Sherman, 1968), teaching mute schizophrenics to talk (Issacs, Thomas and Goldiamond, 1960), teaching childhood schizophrenics to cooperate with other children (Hingtgen, Sanders, and DeMeyer, 1965), increasing interpersonal responsiveness in severely withdrawn schizophrenics (King, Armtage, and Tilton, 1960), and establishing complex skills in retarded children (Bensberg, 1965; Bensberg, Colwell, and Cassel, 1965).

However, our review up to this point seems to imply that a number of problems may be encountered when utilizing the shaping procedure in organizational settings. Sidman's rules, for example, suggest that regardless of how some people would like it portrayed, the successful shaping of behavior is not an easy task. Little research has been undertaken to provide the manager with useful generalizations as to what would constitute too much or too little reinforcement for each approximation. Too little reinforcement at each step may result in extinction of an approximation to the target response. Too much reinforcement at each step may produce habituation effects with the result that the acquisition of the target response is slowed down. Of course, some individuals might argue that the knowledge about what constitutes too much or too little reinforcement for each successive approximation will develop as the manager becomes more experienced with the use of the shaping technique. This would appear to be a valid argument, for as one becomes more intimately involved with behavioral change efforts, he or she will also become more

[2]From M. Sidman, Operant Techniques. In A. J. Bachrach (Ed.), *Experimental Foundations of Clinical Psychology.* New York: Basic Books, Inc., 1962. Used with permission.

familiar with the parameters within which such change efforts are most effective.

Though it is conceded that some problems in applying the behavioral shaping procedure in organizational settings may be eliminated with experience, more substantive difficulties in its use may still be encountered. First, shaping would appear to be appropriate only in those cases where the first approximation to the target response occurs at a reasonably high operant level. In those situations where the operant is not emitted at reasonably high levels, undue time may be wasted in waiting for its occurrence.

Second, unless a clear, concise behavioral definition or description of each step or successive approximation can be given, the shaping procedure is not likely to be effective. In those situations where such behavioral specification is not attainable, the probability of undesirable or dysfunctional behaviors resulting from the shaping procedure is increased. Such specification is, of course, dependent to a large degree on the sophistication of the trainer. However, some behavioral classifications such as "innovative," "creative," or "inventive" behaviors may prove more elusive in naturalistic settings.

Third, the shaping procedure may take considerable amounts of time and requires patience on the part of the change agent. Although the shaping procedure seems to direct our attention toward the behavior of the trainee, we must not forget that in order for the trainer's behavior to be sustained, it, too, must be reinforced. For most managers or trainers, it is likely that desirable or functional organizational operants on the part of the trainee have acquired the properties of a conditioned reinforcer. Thus, when the shaping of an employee's work behavior takes an inordinately long time, the acquisition of the response is slow, or the time between the initiation of the change process and the employee's emission of component responses (successive approximations) is extended, the trainer's behavior may undergo extinction and decrease as a result. It is possible, of course, to supplement the trainer's reinforcement schedule with verbal reinforcers applied by his or her peers or supervisors. However, this still does not eliminate the fact that some degree of patience and time is required to shape desirable responses—it only moves the problem to a higher level in the organizational hierarchy.

Fourth, because shaping is a gradual process, the procedure will not prove useful in situations where it is necessary to induce the target response immediately or in those cases in which the performance of the successive approximations toward the target behavior would expose the trainer, trainee, or others to dangerous, injurious, or undesirable consequences. For these situations, other methods of behavioral change (which nevertheless, may include shaping) must be utilized.

Finally, it is important to note that most individuals have already developed the basic units of behavior necessary to perform most tasks prior to their entry into the organization. As a result, we are generally more interested in improving or refining the skill properties of the operants individuals can already perform and in bringing them under the control of specific stimulus events, rather than developing them in raw form. Thus, the problem faced by leaders in producing functional organizational behaviors often has less to do with shaping component responses than it does with evoking operants that may be of low probability and bringing them under the control of appropriate stimuli. In these situations, other methods of behavioral change may prove to be much more effective in facilitating the development of functional operant behavior. For example, providing a model for appropriate behaviors has been shown by Bandura (1969, 1971, 1977) to be an effective method of developing new or novel responses or of altering the probability or rate of already learned behaviors. Another technique for evoking functional subordinate behavior involves the use of verbal stimuli in the form of instructions, directions, verbal prompts, and so on. These verbal stimuli, called contingency-specifying discriminative stimuli, may be used quite effectively in evoking rather complex responses once an individual has acquired a verbal repertoire. Even in cases where distinctly new behavior is required, verbal instructions and modeling frequently prove to be more effective methods of behavioral change than shaping. Because of the importance of both modeling and verbal stimuli in human affairs, we will discuss them in greater detail later in this chapter, as well as in Chapters 5, 7, and 8.

SCHEDULES OF REINFORCEMENT

Up to this point in our discussion, we have focused our attention on various contingencies of reinforcement and their effects on behavior. We have seen that much of the behavior individuals exhibit in organizational settings is affected by its consequences. However, we have not discussed the effects that the patterning or timing of reinforcing events has on such behavior.

Research on the effects of varying patterns of reinforcement is generally referred to as the study of *schedules of reinforcement*. A reinforcement schedule is a *rule* that specifies the conditions under which and how often a particular operant is reinforced (Schwartz, 1978, p. 152). The investigation of the effects that various schedules of reinforcement have on behavior has been of interest to behavioral scientists for over three decades. Most of this research has been concerned with the identification of the various possible patterns of reinforcement and their effects on behavior. Though many schedules of reinforcement exist, perhaps the most widely examined are the continuous and intermittent reinforcement schedules.

Continuous and Intermittent Reinforcement Schedules

When a particular response produces or is followed by a reinforcer every time it is emitted, we call this a *continuous schedule of reinforcement* or *CRF*. Research has shown that continuous reinforcement schedules produce reasonably high response rates and are the most efficient way to condition or "shape" new behaviors. However, most reinforcers in natural situations do not occur on a continuous basis. A quarterback rarely completes every pass, nor does the baseball player get a hit each time he or she swings the bat. We may have to make many attempts to solve a complex problem before we are actually successful. And a subordinate is likely to be praised only occasionally for his or her task performance by the supervisor rather than each time he or she completes the task. When a particular response is followed by reinforcement occasionally rather than continuously, we say that an *intermittent* or *partial* schedule of reinforcement is being utilized. The effects of intermittent schedules of reinforcement on behavior are different from, but no less lawful than, the effects of continuous reinforcement. Further, the lawful relationships that result from intermittent reinforcement have important implications for those interested in sustaining operant behavior in organizational settings once it has been shaped and strengthened.

Though there are numerous intermittent schedules of reinforcement that could be examined, we will direct our attention to four basic ones (Fig. 3.5). Two, which are based on the passage of time, are called *interval schedules*. The remaining two, based on the number of responses an individual emits, are called *ratio schedules*.

Fixed-Interval Schedules

In a *fixed interval* schedule of reinforcement, a fixed amount of time must elapse between the prior reinforcer and the next response that produces a reinforcing event. An FI–10′, for example, indicates that 10 minutes must expire from the presentation of the previous reinforcer before a response will once again produce reinforcement. Fixed interval schedules of reinforcement produce behavior that is more resistant to extinction than behavior under the control of a continuous schedule. Thus, behavior reinforced on such a schedule is difficult to eliminate once it has been conditioned.

Because the regularity of reinforcement in fixed interval schedules makes it possible to develop a temporal discrimination, individuals reinforced on these schedules are often found not to respond immediately after the delivery of a reinforcing event. However, they increase the frequency of their responses as the time for the reinstatement of the reinforcement contingency draws nearer. This alternation of behavior, from "breaks" after the presentation of a reinforcer to high rates of response just prior to the end of the interval, creates the deep "scallops" in the rate of responses often associated with FI schedules that have long intervals between reinforcers. In the extreme case, where the intervals are "stretched" too far and great periods of time are required between reinforced responses, interval "strain" may result. In such instances, the worker is likely to decrease his or her production or quit his or her job.

Weekly, biweekly, or monthly pay periods, as well as scheduled "work-breaks," are frequently described as examples of fixed-interval schedules of

Schedule of Intermittent Reinforcement	Illustration of Schedule	Characteristics and Effects of Schedule
FIXED INTERVAL (FI) A fixed interval of time must elapse between the prior reinforcer and the next response that produces reinforcement	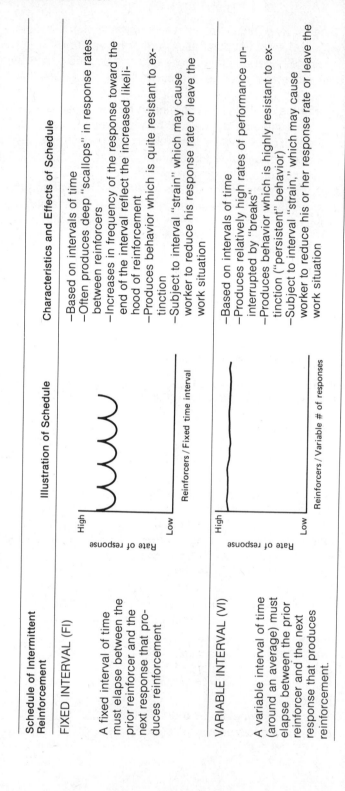 Rate of response — High / Low Reinforcers / Fixed time interval	—Based on intervals of time —Often produces deep "scallops" in response rates between reinforcers —Increases in frequency of the response toward the end of the interval reflect the increased likelihood of reinforcement —Produces behavior which is quite resistant to extinction —Subject to interval "strain" which may cause worker to reduce his response rate or leave the work situation
VARIABLE INTERVAL (VI) A variable interval of time (around an average) must elapse between the prior reinforcer and the next response that produces reinforcement.	Rate of response — High / Low Reinforcers / Variable # of responses	—Based on intervals of time —Produces relatively high rates of performance uninterrupted by "breaks" —Produces behavior which is highly resistant to extinction ("persistent" behavior) —Subject to interval "strain," which may cause worker to reduce his or her response rate or leave the work situation

FIXED RATIO (FR)

A fixed number of responses must occur between the prior reinforcer and the next response that produces reinforcement

—Based on the number of responses
—Reinforcement often followed by a short postre-inforcement "pause"
—The more rapidly an individual works—the more reinforcers he or she obtains
—Problem—"stretching" of schedule may cause worker to slow his or her responding or leave the work situation

VARIABLE RATIO (VR)

A variable number of responses (around an average) must occur between the prior reinforcer and the next response that produces reinforcement

—Based on the number of responses
—Produces high, consistent performance levels
—The more rapidly one works, the more reinforcers he or she obtains
—Problem—"stretching" of schedule may cause worker to slow his or her responding or leave the work situation

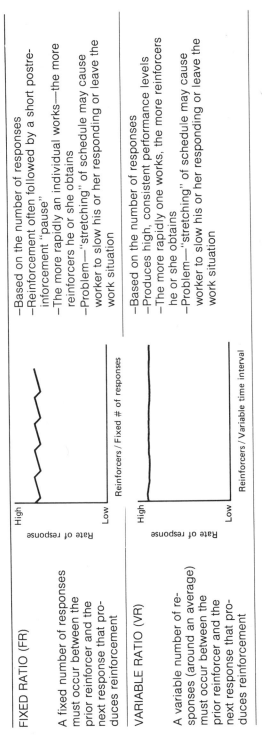

Figure 3.5 Intermittent schedules of reinforcement.

reinforcement. Most organizational reinforcers, however, are administered on the basis of a combination of response and time requirements so that their effects are more complex than that produced by simple fixed-interval schedules. For this reason, managers should not expect to find the behavior of subordinates produced by set pay periods to be completely analogous to that produced by fixed-interval schedules.

Variable-Interval Schedules

The interval of time between reinforcers need not be fixed. With variable-interval schedules of reinforcement, a variable amount of time must elapse between the prior reinforcer and the next response that produces reinforcement. A *VI–2'* means that, *on the average*, a reinforcer follows or is produced by a response every two minutes. Typically, variable interval schedules produce behavior that may be said to be extremely resistant to extinction, and individuals performing tasks while on variable-interval schedules perform at relatively high, uniform rates with few "breaks" in the response rate between reinforcers.

Fixed-Ratio Schedules

Some schedules of reinforcement are based on the number of responses emitted rather than on the passage of time. A fixed-ratio schedule is characterized by a fixed number of responses between the prior reinforcer and the next response that produces a reinforcing stimulus. The more rapidly one responds on a fixed-ratio schedule, the more reinforcement he or she obtains. Among the most frequently cited industrial examples of a fixed-ratio schedule of reinforcement is the administration of pay on a piecework basis. For example, an *FR–10* would imply a worker is paid a given amount of money each time he or she produces 10 units. In reality, in most cases in industry where piecework pay (fixed ratio) is said to control behavior, it is actually the proposition to the employee that he or she will be reinforced on a piecework basis that exercises the control over the employee's behavior. Even though the behavioral effects may be similar, the distinction between *contingency-specifying* and *experientially developed* discriminative stimuli is one that should not be overlooked and will be returned to in a later discussion.

Fixed ratios produce relatively high levels of performance, typically interrupted by small postreinforcement "pauses." These pauses are revealed graphically as shallow "dips" in the frequency of responding. As with interval schedules, one difficulty frequently encountered in the use of fixed ratios in industry is the tendency of some managers to "strain" the ratios. Up to a point, employees maintain their production level when the requirements or the number of responses per reinforcement is increased. In fact, "stretching" the ratio (or interval) is necessary in order to maintain employee performance without utilizing continuous reinforcement. However, as in the case of an interval schedule, when a ratio is "strained" (number of responses per reinforcement made too high, too quickly), employees may (1) decrease their production, (2) seek the protection of employee associations (i.e., unions), or (3) seek other employment possibilities. Therefore, although fixed ratios may produce relatively high performance levels, caution must be employed in their use.

Variable-Ratio Schedules

Just as with interval schedules, ratio schedules of reinforcement may be applied on a variable basis. In variable-ratio schedules, a variable number of responses must be emitted between the prior reinforcer and the next response that is followed by a reinforcing event. A VR–10 would indicate that, on the average, 10 responses must be emitted to produce the reinforcer. Variable ratios have been found to produce extremely high levels of performance, because as in the case of fixed ratios, the more rapidly one responds, the more reinforcement he or she will obtain. Numerous examples of variable ratio schedules occur in everyday situations. The behavior of a baseball batter is, in part, controlled on a variable-ratio schedule. Few players actually get a "hit" each time they are at bat. Even in those instances when they actually connect with the baseball when they swing, the ball may go "foul" or be caught, or they may be thrown out before reaching first base. Most people who have observed baseball players know that the variable ratio of "hits" generally ensures that the batter's behavior will not extinguish rapidly. Even when reinforcement is not forthcoming for some time (and the player is said to be in a "slump"), he or she will often continue to play baseball for some period of time. Similar effects can be seen in the behavior of the basketball player who does not make every field goal, the fisherman who does not catch a fish every time (s)he casts the line, or the door-to-door salesperson who does not make a sale with every customer. However, perhaps the most dramatic evidence of the influence of VR schedules is the effect slot machines and other gambling devices have on human behavior. Because it is always the case that the next "pull" on the slot machine may produce the reward, the behavior of many players often remains consistently high and is difficult to extinguish.

It is evident that intermittent schedules of reinforcement are of considerable importance to management practitioners. Beyond the fact that partial reinforcement is more prevalent in naturalistic environments than is continuous reinforcement, it would also appear that behavior can be sustained at very high rates by intermittent schedules of reinforcement. A practicing manager need not, therefore, be present to reinforce appropriate or desirable behavior each time it occurs. However, caution must be exercised when utilizing the various schedules and their combinations if optimal results are to be achieved. Though it is true that practicing managers nearly always revert to some sort of intermittent schedule once an employee has been trained (i.e., required operants have been appropriately strengthened), a perennial problem is too much "stretch" and "strain" in the application of positive reinforcers. Of course, insofar as monetary reinforcers are concerned, practitioners are not likely to modify current schedules to a large extent. Nevertheless, the application of evaluative reinforcers such as praise and recognition is, in many instances, as important in controlling the behavior of subordinates as is money and for that reason could be scheduled more effectively than such reinforcers normally are. Moreover, we should not forget that intrinsic reinforcers may be effective in sustaining task behavior even in the face of ineffective schedules of extrinsic reinforcers. It would be best, of course, if all reinforcing events were effectively scheduled.

DISCRIMINATED OPERANT BEHAVIOR

The conditioning of operant behavior may be described without any reference to stimuli that precede the occurrence of an operant response (Skinner, 1953). Nevertheless, operant behavior does come under the control of antecedent stimuli. Any stimulus that precedes an operant or is present when that response is followed by the presentation or withdrawal of a reinforcing or punishing event will acquire some control over responses of that operant class. The antecedent stimulus is called a *discriminative* stimulus or an S_D. It does not elicit or automatically produce the operant. Rather, we say that the discriminative stimulus evokes or *sets the occasion* for an operant that is followed by reinforcing consequences. Operant responses that are under the control of an antecedent stimulus are called *discriminated operants*.

Examples of discriminated operant behavior abound in naturalistic settings. When we are allowed to pick between two large, red, ripe apples, for example, we pick the one without the worm hole in it. In purchasing a suit, we select the "plaid" one. A child's ability to pick out her father from all other men is a form of discriminative stimulus control. For it is the special stimulus properties that are differentially associated with her father that distinguish him from all other members of the stimulus class we call "males." The control exercised over our behavior by gestures and voice inflections that accompany vocal operants also identify these stimuli as discriminative. Bem (1964, 1967, 1972) has pointed out that we often make inferences about the emotions or attitudes of ourselves (as well as others) from environmental stimuli present at the time that the behavior is observed.

In industry, discriminated operant behavior is often demonstrated by the experienced quality controller who, on the basis of but a few stimulus differences (or imperfections), must accept or reject a finished product. Similarly, discriminative stimulus control is evident from the behavior of scientists such as the botanist who distinguishes between various plant species on the basis of their leaf structure, leaf configuration, or the area in which the plant grows; or the meteorologist who differentiates between cumulus, cumulonimbus, cumulocirrus, and cumulostratus clouds on the basis of their altitude and shape; or the lepidopterist who comes to discriminate various species of butterflies or other insects on the basis of what would be considered by most individuals to be very subtle and complex stimulus events that can come to control a scientist's behavior. Indeed, one might suggest that one of the main differences between the scientist and the "person on the street" is the fact that the scientist's behavior is often under the control of much more subtle properties of stimuli in the field in which he or she is considered an expert.

The Discrimination Training Procedure

Regardless of whether the control exercised by a stimulus is based on easily observable or rather subtle properties, the basic process by which antecedent environmental events acquire the ability to affect our behavior subsequently is the same. This process results from the discriminative training procedure (see Fig. 3.6).

As an example of how stimuli acquire discriminative properties, let us assume that an employee's supervisor, as well as a fellow worker named Mary Beth, serve as the antecedent stimuli for the employee's behavior in which we are interested. Suppose that, in the presence of the supervisor, the worker's task behavior is frequently reinforced by approval ($Sc+$). However, in the presence of Mary Beth, such behavior is not reinforced ($\overline{Sc}+$) because Mary Beth prefers to talk and expects her audience to listen and not to work. With regard to the supervisor, we say that the worker is differentially reinforced for task behavior. The supervisor, therefore, becomes a discriminative stimulus that signals positive reinforcement ($S_{D_{PR}}$) and that sets the occasion on which the worker's on-task behavior is likely to be reinforced ($S_{D_{PR(1)}} : R_1 \equiv Sc+$). Thus, in the supervisor's presence, performance should increase.

In the presence of Mary Beth (S_2), however, approval is not likely to follow behavior that leads to high levels of performance. Mary Beth, therefore, becomes a discriminative stimulus that signals extinction ($S_{D_{EXT(2)}} : R_1 \equiv \overline{Sc}+$). Thus, when Mary Beth is present, performance will normally decrease.

The occurrence of the discriminative training procedure in other organizational contexts, of course, produces other examples of $S_{D_{PR}}$'s and $S_{D_{EXT}}$'s. "Horseplay" on the part of a worker in front of his or her peers may be reinforced by their laughter whereas horseplay in front of the boss is unlikely to produce much merriment. A supervisor's "good mood" may indicate the time is "ripe" to ask for a raise; his or her "bad mood" may signal that discussion of the raise is best held for later. Discussions about management abuses will be reinforced by the attention of striking workers whereas apathy may be expressed by "scabs" or strikebreakers.

Of course, stimuli that set the occasion on which a response is to be reinforced or on which reinforcement is to be withdrawn do not exhaust the events that may acquire discriminative properties. A stimulus may also become an S_D if it is differentially associated with either the presentation or the withdrawal of an aversive stimulus. In the first case, the stimulus comes to set the occasion on which a particular response class (Ry) is punished ($Sc-$) and, therefore, becomes a discriminative stimulus that signals punishment (an $S_{D_{PUN}}$). Warning signs such as "Beware of Dog" or "Danger—Radioactive Material,"

ENVIRONMENTAL STIMULI *PRIOR TO* DISCRIMINATION TRAINING PROCEDURE

Two environmental stimuli that have not previously been associated with the operant response of interest and its consequent stimuli

S_1

S_2

OPERANT RESPONSE *PRIOR TO* DISCRIMINATION TRAINING PROCEDURE

One operant response

R_1

ENVIRONMENTAL STIMULI AND OPERANT RESPONSE *DURING* DISCRIMINATION TRAINING PROCEDURE

In the presence of one environmental stimulus (S_1), the operant response (R_1) is reinforced, whereas in the presence of the other environmental stimulus (S_2), the reinforcement is withdrawn when the operant response (R_1) is emitted. Thus, S_1 becomes a $S_{D_{PR}}$, and $S_{(2)}$ becomes a $S_{D_{EXT}}$.

$S_{(1)}$: R_1 ≡ $Sc+$ $\qquad$ $S_{(1)}$ $S_{D_{PR(1)}}$

$S_{(2)}$: R_1 ≡ $\overline{Sc}\pm$ $\qquad$ $S_{(2)}$ $S_{D_{EXT(2)}}$

EFFECT OF $S_{D_{PR(1)}}$ AND $S_{D_{EXT(2)}}$ ON THE *PROBABILITY* OF R_1, *AFTER* THE DISCRIMINATION TRAINING PROCEDURE

$S_{D_{PR(1)}}$ $(R_1 \uparrow\ )$ As a result of the training procedure, $S_{D_{PR(1)}}$ has become a discriminative stimulus, in the presence of which the probability of R_1 is increased.

$S_{D_{EXT(2)}}$ $(R_1 \rightarrow\ )$ As a result of the training procedure, $S_{D_{EXT(2)}}$ has become a discriminative stimulus, in the presence of which the probability of R_1 is decreased.

Figure 3.6 Schematic of the discrimination training procedure.

as well as threats and other verbal stimuli that precede a response and signal that it will be punished if it is emitted, are examples of stimuli that may become $S_{D_{PUN}}$'s.

Finally, an antecedent environmental event may acquire some control over a response if, when the response is emitted in its presence, it is differentially associated with the withdrawal of an aversive stimulus. Such a situation might occur when, in the presence of a particular supervisor, a request by an individual to work inside on a hot, humid day is granted. In this situation, the supervisor becomes a discriminative stimulus who signals negative reinforcement ($S_{D_{NR}}$) and in whose presence the request is followed by the withdrawal of the aversive stimulus of having to work in the hot sun. We would expect that the worker's requests to work inside will increase in the presence of this supervisor under similar conditions in the future.

When requests are made by a worker in order to *prevent* the occurrence of the aversive event (such as having to work outside on a hot day), they become a form of *avoidance behavior*. Other forms of avoidance responses are also prominent in organizational settings. On noting the approach of a fellow employee who has annoyed us, for example, we may make a "quick exit." In the presence of a supervisor who has shown her disgust with employees who talk while they are working, the employees may avoid discussion. Putting on a pair of safety goggles before lighting a cutting torch provides protection from the possible injury we may receive from flying sparks.

The reader may have recognized the similarity between avoidance behavior and the forms of escape behavior that we discussed earlier. Both of these types of behavior increase as a result of the occurrence of aversive stimuli. Avoidance behavior is made possible because a discriminative stimulus temporally precedes and, in a sense, signals that the terminal aversive event is forthcoming. Avoidance behavior is, therefore, associated with an $S_{D_{PUN}}$ that temporally precedes the response whereas escape behavior is not.

Experientially Developed Discriminative Stimuli

As indicated by a number of our previous examples, many stimuli acquire discriminative procedures as a result of prior reinforcement histories. Such stimulus events may be called *experientially developed* discriminative stimuli. Though experientially developed discriminative stimuli affect the way we respond in social settings (in the presence of supervisors, peers, subordinates, etc.), nonsocial environmental events also may acquire discriminative properties in this fashion. Thus, as a result of his experience, extremely "wet" mortar becomes a stimulus for a bricklayer to "roll" rather than to "pack" it. Open-grained wood becomes S_D for the wood finisher to use a filler before a stain is applied. And, to a welder, aluminum becomes a stimulus for different welding techniques than those used for iron.

A special case of a discriminative stimulus that is experientially developed and that frequently results from social interaction deserves special mention here because it may be used to facilitate the shaping as well as the emission of behavior that may otherwise occur at low operant levels. These stimuli have their characteristic effects on our behavior because we learn that the behavior of others frequently sets the occasion on which similar behavior on our part is likely to be reinforced. A young boy, for example, who sees his brother rewarded with candy by an uncle for turning a somersault may imitate his brother's behavior because he has learned that such behavior on his part is also likely to be rewarded by his uncle. In this particular situation, the behavior of his brother has become a stimulus that has acquired discriminative properties in such a way that it sets the occasion on which *imitative* behavior is likely to be reinforced. In other words, the behavior of the boy's brother has become a $S_{D_{PR}}$ for imitative operants. This, of course, is not the limiting case. The behavior of a model, as well as the consequences of that behavior, may also come to signal to an observer that imitative behavior on his or her part is likely to be followed by punishment ($S_{D_{PUN}}$), the removal of an aversive stimulus ($S_{D_{NR}}$), or the removal of a positive reinforcer ($S_{D_{EXT}}$). Because of the usefulness of imitative processes in language acquisition and in leadership, we will discuss them in greater depth in Chapters 5 and 8.

Contingency-Specifying Discriminative Stimuli

Not all stimuli acquire discriminative properties because of our direct experiences with them. We often respond to certain situations in characteristic ways because the contingencies have been pointed out or described to us. These descriptions serve as discriminative stimuli that specify the conditions under which a particular response will be reinforced or punished. Such discriminative stimuli may be called *contingency-specifying* discriminative stimuli.

As an example of a discriminative stimulus that specifies behavior, we may consider the situation in which a supervisor tells an employee, "In the presence of a red light on panel A, press button number 1 down to release the pressure so that the boiler does not explode." In this example, the contingency-specifying stimuli takes the form of a verbal instruction (as well as a warning or threat) on how to respond in order to avoid an aversive situation. Instructions comprise an important and widely used class of contingency-specifying discriminative stimuli for organizational behavior. Other important forms often utilized in organizational settings include policy statements, written procedures, directions on how to perform a task, job descriptions, and the advice of peers. Each of these is utilized in organizations to specify responses and, perhaps, their associated consequences. A job description, for example, specifies the behaviors considered necessary to perform a task properly. Advice from one's peers may provide suggestions on how to behave in the supervisor's presence or how to do a job more effectively. Threats may be used by a supervisor either to increase desirable task behavior ("If you don't increase your productivity, I'll have to let you go") or to decrease undesirable organizational behaviors ("Unless you stop disrupting your fellow workers, action will be taken to move you to another department").

Unfortunately, some supervisors use verbal warnings or threats of firing an employee as their *primary* forms of contingency-specifying stimuli. Numerous problems may result from this tactic. First, threats frequently produce emotional responses on the part of the individual who has been threatened. These emotional responses may, in turn, be incompatible with the desired behavior. Employees who are "upset" by a supervisor's threat are unlikely to be able to perform at their best. Second, the supervisor who frequently uses such tactics may become a conditioned aversive stimulus. In these cases, the employee may perform the desired behavior but only as an avoidance response when the supervisor is present. In the extreme case, we might expect the individual to avoid all contact with the supervisor by quitting his or her job or asking to be transferred. Finally, the employee may become aggressive when threatened. We are all aware of the aggressive behaviors that result when someone is "pushed too far." This type of behavior is, of course, not conducive to effective forms of organizational behavior.

Not all contingency-specifying discriminative stimuli are, of course, constructed for us by others. Once an individual has acquired a verbal repertoire, his or her own verbal responses may serve the function of a stimulus that acquires some control over other behaviors he or she emits. These contingency-specifying discriminative stimuli generated by the individual *may* be expressed as overt, vocal forms of verbal behavior. In many cases, however, they appear only at the covert level and are associated with our processes of "thinking." The importance of these covert forms of verbal behavior to other complex behavioral processes such as problem solving and decision making cannot be overlooked. For, in some situations, it is only through the process of generating discriminative stimuli that control our own subsequent behavior that we can maximize our reinforcers, minimize our punishments, and reduce the aversiveness that often accompanies the indecision as to what to do.

Stimulus Generalization

Individuals who are conditioned to behave in a given way in the presence of a specific stimulus tend to behave that way in the presence of other stimuli as well. These are normally stimuli that have a feature in common with the stimulus that has become an S_D or that differ from it only in a specific dimension such as size, location, or wavelength (Dinsmoor, 1970). The induction of the effects of one stimulus to another is called *stimulus generalization.*

A study conducted by Guttman and Kalish (1956) provides a good example of the basic form of stimulus generalization. These researchers divided 24 pigeons into four equal groups and trained the pigeons in each group to peck at a light that had a wavelength of either 530, 550, 580, or 600 millimicrons (Mu's) in order to receive food on a variable-interval schedule of reinforcement. As a test to determine whether generalization to wavelengths of light

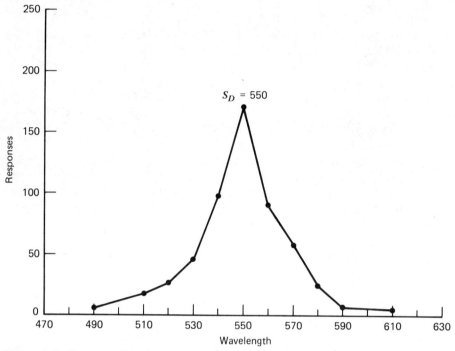

Figure 3.7 Example of stimulus generalization. The mean number of pecks occurring in the presence of each test stimulus after a training session in which pigeons were reinforced on a variable-interval schedule in the presence of a 550-millimicron light. *Source:* Adapted from Guttman and Kalish, 1956.

other than the one the subjects were trained on had occurred, the pigeons were exposed during various extinction periods to different wavelengths of light, and the number of responses made to each of these wavelengths was recorded. The resulting *generalization gradient* for subjects who were origi-nally trained at 550 millimicrons is shown in Figure 3.7. From this figure, it is evident that the key pecking response was evoked by other wavelengths of light (which ranged from 490 to 610 millimicrons) and that the closer in wave-length and stimulus presented in the extinction trial was to the one originally trained on, the greater the number of key pecks emitted by the pigeon.

The process of stimulus generalization is also observable in human affairs. Children who are learning to talk, for example, often use the response "Doggy" or "Kitty" to describe animals of just about any size or shape—including monkeys, ponies, and other small animals. Similarly, the word "Daddy" is often used to refer to all adult males whereas the response "Car" may be used for anything from a motorcycle to a diesel truck. Of course, children are not the only ones who "overgeneralize." Examples are evident in adult behavior also. The worker who had been reinforced for joking with his or her old supervisor may behave in the same manner in the presence of a newly appointed one. And the individual who is reinforced for "talking shop" with his or her fellow workers may also continue to carry on these discussions with family and friends outside of work.

The errors made by children or the tendency of some adults to over-generalize supply the most obvious instances of stimulus generalization. However, it is inappropriate to provide only what would appear to be undesirable examples of generalization. Generalization is an adaptive process that affects much of our behavior. No two stimulus events or situations we encounter are precisely the same. Generalizations allow us to respond to new or novel situations without having to learn new responses each time and, thus, save us much time and energy in the interactions we have with our environment. Generally, the more similar two stimuli are or the more common properties they share, the greater the generalization that will result.

Discriminative Stimuli and Conditioned Reinforcement

Discriminative stimuli are important to our analysis because of the control they acquire over operant responses. Once a discrimination has been established, the presentation of an $S_{D_{PR}}$ or $S_{D_{NR}}$ will increase the probability of a response whereas the presentation of an $S_{D_{EXT}}$ or $S_{D_{PUN}}$ will decrease the probability of a discriminated operant. However, such stimuli are of further import because they frequently acquire other characteristics. When an environmental event serves as a discriminative stimulus that sets the occasion for a response to be reinforced, that stimulus may—because of its pairing with the terminal reinforcing event—also become a conditioned positive reinforcer.

Cowles (1937) was among the first to demonstrate directly that a discriminative stimulus consistently associated with the acquisition of a primary reinforcer could itself acquire reinforcing properties. In one of his experiments, hungry chimpanzees were trained to put a token into a vending machine that would dispense food for each token that was inserted. In this fashion, tokens, which were neutral stimuli for the chimpanzees before the experiment began, were classically paired with food, a primary reinforcer. Following this and other training procedures that required the subjects to work for tokens that they could then exchange for food the chimps were found to learn new responses when the only immediately produced stimuli were the tokens. Thus, the tokens themselves had become conditioned reinforcers.

Additionally, indirect evidence that discriminative stimuli may acquire the characteristics of reinforcing events has been supplied bt Byrne and his colleagues (Byrne, 1971; Byrne and Clore, 1970; Kaplan and Olczak, 1970; and McDonald, 1962) in their analysis of factors that affect our interpersonal attraction or "liking" for others. In general, their research findings suggest that our liking or attraction for individuals who mediate reinforcers (which, as we have seen in Chapter 2 are generally described as being "liked") tends to increase whereas our liking and attraction for individuals who mediate punitive events (which are generally described as being disliked) tend to decrease. These results are what would be expected if neutral stimuli associated with reinforcing events become conditioned positive reinforcers and neutral stimuli associated with the presentation of aversive events become conditioned aversive stimuli or negative reinforcers.

Of course, even greater conditioning effects would be expected to result from those instances in which a discriminative stimulus is associated with a large variety of reinforcing events. In such cases, the discriminative stimulus not only affects the probability of subsequent behaviors but may also serve as an effective generalized reinforcer. As noted earlier, money is perhaps the prime example of a discriminative stimulus that can acquire the characteristics of a generalized positive reinforcer. Money reinforces behavior that produces it and also sets the occasion for other types of behavior to be reinforced. Thus, with money in hand, we can perform a number of responses— each of which has its own reinforcer.

On the other side of the coin, we generally find that negative evaluations such as criticism, ridicule, lack of acceptance by others, or indications of failure acquire the properties of generalized negative reinforcers. Thus, these stimuli often come to perform the dual functions of decreasing the probability of behavior that precedes them as well as serve as cues that the behavior that is emitted after their occurrence is also likely to be followed by punishment. As with generalized positive reinforcers, generalized negative reinforcers are relatively independent of the momentary deprivation levels of the individual and, therefore, serve as rather effective punitive events in organizational settings.

FOUR
THEORIES OF REINFORCEMENT

The principles of operant behavior discussed in Chapter 3 describe relations between the behavior of individuals and environmental events we call reinforcers. For many practical purposes, these principles are useful to management practitioners even though they may not know *why* a particular environmental event has the effects it does. For example, the practitioner can come to understand a great deal about the behavior of individuals in organizations by simply observing the frequency of a given operant response and then establishing a contingency between that response and a particular environmental event while noting any change in the frequency with which the response is emitted. If a stimulus event that follows a response increases the probability of the response's occurrence, that stimulus is a positive reinforcer. Conversely, a stimulus that follows a response and decreases the probability of its occurrence is a negative reinforcer.

Having determined by such a functional analysis that certain environmental events are reinforcing, an organizational leader can predict the effects these events will have on functionally equivalent operants under similar organizational conditions. Moreover, when it has been demonstrated that particular stimuli have effects on the individual's behavior under differing conditions (e.g., their reinforcing effects are demonstrated in other situational contexts), the practitioner may begin to develop a catalogue of events that serve a reinforcing function for that individual. Finally, recording those events that prove reinforcing to many individuals across numerous settings may provide an organizational leader with a list of reinforcers that will be effective in behavioral change efforts with a wide range of people in almost any organizational setting. To the degree that practitioners can manipulate these events, they will, of course, be able to influence or control the behavior of others.

As the preceding discussion suggests, we can learn a great deal about behavior in organizations and those environmental events that control it without worrying about *why* reinforcers have their characteristic effects. And one might make the assumption that reinforcing events have little in common apart from their power to reinforce the responses they follow. It is, however, both theoretically and practically important to determine why and how reinforcers work. Then, as noted by Berlyne (1967), we can increase our ability to identify reinforcing events before we have tried them out and can learn more about the conditions that make them effective.

> ... psychology will presumably not have finished its work until we can say what all reinforcing events have in common to make them capable of supplying reinforcement, so that we can predict whether or not an event will reinforce a response, and how powerfully, before we try it out. This is not only desirable from a theoretical point of view so that we can feel that we understand the phenomena in question. It may also have considerable practical importance. We are often told that current practices in child rearing, education, (business[1]), penology, and psychotherapy are less successful than they need to be because they schedule reinforcement inefficiently. An improvement in the timing of familiar reinforcing events can, according to proferred evidence, work wonders. But if we know more about how reinforcement works, we might be able to bring about desirable changes in behavior more successfully by using the most potent reinforcing agents as well as scheduling them appropriately [Berlyne, 1967].

Berlyne's point is well taken. The practitioner who not only understands the functional relationships between various environmental events and behavior, but who can also identify those events that are likely to prove reinforcing *prior* to their occurrence, would appear to be in a superior position with regard to effecting behavioral changes. The reinforcing properties of any stimulus are, of course, determined by the individual's genetic background, his or her prior conditioning history, and the reinforcing events presented or withdrawn just prior to—as well as concurrently with—the environmental event of interest. Only by examining the factors that determine why reinforcing events have their characteristic effects will the management practitioner come to understand more fully the rich complexity of the reinforcement process and the properties common to reinforcing events that distinguish them from other stimuli that do not effectively modify behavior.

CONTEMPORARY REINFORCEMENT THEORIES

Although a great deal of speculation as to the essential properties of reinforcing events has occurred over the years, the most widely recognized contemporary theories of reinforcement may be divided into three categories: need-reduction theories, response-based theories, and arousal theories of reinforcement. Each of the theories that fall into these general categories is useful in accounting for the reinforcing effects of some environmental events, and to that extent each contains a bit of useful information. However, few reinforcement theories are as comprehensive in their explanation or encom-

[1]Words in parentheses were added by the authors.

pass as many of the known facts about reinforcing events as an arousal theory does. Therefore, though we will briefly discuss some selective representatives of both need-reduction and response-based theories, we will concentrate primarily on an arousal interpretation of reinforcement in this chapter.

Need-Reduction Theories

Historically, need, or drive-reduction theories have been among the most widely utilized explanations of the reinforcement process. Proponents of these theories assert that the property common to all reinforcing events is that they reduce an individual's needs or drives. Early need theories focused on the reduction of *biological* or *tissue* needs as the defining properties of reinforcing events. In this formulation, needs were taken to be physiological imbalances, and reinforcers were described as those stimulus events that minimized or reduced these imbalances (Timberlake, 1980).

The basic simplicity of tissue and need-reduction models of reinforcement is quite appealing. These models suggest that when biological imbalances exist, any event that reduces this imbalance or that is associated with stimuli that reduce the imbalance will serve a reinforcing function. The greater the imbalance, the greater the need and, subsequently, the greater the reinforcing potential of the stimulus associated with the need's satisfaction.

Despite their intuitive appeal, need theories based on tissue imbalances have fared rather poorly when compared with the available empirical evidence. There are numerous stimulus events that have been known to produce reinforcement effects even though they violate tissue need-reduction assumptions. For example, several studies have shown that stimuli with no apparent biological need-reducing value may serve as reinforcing events. Saccharin, which is a nonnutritive sweetener that has no apparent biological value (and indeed may be carcinogenic), has been shown to be as effective a reinforcer for some species as food (Sheffield and Roby, 1950) or a nutritive (need-reducing) solution (Sheffield, Roby, and Campbell, 1954). These findings suggest that tissue need reduction is not a *necessary* condition for reinforcement. Other evidence has shown that biological need reduction is also not a *sufficient* condition for reinforcement. Richter (1942), for example, found that reinforcement did not necessarily occur even when tissue needs were reduced. These findings are difficult to reconcile with theories of reinforcement based on the assumption that tissue need reduction is both necessary and sufficient for reinforcement.

The hypothesis that reinforcers may be identified as those events that reduce biological needs or drives also has difficulty in accounting for the findings of experiments performed by Premack and his colleagues (Premack, 1959, 1962; Bauermeister and Schaeffer, 1974) and by Timberlake and Wozny (1979). These researchers have demonstrated that the reinforcement relationship between events considered to have need-reducing properties and other events that are not supposedly need-reducing could be reversed. That is, behavior associated with a specific need (e.g., eating) could be reinforced by an event with no specific need associated with it. However, perhaps the most frequently cited evidence against the tissue need-reduction hypothesis are studies that demonstrate that biologiclly "indifferent" events such as changes in illumination (Kish, 1955, 1966; Berlyne, 1967) and novel or complex stimuli (Berlyne, 1960, 1967), as well as the electrical stimulation of various neural structures in the lower parts of the brain (cf. Berlyne, 1967; Scott, 1966), could produce reinforcement. Because these stimulus event serve no obvious need or drive-reduction function and in many cases appear to involve *increases* rather than decreases in drive, they present considerable problems for biological need-reduction theories.

The difficulty posed for the early need-reduction theories led several researchers to become quite skeptical about the ability of these approaches to explain the reinforcement process. However, this is not to say that need-reduction theories were totally abandoned. There are several contemporary theories of human behavior and motivation that still incorporate need-reduction assumptions. Perhaps recognizing the problems encountered by early need-reduction approaches, most of these contemporary theories have judiciously avoided limiting the definition of needs to biological entities and have included under the rubric of needs various social and psychological entities as well. Maslow's (1943, 1954) theory of human motivation, for example, asserts that human needs may be classified not only into physiological and safety needs (which presumably are largely related to the biological requirements of the individual), but also into social, self-esteem, and self-actualization needs, which are social and psychological in nature. Similarly, Alderfer's (1972) redefinition of Maslow's needs into existence, relatedness, and growth needs also suggest an expansion of needs categories beyond the biological requirements of the individual.

Unfortunately, these more recent versions of need-reduction models are not without their own problems (Salancik and Pfeiffer, 1977). First, though many of the needs identified in these models are more complex than simple tissue needs, they also are more ambiguously defined and operationalized. Moreover, in many cases, there has been little effort made to describe the origins of these more complex needs or how they develop. Finally, as was the case with many of the simpler needs theories, the available empirical evidence has not been very supportive of many of the assumptions of the more elaborate need-reduction models.

Response-Based Theories

Though many of the early attempts to explain reinforcement favored the need-reduction hypothesis, some researchers felt that reinforcement effects might be better interpreted in terms of properties of the responses individuals make in various environmental settings. In general, these theorists suggest that the amount of time an individual spends performing a response when his or her behavior is unconstrained (e.g., when the individual is allowed free access to a particular environmental setting) is a measure of the relative value of that response as a reinforcing event for that individual.

David Premack was among the first proponents of a response-based theory of reinforcement. Premack's interest in the reinforcement process began while he was attempting to teach a visual language to cebus monkeys (Premack, 1976, p. xi). Quite by accident, he discovered that he could reinforce responses that were emitted by his subjects at a low rate with responses that were emitted at a high rate as long as a contingency was established that required the subjects to perform the lower probability behavior before they were allowed to perform the higher probability behavior. In subsequent research, Premack found that the relationship between the relative probabilities of various responses could also be used to produce reinforcement effects with human subjects. For example, in one study, Premack (1959) gave children the choice of eating candy or operating a pinball machine. He found that many of the children spent more time playing the pinball machines than eating candy. He then required these children to eat candy in order to play pinball. According to his theory, such a contingency should increase candy consumption. Consistent with this expectation, his findings showed that children who preferred playing with the pinball machine would increase their consumption of candy if playing pinball was made contingent on eating.

Further examination of these and other experimental findings led Premack (1959, 1965) to propose what has come to be called the prepotent-response or probability-differential hypothesis. This hypothesis states that *any* response in a particular situation that is relatively more probable, dominant, or prepotent will reinforce *all* less probable responses when the performance of the more probable response is made contingent on the performance of the less probable response. This hypothesis suggests that (1) virtually any response could be reinforced as long as a higher probability response was made contingent on its occurrence, (2) a lower probability response could not be used to reinforce a higher probability response, and (3) if the relative baseline probabilities of two responses could be reversed, their reinforcement relationship could also be reversed.

A sizable amount of evidence from research with both animal and human subjects has been presented in support of each of the above postulates of Premack's theory (cf. Premack, 1959, 1965, 1971). Nevertheless, the probability-differential hypothesis does not appear to be without its problems. The evidence cited earlier, (pp. 69–70) which shows that some events such as changes in illumination or electrical brain stimulation may produce reinforcement effects when they are made contingent on a particular response, is not easily explained by Premack's theory because few of those events have readily observable responses associated with them. Moreover, the findings of numerous researchers (e.g., Allison and Timberlake, 1974; Eisenberger, Karpman, and Trattner, 1967; Heth and Warren, 1978; Podsakoff, 1982), which show that a lower probability response can be used to reinforce a higher probability response under certain conditions and that the probability-differential condition is neither a necessary nor sufficient condition to produce reinforcement, make any speculation about the nature of reinforcement based on the probability-differential hypothesis questionable. Thus, even though Premack's hypothesis provides a novel and interesting account of reinforcement and is the predecessor of other response oriented theories (cf. Allison, 1976; Timberlake and Allison, 1974; Rachlin and Burkhard, 1978; Staddon, 1979) that have provided additional insights into the reinforcement process, it would appear that the probability-differential hypothesis does not provide an adequate account of reinforcement.

Arousal Theories of Reinforcement

Owing in part to the inability of need-reduction and response-based theories to encompass the great diversity and number of events that can produce reinforcement and in part to research that indicates the importance of various neural structures in the reinforcement process, a number of researchers in recent years have become interested in an arousal theory of reinforcement. Basic to this theory is evidence that suggests that different type of reinforcers produce similar neurophysiological effects and that the effects that reinforcers have are apparently mediated through a common mechanism—the reticular activating system—located for the most part in the lower portions of the brain. In general, it appears that an arousal theory is a better account of reinforcement than either the need-reduction or probability-differential approaches. We will, therefore, discuss the postulates of an arousal theory in some detail and point out some of this theory's implications for those interested in organizational behavior. In order to accomplish this, however, we must first examine some of the neurophysiological structures of the reticular activating system and the functions they serve.

THE RETICULAR ACTIVATING SYSTEM

The reticular activating system (*RAS*) is a primitive brain structure that starts to develop rather early in the life of a human embryo. It is located just above the spinal cord and, as shown in Figure 4.1, includes the medulla, pons, midbrain, and portions of the thalamus and hypothalamus. Numerous neural fibers that conduct nerve pulses outward from and inward to the reticular structure connect the RAS directly or via relays to parts of the cerebellum, spinal cord, limbic system, and the upper portions of the brain. This diffuse neural network (or reticulum) can be distinguished from the classical sensory pathways that transmit neural activity in a point-to-point fashion from the primary receptors (i.e., the skin, eyes, ears, nose, viscera, etc.) to relays located in the thalamus and then on to the principal sensory regions of the neocortex. Anatomically, the reticular formation is comprised of a dense network of neurons with multiple branches or relays that conduct activity from one neuron to another throughout the structure.

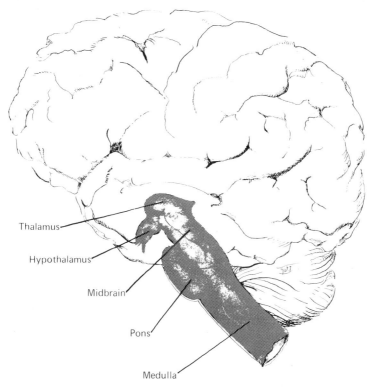

Figure 4.1 Illustration of the left side of a human brain depicting the medulla, pons, midbrain, thalamus, and hypothalamic portions of the brain stem reticular formation.

The reticular activating system receives neural connections from the classical sensory pathways (see Figure 4.2) and is activated when an environmental event elicits activity in any of our sensory receptors. Any stimulus activity received from the auditory, visual, olfactory, proprioceptive, or visceral receptors or a combination of them will travel up the neuron chain of the classical sensory pathways to the thalamic relays and on to the specific neocortical regions of the brain associated with that particular receptor. Activity in these pathways will continue only for as long as the receptor is stimulated. This activity in the specific projection system, however, will produce diffuse excitation in the reticular formation that continues for some time after the removal of the stimulus event.

The Functional Properties of the RAS

Reviews by Berlyne (1960, 1967), Samuels (1959), and Scott (1966) of various empirical findings have helped to identify the functional properties of the reticular activating system. A brief summary of these findings will prove useful in our present analysis. First, the reticular formation is the neural structure that is primarily involved in behavioral and neural activation (or arousal).

Specific neocortical receiving
area of the auditory receptor (ear)

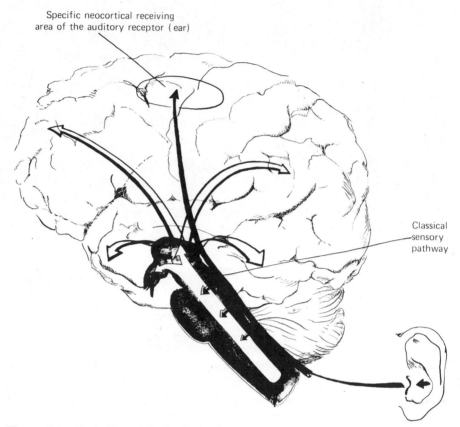

Classical
sensory
pathway

Figure 4.2 Illustration of the brain depicting how sensory input into a receptor (the ear) travels up the classical sensory pathways to a specific neocortical receiving area and via collaterals into the reticular formation from which diffuse neocortical activity is sustained beyond the presentation of the stimulation.

Moruzzi and Magoun (1949) were among the first to discover that electrical stimulation of the reticular formation changed the electroencephalograph (EEG) pattern characteristic of sleep to one corresponding to activation or alert wakefulness. Then Lindsley, Bowden, and Magoun (1949) found that when the reticular formation was surgically eliminated, the electroencephalograph recording changed to that of deep sleep or somnolence.

With all the reticular activating system intact, a sleeping animal may be aroused by electrical stimulation of the reticular formation, and at somewhat higher voltages the animal will awake, vocalize, and show signs of negative affect. With further increases in voltage, the animal will show abrupt arousal, extreme agitation, escape responses, and behavioral disorganization (Worden and Livingston, 1961). Conversely, studies by Lindsley et al. (1949) and French and Magoun (1952) have shown that lesions in the RAS with the classical sensory pathways intact produce a chronically comatose animal that cannot be aroused. Under this condition impulses from the various sensory modalities reach the cortex via the classical pathways, but EEG recordings indicate that this activity does not outlast the presentation of the stimulus. With the classical sensory pathways cut and the reticular formation intact, direct electrical stimulation of the reticular formation or its excitation by the stimulation of any peripheral nerve (auditory, proprioceptive, visceral, etc.) will produce behavior arousal that persists after stimulation has stopped (French, Amerongen, and Magoun, 1952; French and Magoun, 1952; Lindsley, Schreiner, Knowles, and Magoun, 1950).

Studies reviewed by Lindsley (1957, 1961) and Samuels (1959) have shown that neural connections from the ascending classical sensory pathways come together at the reticular activating system and that any receptor can produce an increase in reticular activity and, in turn, a diffuse activation pattern in the cortex. Further, reseach by French, Hernandez-Peon, and Livingston (1955) demonstrates that the stimulation of peripheral receptors (i.e., auditory, visual, tactile, etc.) is not the only way of producing increases in neural activity. Their findings indicate that stimulation of specific cortical areas also produces arousal. Thus, as Figure 4.3 indicates, projections from the cortex descending

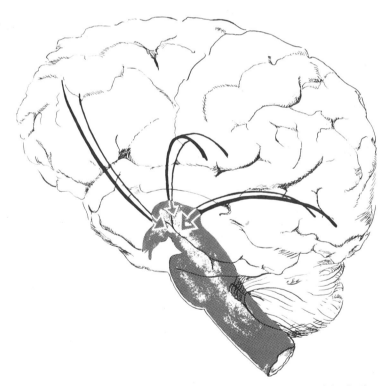

Figure 4.3 Illustration of how neocortical activity may initiate activity in the reticular activating system (RAS) and other related subcortical mechanisms.

down into the reticular formation provide a means for cortical influence on arousal.

> It is known, too, that the cortex itself sends many neural projections back down to the RAS (reticular activating system), and these interbrain connections can keep the activity in the RAS at a level sufficient for consciousness. We are all familiar with the fact that we can "think" ourselves into an excited state, or that thinking can keep us awake even when we have successfully shut off most sources of sensory stimulation [Hilgard and Bower, 1966, p. 441].

The "Pleasure" and "Punishment" Areas in the Brain

Discoveries by Olds and Milner (1954) imply that the neural activity (arousal) that results from stimulation of the reticular formation may also be the crucial factor in determining whether a stimulus event serves as a positive or negative reinforcer. Utilizing sophisticated equipment to implant electrodes into various neural systems in the brain, Olds and Milner (1954) discovered that when certain brain structures were stimulated, the stimulation produced a behavioral effect similar to that of positive reinforcement. For example, rats with electrodes implanted in certain localized areas of the hypothalamus would continue to depress a lever to get electrical stimulation. Working independently of Olds and Milner, Delgado and his associates (Delgado, Roberts, and Miller, 1954) demonstrated that the effects of such stimulation could also serve as a negative reinforcer (removal of which would increase response rates). With further technological improvements, Olds and his colleagues (Olds, 1956; Olds and Olds, 1963) proceeded to map the effects of electrical stimulation at various levels of the brain. They discovered that though stimulation of the upper cortical regions of the brain has almost no effect on subsequent behavior, implants in neural structures just above the reticular formation allowed the researchers to identify centers that mediate pleasure and pain. These structures, called the *medial forebrain bundle* (more commonly referred to as the reward center) and the *periventricular system* (more commonly referred to as the punishment center) are contained in the limbic system of the brain, which is comprised of the hypothalamus, the amygdala, the hippocampus, and the septal regions and which has a number of connections with the RAS.

Berlyne (1967) has noted the possible effects of the limbic system, the reward center and the punishment center in the reinforcement process. He suggests that there is a mutually inhibitory relationship between the reward center and the punishment center. Activity in the punishment center, which mediates feelings of pain or discomfort, for example, will suppress activity in the reward center, which mediates feelings of pleasure. When activity in the punishment center subsides, "rebound" activity will occur in the reward center. Quite possibly this "rebound" effect is responsible for the feelings of elation or relief we experience when an aversive stimulus is withdrawn or its intensity is decreased. Though the limbic system does not generate positive reinforcement directly, certain patterns of activity in this system appear to inhibit activity in the punishment center and, therefore, initiate neural responses in the reward center via disinhibition. Moderate stimulation of the reticular formation seems to produce a synchronized pattern of activity in certain areas of the limbic system. Although this activity is somewhat slow and rhythmic, it is accompanied by an arousal pattern in the cortex, and it also appears to inhibit activity in the punishment region of the limbic system. Positive affective feelings (joy, elation, pleasure, etc.) are likely to be the result. Intense stimulation of the reticular formation, on the other hand, appears to disrupt this rhythmic activity. At the same time, the punishment center, which is no longer inhibited by activity in the hippocampal region of the limbic area, becomes active, thereby inhibiting activity in the reward center. Negative affect, which is often correlated with pain, discomfort, or anxiety, is likely to be produced in such a condition. Although the evidence is less direct, extremely low levels of activity in the reticular formation also seem to produce similar kinds of negative affective feelings. We might speculate, therefore, that under conditions of restricted stimulation the pattern of hippocampal activity is also disrupted and again produces resultant activity in the punishment center of the brain.

Habituation Effects

A number of studies have demonstrated that the habituation phenomenon may also result from mediational processes in the reticular activation system (Groves and Lynch, 1972; Groves and Thompson, 1970; Sharpless and Jasper, 1956). That is, stimulation of any receptor that produces an increase in arousal will be followed by a subsequent decline when the stimulus is repeatedly presented. Sharpless and Jasper (1956), for example, found generalized cortical arousal to diminish rapidly with repeated presentations of auditory stimuli. After habituation had been established, increases in the arousal level could be obtained with changes in the frequency or pattern of the auditory stimulus or after a period of rest following discontinuation of the stimulus. Further studies reviewed by Worden and Livingston (1961) have indicated that habituation effects are primarily a function of the reticular formation. These researchers found that once habituation has been established, an anesthetic that acts on the RAS could be used to eliminate the habituation effect, and that once the animal recovers from its anesthetized condition, habituation effects are reinstated. Moreover, recent evidence from research performed by Groves and Lynch (1972) suggests that habituation phenomena may be traced to a form of synaptic depression in the RAS and that sensitivity to incoming stimulation will increase after the stimulus has been withdrawn for a period of time.

These habituation effects in the reticular formation may help to explain why environmental events that initially prove to be reinforcing will often lose their reinforcing properties with repeated presentations. For example, though movement in one's environment usually proves to be reinforcing, when those movements are repeated over and over within a short time period, the stimulation that those movements produce loses its reinforcing powers. This does not imply that all environmental events lose their arousal-producing or reinforcing properties in a similar fashion when administered repetitiously. For, as Duffy (1962) has pointed out, complex stimulus events, as well as those that prove to be of special significance to the individual, may actually increase arousal levels with repeated presentations. Generalized reinforcers, for example, that have been paired with a number of other reinforcing events and do not depend on the momentary condition of the individual to be effective, may retard habituation effects. Furthermore, extremely novel stimuli or intense stimuli that induce pain have also been shown to be quite resistant to habituation effects (Fiske and Maddi, 1961).

Primitive Approach and Avoidance Behavior

Finally, activation in portions of the upper brain stem has been suggested as the mediator of primitive approach and avoidance responses elicited by certain stimuli. Glickman and Schiff (1967) have pointed out the possibility that the evolutionary history of various organisms (presumably including human beings) has promoted the development of neural pathways that are uniquely sensitive to certain properties of stimuli external to the organism. They note that stimulation of certain portions of the upper brain stem will elicit primitive approach patterns such as investigatory and manipulatory activities as well as feeding, drinking, and sexual behavior if appropriate stimulus objects are available (e.g., water in the case of stimulation of those regions that elicit drinking responses). Stimulation of other nearby areas will produce defensive patterns such as freezing and withdrawl responses. Based on these and other observations, Glickman and Schiff suggest that primitive approach and withdrawal patterns are organized in some "preformed" state in the upper brain stem—quite possibly the medial forebrain bundle (or reward center) and the periventricular system (or punishment center). They conclude on the basis of their observations that the necessary and sufficient condition for reinforcement is activity in the neural systems described above. They also note that although peripheral reflex activity is often observed in the presence of certain reinforcers, it is not a necessary condition for reinforcement effects.

All in all, our brief summary suggests that the reticular activating system possesses a number of important functional properties. First, the reticular formation has been implicated as a necessary mediator of various types of behavioral arousal or activation. Second, arousal in the reticular formation and some related neural structures may be the crucial factor in determining the reinforcing properties of an environmental event. Moreover, the reticular formation also appears to be an important mechanism in habituation phenomena. The present evidence suggests that habituation may result from a form of synaptic depression in the reticular formation and that increased sensitivity will occur when the stimulus is withdrawn for a period of time or the parameters of the stimulus (e.g., its intensity) are altered. Finally, it has been suggested that neural activity in regions just above, but connected with, the upper portions of the reticular formation (quite possibly in the medial forebrain bundle and the periventricular system), mediate various forms of primitive approach and avoidance responses.

POSTULATES OF AN AROUSAL THEORY OF REINFORCEMENT

Based on the extensive investigations and evidence regarding the reticular formation and its associated neural activity, a number of postulates may be suggested regarding relationships between environmental events, arousal levels, and reinforcement processes. For the most part, these postulates refer to events or responses that occur beneath the skin, but that are, nevertheless, observable with proper instrumentation.

We shall begin with a postulate about the concept of arousal itself. For our purposes, it is most fruitful to conceive of arousal as the degree of generalized excitation in the reticular formation of the brain. As such, arousal may be said to exist along a neurophysiological continuum from low through moderate to high levels. Such neural activity often is associated with various behavioral manifestations ranging from comatose states through alert attentiveness to extreme forms of agitation and possibly convulsions as activity in the reticular formation varies from minimal to maximal levels. This has led at least one researcher (Duffy, 1957, 1962) to suggest that a definition of arousal should include both behavioral as well as neurophysiological responses. However, because no organism is equally activated in all of its parts and because the correlaton between neurophysiological and specific behavioral responses is seldom very high, we prefer to limit the definition of arousal more precisely to that activity or excitation that occurs in the reticular activating system. The definition of the term *arousal* utilized here is, therefore, in close accord with those given by Fiske and Maddi (1961), Malmo (1959), and Scott (1966).

Our second postulate concerns the variables that produce changes in arousal levels. Many of the studies reviewed up to this point suggest that an individual's level of arousal at any particular point in time will be determined by the amount or type or both of interoceptive, exteroceptive, and cortical stimulation he or she receives during that period. Thus, an individual's arousal level will be expected to change from moment to moment depending on the nature of the stimulation the reticular formation receives from sensory and cortical sources. Low levels of arousal will result when stimulation is limited, restricted, or repetitious. Intermediate levels of arousal are produced from moderate stimulation, and high arousal levels result when the reticular formation is excessively stimulated.

In addition to the rather immediate effects it has on arousal levels, incoming stimulation may also have an indirect influence on subsequent levels of neural activity in the reticular formation. For example, the neural excitation provided by an external stimulus such as a loud, unexpected noise may produce a number of "emotional" and primitive avoidance responses that continue to provide internal stimulation and thus maintain arousal at a high level even after the initial stimulus has subsided. Similarly, novel or complex stimuli—or those that have acquired special significance to the individual because they have been paired with other arousal-inducing events—may maintain or even increase the level of arousal for some period of time after the original source of stimulation has been removed.

Previously received stimulation may also have indirect effects on the arousal-producing ability of current stimuli. Owing to the habituation phenomena, the ability of most continually presented stimuli to sustain neural excitation is limited. When first administered, a particular stimulus may produce high levels of arousal. However, with repeated presentations of this stimulus, arousal levels will gradually decline from high through moderate to low levels if no other form of stimulation is forthcoming. Repetitiously presented stimuli, therefore, generally have a steadily decreasing effect on arousal level and will not sustain a given level for very long periods of time without additional stimulation.

Other variables, of course, affect the sensitivity of the reticular formation and the changes that occur in any particular individual's arousal level. A person's genetic makeup, for example, undoubtedly affects the biochemical composition of the reticular structure and, thus, its sensitivity to incoming stimulation. Moreover, this structure is also subject to enduring and perhaps major modifications after this period as a result of the individual's conditioning history. Of course, lesions of the reticular formation produced by an accident, injury, or operation could permanently modify its sensitivity, and the use of some drugs may produce sizable but temporary modifications in this neural structure. Furthermore, the diurnal patterns of sleep and activity could also affect relatively small cyclical modifications in the sensitivity of the reticular formation to arousal level changes; that is, continued activity may produce true neural fatigue and decreases in sensitivity whereas sleep would restore it to its original level.

Finally, it may be postulated that stimulus events characterized as positive or negative reinforcers have these properties by virtue of their effects on the level of activity in the RAS and surrounding structures. More specifically, stimuli producing intermediate levels of arousal act as positive reinforcers by virtue of their presumed ability to elicit neural activity in both the hippocampal region and in the reward centers of the brain. Stimuli that are identified as positive reinforcers, in other words, are positively reinforcing because they produce intermediate levels of arousal. In general, these stimuli will increase the probability of behavior upon which they made contingent; evoke approach responses; and are often described as pleasant, enjoyable, or satisfying by the individual. On the other hand, environmental events producing either high or low levels of arousal act as aversive stimuli by virtue of their presumed ability to produce activity in the periventricular system (punishment center) and to inhibit activity in the medial forebrain bundle (the reward center). These stimuli will generally decrease the probability of responses that follow them; evoke escape and avoidance behavior; and are frequently described as painful, annoying, or distasteful. Escape from aversive stimuli is postulated to be reinforcing (a negative reinforcement effect) because it reduces activity in the punishment center and produces "rebound" activity in the reward center. Finally, we postulate that the removal or withdrawal of a positive reinforcer is punishing because it reduces activity in the reward center of the reticular activating system.

An important corollary of the postulate that environmental events are reinforcing by virtue of their ability to elicit neural activity in the reticular formation is that the efficacy of a stimulus as a reinforcing event is subject to modification as our exposure to it increases. A moderately novel or new task that an individual is asked to perform, for example, may initially produce intermediate levels of arousal and, therefore, be reinforcing even if it is relatively simple and requires repetition. However, as the individual becomes familiar with his or her surroundings and continues to behave in a repetitive fashion, activity in the reticular formation declines to a low level, and task performance may become rather aversive unless supplementary stimulation is provided. The expressions of boredom or monotony made by some assembly-line workers after only a few weeks on the job are perhaps among the best examples of the verbal reports that may accompany repetitious tasks and, presumably, low arousal levels.

Stimulus Determinants of Arousal

Having outlined the fundamental postulates of an arousal interpretation of reinforcement, we are now in a better position to examine in greater detail the relationships between environmental stimuli and arousal levels. Our second postulate suggests that the characteristics or properties of environmental stimuli are among the most important determinants of neural excitation in the reticular activating system. To a large extent, much of the literature reviewed up to this point suggests which stimulus properties are most important in producing arousal. Nevertheless, the analysis of these properties by themselves is of some value.

The reticular formation receives collateral neural tracts from the classical sensory pathways, and, as we know, stimulation of any receptor produces changes in arousal. We might, therefore, expect that virtually *any* stimulus could act as a reinforcer under suitable conditions. Support for this proposition is offered by a host of studies in the field of sensory reinforcement that have shown that light onset (and offset), auditory, kinesthetic, gustatory, and tactile stimulation will reinforce responses on which such stimuli are made contingent (Kish, 1966). Furthermore, Kish has noted, as have others, that prolonged exposure to a sensory stimulus such as light onset leads to a weakening of its reinforcing properties, which recover again when the stimulus is withdrawn for some period of time. Reversal effects have also been observed. That is, a stimulus event will function as a reward *or* as a punisher depending on the subject's prior exposure to it and the intensity of the stimulus. Similar effects have been observed in the case of conventional reinforcers (Berlyne, 1967; Fowler, 1971; Premack, 1971). A given food stimulus, for example, will not act as a reinforcer for animals that have recently been fed. Moreover, mild electric shocks have been found under some conditions to serve as positive reinforcers. It is obvious, therefore, that the reinforcing potential of conventional reinforcers is not a fixed value and that the factors that affect the reinforcing potential of conventional rewards are similar to those that determine the reinforcement value of sensory stimuli.

Though it seems plausible to conclude that all reinforcing stimuli work through their ability to effect changes in arousal level, it does not appear that all stimuli are equally effective in doing so. As a consequence, a number of writers (e.g., Berlyne, 1967; Fiske and Maddi, 1961; Kish, 1966) have attempted to delineate the variables that affect the arousal-producing properties of stimuli. Quite naturally, their proposals reflect the evidence presented in the earlier parts of this chapter and in a sense summarize it.

Stimulus Novelty.   It seems clear that one variable that determines the degree of arousal produced by a stimulus and, therefore, its reinforcing value is its *novelty* at the time of presentation. A stimulus can be absolutely novel, never before encountered by the subject, or relatively novel, depending on the amount of time since it was last encountered. Relatively novel stimuli generally evoke approach behavior suggesting intermediate levels of arousal. By our definition, such stimuli are positively reinforcing. Stimuli that are absolutely novel to the subject have been found to evoke withdrawal reactions and behavior suggesting a high degree of arousal. By our definition, such stimuli are aversive. However, with continued exposure, absolutely novel stimuli lose their aversive properties, taking on positive reinforcement value that gradually diminishes as exposure is prolonged. In view of the role of the reticular formation in stimulus habituation affects, novelty appears to be one of the more straightforward variables influencing the degree of arousal produced by a stimulus and may merely express the degree to which prior exposure to the stimulus has led to habituation.

Stimulus Intensity.   The physical *intensity* of a stimulus, at least in the cases where it can be readily assessed, is another variable influencing the degree of arousal produced by a stimulus. As in the case of novelty, high levels of intensity are aversive. Few of us would find the sound of church bells positively reinforcing if we were standing right next to them and received the full force of their sound when they were chimed. Heat from the sun may not prove enjoyable—even to the sun worshiper—when the temperature is 125° F. Like-wise, a dip in a spring that is 33° F. will not prove rewarding to most people. However, the sound of bells, the warmth of the sun, and cool water do prove reinforcing for many individuals when they are presented at intermediate levels of intensity.

Stimulus Complexity.   The *complexity* of a stimulus is another property thought to influence arousal level and, consequently, its reinforcement poten-tial. If, as Berlyne (1966) has suggested, complexity increases with the num-ber of distinguishable elements comprising the stimulus and the dissimilarity between those elements, then habituation should proceed more slowly with complex stimuli. However, that may not inevitably be the case, and there is the possibility that a complex stimulus is simply more likely to be novel or that it may impact on more that one sensory modality. Therefore, it seems to us that a satisfactory conceptual analysis of complexity remains to be accomplished. If such a conceptualization of complexity can be achieved, we would expect that moderate levels would prove positively reinforcing whereas high levels would prove aversive.

Sensory Modalities.   It also appears that stimulation of the various *sensory modalities* produces differential arousal effects. Bernhaut, Gelhorn, and Ras-mussen (1953) have reported that proprioceptive stimulation elicits wide-spread cortical arousal followed by auditory and visual stimuli in that order. Though to our knowledge it has not been reported, it seems probable that tactile stimuli of moderate intensity would rank near proprioceptive stimula-tion in their arousal effects, for many skin receptors resemble proprioceptors and send information to the central nervous system through the same routes (Milner, 1970).

Commonsense observations suggest that there are classes of stimuli that have more powerful reinforcing effects than the so-called sensory reinforcers and do not as readily exhibit habituation or reversal effects with prior expo-sure. For example, very intense tactile stimuli, strong enough to elicit pain (Casey, 1973), do not habituate as quickly as mild tactile stimulation, nor do they readily become positive reinforcers with repeated exposure. And con-ventional food rewards for animals do not often serve to suppress responses on which they are made contingent, even with prolonged deprivation, and they appear to habituate more slowly with prolonged exposure than most kinds of sensory stimuli. Quite possibly, conventional reinforcers are more powerful and habituate less readily than sensory stimuli either because they occur at a given level of intensity or are stimulus compounds or both. Most foodstuffs that serve as effective positive reinforcers, for example, are mild visual stimuli, olfactory stimuli, and, when manipulated and ingested, tactile, proprioceptive, and gustatory stimuli. Similarly, conventional or formal organi-zational reinforcers such as money may be more effective than sensory rein-forcers because they have been paired with any of a number of visual, olfactory, tactile, and gustatory stimuli of moderate complexity, intensity, and novelty or because they set the occasion on which various behaviors may be performed that produce stimuli possessing such properties. A sensory stimulus such as a light source, on the other hand, rarely gives off odors (as does food), nor is it usually associated with tactile, proprioceptive, or gustatory stimuli.

In summary, evidence from a wide variety of sources indicates that though stimuli vary in their reinforcing potential, virtually any stimulus can serve as a reinforcer under suitable circumstances. The reinforcing potential of a stimulus is variable, however, and depends on its intensity, novelty, and complexity at the time it is introduced. Prolonged exposure to a reinforcing stimulus reduces its reinforcing effectiveness and may even reverse its effects, and the withdrawal of the stimulus for significant periods of time will serve to reinstate its reinforcing effects.

ELICITING PROPERTIES OF REINFORCING EVENTS

Our preceding analysis suggests that one property common to all reinforcing events is that they elicit psychoneural activity; that is, neural activity in the reticular activating system and activity in the reward and punishment centers of the hypothalamus. This psychoneural activity is often accompanied by other forms of respondent activity, including changes in autonomic responses such as salivation, sweat gland activity, and heart and respiratory rates and is sometimes accompanied by species-typical approach and consumatory responses or escape and defensive responses. As noted earlier, these psychoneural, species-typical and autonomic respondents do not necessarily vary together in a fixed pattern, and, in fact, a stimulus may be a powerful reinforcer even when it does not elicit respondent behavior that can easily be observed at the periphery of the body. But we can be certain that a reinforcing event will elicit respondent behavior, and for that reason we must expand the basic three-term contingency described in Chapter 3 to include a fourth term. Thus, we have:

$$Ss : Rx \equiv Sc \rightarrow r$$

where r refers to the respondent or respondents elicited by ($\rightarrow$) the Sc.

Ramifications of the Four-Term Contingency

The addition of the fourth term (r) into our analysis of the principles of human behavior has several important ramifications. The most obvious one is that when an operant (Rx) is followed by a reinforcing event (Sc), certain features of the setting (Ss) will be effectively paired with the Sc. For that reason, various features of the Ss will come to elicit some portion of the respondent pattern (r) elicited by the Sc. For example, if the behavior (or the results of the behavior) of a group member is especially reinforcing for the leader, the behavior of that group member and other features of the setting will come to elicit respondents in the leader that could be described as feelings of satisfaction, admiration, or attraction toward the group member. If the leader, in turn, administers positive consequences to the group member, the leader's presence will elicit the same sort of respondent reactions in the goup member. Conversely, if the group member's operants or the results of his or her operants are aversive to the leader, the mere presence of the group member and other features of the setting will come to elicit respondents in the leader that could be described as tension, anger, and dislike of that group member. The leader will not readily approach the group member and may show a tendency to turn away from, avoid, or agress against him or her, though the latter behavior is likely to be learned operant behavior rather than elicited respondent behavior. If the leader administers aversive events (negative reinforcers or punishment) to the group member, then the leader may be one who is avoided and who will otherwise elicit the same pattern of respondents in that group member. (An effective leader will be required to administer punitive consequences on occasion, but, as we shall note in Chapter 8, this can be accomplished without establishing strong or long-lasting respondent reactions that could be described as tension, anger, or avoidance).

The conjunction of behavioral and environmental events we have just described may lead one to the conclusion that features of the setting, including the presence of others, come to elicit conditioned respondents that serve as "causes" of operant behavior. Laymen and scientists alike have from time to time proposed that satisfaction or attitudes cause performance. However, we know that is not the case. Conditioned respondent behavior has been observed to occur after and during operant behavior as well as before it occurs. In some of these instances, elicited respondents may have little or no effect on operant responding. But the fact that conditioned respondents are merely collateral responses does not mean that important interactions do not occur. Respondent behavior elicited by reinforcing stimuli or features of the setting in which those stimuli are introduced may be compatible with and facilitate ongoing operant behavior. In these instances, the features of the setting may eventually not only come to set the occasion for operants of a particular class to be emitted but also will elicit respondents that facilitate the emission of those operants.

On the other hand, respondent behavior, conditioned or otherwise, may be so prominent or incompatible with operant responses that these disrupt or interfere with its emission. Many of us have experienced a situation in which an extremely aversive stimulus, such as a quickly approaching automobile, a snake in our path, or a sudden fright has caused us to "freeze" or be paralyzed with emotion. These examples are, or course, extreme. Nevertheless, one of the major effects of many punitive stimuli is to cause respondents to be elicited that are incompatible with the emission of a large variety of operant behaviors. Potent reinforcers, or course, may also disrupt rather than enhance the occurrence of operant responses. For example, the elation experienced by a mother who finds her lost child may prove so strong that all she can do is "cry for joy." However, whether the situation includes potent reinforcing or aversive stimuli, when respondents are elicited that are incompatible with operant responding, such respondents may preclude or interfere with the operant's occurrence.

IMPLICATIONS OF AN AROUSAL THEORY OF REINFORCEMENT

Arousal Theory and Task Behavior

An arousal theory of reinforcement points to the significance of certain stimulus events heretofore unrecognized as having reinforcing potential. Many such events are an integral part of tasks and the manner in which they are designed and as such may be called "intrinsic" reinforcers. When such reinforcing events are low in number or when they are repeatedly presented, behavioral quality (i.e., performance) should suffer. The behavioral consequences of tasks that require the constant repetition of a limited number of responses can, therefore, be anticipated.

As an individual becomes familiar with his or her task surroundings and learns the responses required in a repetitive task, a decline in arousal level is expected. If arousal decreases to a low level, the individual will generally experience negative affect and may attempt to increase arousal via various forms of *impact-increasing* behavior (Fiske and Maddi, 1961; Scott, 1966). If he or she is prevented from engaging in impact-increasing behavior, the result will most likely be a continuous decline in performance. When confronted with these circumstances, the individual may temporarily or permanently leave the task situation if these alternatives are readily available. If, however, the individual is successful in increasing stimulus impact, the result would be an increase in the arousal level and positive affect. The quality or quantity of performance or both may then be restored to the original level depending on the nature of the impact-increasing behavior.

It may be noted that any of the wide range of impact-increasing behaviors may be utilized to change arousal levels. The individual may increase proprioceptive stimulation and thus sustain arousal levels by stretching, alternating positions, or otherwise varying his or her position at the task site. Leaving to visit the water fountain, another department, or the rest room not only increases proprioceptive stimulation but also results in greater stimulus variation. Additionally, cortical stimulation resulting from thoughts of an anticipated fishing trip, the recall of a recent encounter with a sexual partner, or "daydreaming" about possible future encounters may similarly offset a decline in arousal level. Social activities, including conversation with fellow employees, the development of complex group relationships, gambling, and horseplay, also introduce variation in the task environment that may serve to increase one's arousal level.

It should be obvious that much of the impact-increasing behavior that is described above and that is generally available to the individual is extrinsic to the task and may be incompatible with task performance. If the impact-increasing behavior is incompatible with task performance, we have the possibility of obtaining sustained arousal levels and "high morale" but low performance. If, on the other hand, the impact-increasing behavior does not interfere with task performance, we have the possibility of attaining a successful adaptation to a repetitive task.

The individual may also introduce variation into the task itself. Individuals confronted with a repetitive task of long duration may be observed dividing the total task into discrete units and then responding until each unit is complete. The experience seems to be pleasant and associated with a feeling of reduced effort (Baldamus, 1951, p. 42). This type of variation is probably most effective where the individual can arbitrarily set intermediate goals, can obtain immediate feedback regarding progress as responding continues, and can be reasonably certain of a change in activity such as a rest period when the goal is reached. This is only one example of what must be a wide variety of ways of increasing functional variation by modifying the task itself. If the individual is successful, the effect may be to sustain arousal level over a long period of time, in which case there is the possibility of continued high performance and moderately high morale in what is otherwise a repetitive task.

Managers may also introduce variation extrinsic to the task. The anticipation of monetary rewards or a promotion may effect some changes in activation level as may rest periods or the introduction of music into the work setting. However Scott's (1966) review of the literature suggests that the effects of introducing variation extrinsic to a repetitive task may not be as effective as introducing variations into the task itself.

From an arousal interpretation, it may be anticipated that as more variation is introduced into a repetitive task, the result would be a reduction in habituation and a sustained arousal level closer to that required for optimal behavioral efficiency. If the increase in variation results in an intermediate level of arousal or perhaps just above that level so that responding to the task results in consistent shifts back to the norm, increases in performance and positive affect could be expected. Thus, in repetitive tasks that typically produce low levels of arousal, variation intrinsic to the task that requires the individual to attend to stimulation of greater variety or complexity or both should have more potential for effecting long-run productivity and satisfaction than variations extrinsic to the task.

Arousal Theory and Accident Behavior

Another important variable in organizations that may be accounted for by an arousal interpretation of reinforcement is accident behavior. Behavior on the part of an individual that leads to injury to himself or herself or others or to damage to the equipment or products he or she is working on is often found to occur with greater frequency when an individual is asked to perform a very novel or complex task, when environmental stressors are present, or after the individual has performed a repetitive task for an extended period of time. Though each of these types of increases in accident frequency could possibly be accounted for by a separate theory, an arousal interpretation of these events provides a more parsimonious explanation.

When an individual is assigned to a new job or jobs, he or she often encounters a number of rather novel or complex stimuli or both in the form of new tasks and unfamiliar people and surroundings. As is the case with other novel and complex stimuli, those associated with new tasks and their physical and social environments will often produce high levels of arousal. The behavioral accompaniments of these high arousal levels may include slower reaction times, responding inappropriately to various task and environmental cues, and, in the extreme, some loss of muscular control—all of which are likely to increase the probability of an accident. This is especially likely in those situations where machinery is being used that requires the individual to perform a rather complex chain of responses in order to complete his or her tasks.

With continued exposure to the novel or complex stimuli that comprise the new tasks, an individual's arousal may, of course, decline toward an intermediate level. If arousal is kept at or around this level, we should expect an improvement in behavioral efficiency (i.e., faster reactions times, an improved ability to make appropriate discriminations, etc.), and, therefore, a reduction in the number of accidents. If, however, the new tasks or their environmental surroundings acquire aversive properties because they have been paired with actual injury to the individual or with reprimands from his or her supervisor for damage to company equipment, carelessness, or an inordinately high percentage of rejects, high levels of arousal may be sustained over long periods of time with the result that accidents will continue to occur with a relatively high frequency.

As in the case of extremely novel or complex task environments, both temporary and long-term environmental stressors such as intense heat and humidity and loud noises also have been found to produce high arousal levels (Teichner, 1968) and performance decrements (Wilkinson, 1969). The effects of any particular stressor may, of course, be moderated by factors such as the length of time one has undergone stress while performing the task, the individual's familiarity with the work he or she is to perform, and the presence of other stressors in the work situation (Wilkinson, 1969). Nevertheless, from our present point of view, environmental stressors and extremely novel and complex tasks are similar in that they are both associated with high levels of arousal and are, therefore, negative reinforcers that elicit emotional behavior that may be incompatible with functional operant responses. With the introduction of environmental stressors into an individual's task environment, therefore, we would expect arousal levels to increase and behavioral efficiency to decrease. Under these conditions, accidents are likely to become more numerous and remain at relatively high levels until habituation to the stressor has occurred or until the stressor has been removed from the task environment. At that time, the individual's arousal level should decline, and behavioral efficiency should move closer to an optimal level, producing a decrease in the number of accidents.

Managers may, of course, develop methods for eliminating the undesirable effects that environmental stressors and novel tasks have on accident behaviors. As a first step they can identify and remove environmental stressors from the working environment. When this is not possible, providing the employee with protective devices such as earplugs or insulated clothing may be effective. And where the novelty or complexity of the task environment is of concern, training programs aimed at familiarizing the individual with his or her surroundings may be helpful.

Accident behaviors also have been found to increase in frequency under conditions of low arousal that may result from those situations in which an individual is required to perform a repetitive task that has little stimulus variability. In a series of studies on worker efficiency, for example, Bills (1931) found that individuals engaged in repetitive work show lapses in attention that resulted in performance decrements and an increase in the likelihood of accidents. Based on an arousal interpretation of reinforcement, we might predict that accidents are more probable in repetitive task environments not only because low arousal levels are often accompanied by lapses in attention or by a lack of alertness and relatively inefficient behavior but also because much of the impact-increasing behavior that is likely to occur under these conditions (e.g., daydreaming, horseplay, leaving one's work station for a period of time, etc.) is not compatible with safe task performance. In these instances, an arousal interpretation of reinforcement would predict that increasing arousal to an intermediate level by the introduction of greater task variety or scheduling stimulus events more effectively or both should have a favorable effect on decreasing accidents.

Arousal Theory and Employee Performance and Satisfaction

An arousal interpretation of reinforcement may also facilitate our understanding of the relationship between employee performance and satisfaction. There has been a long-standing interest among behavioral scientists regarding the relationship between employee productivity and job satisfaction (cf. Kornhauser and Sharp, 1932; Brayfield & Crockett, 1955; Kahn, 1960; Greene, 1972). Traditionally, it has been assumed that the individual who is satisfied or whose morale is high will produce more than the individual who is dissatisfied or whose morale is low. In other words, much conventional wisdom suggests that satisfaction causes performance. This presumed causal relationship between satisfaction and performance is, however, not obvious to those researchers who have submitted these phenomena to an empirical test. Nevertheless, a number of current speculations and theories of organizational behavior reviewed by Schwab and Cummings (1970), Greene (1972), Organ

(1977), and Salancik and Pfeffer (1977) still imply that satisfaction and task performance are related in a causal fashion although, in some cases, the presumed cause has now become the effect.

In contrast to these speculations, an arousal interpretation suggests that there is no inherent relationship between satisfaction and performance and that, as a matter of fact, one can produce just about any relationship between self-reports of satisfaction and performance one wishes. Briefly speaking, our analysis suggests that reinforcing events may be administered contingent on performance, in which case their occurrence serves to influence subsequent performance. When administered shortly after the emission of desirable task behavior, for example, positive reinforcers increase the probability of that behavior in the future. But whether reinforcement is contingent or *not,* it is also true that the occurrence or withdrawal of reinforcers produces changes in an individual's arousal level and other respondent behaviors. The presentation of a positive reinforcer or the withdrawal of a negative reinforcer, for example, produces movement toward an intermediate level of arousal and may be accompanied by self-reports of pleasure or satisfaction. The presentation of a negative reinforcer or the removal of a reward, on the other hand, usually results in high arousal levels that are accompanied by self-reports of anxiety, fear, and, in the extreme, pain.

Following this line of reasoning, we may conclude (1) that there is no inherent relationship between employee satisfaction and performance; (2) that variations in arousal and, therefore, in satisfaction are caused by the occurrence, nonoccurrence, and other properties of the reinforcing stimulus; and (3) that one can produce varying degrees of covariation between satisfaction and performance by varying the contingencies between performance and reinforcing events. Put more simply, rewards—whether contingent or not—cause satisfaction whereas rewards based on current performance produce subsequent performance.

Cherrington, Reitz, and Scott (1971) were among the first to test empirically the relationships between monetary rewards, satisfaction, and performance in a laboratory study. These researchers had subjects perform a task for two pay periods in which they were told they could receive a bonus (reward) if they performed well, thus suggesting that high performers would receive a bonus and low performers would not receive a bonus. In actual fact, however, Cherrington, et al. (1971) administered the bonus on a random basis at the end of the first pay period so that both high and low performers had an equal probability of receiving it. This meant that some subject were rewarded according to *appropriate* contingencies (e.g., high performers who actually received the bonus or low performers who did not receive the bonus) whereas other subjects were rewarded *inappropriately* (high performers who did not receive the bonus or low performers who did receive the bonus).

Based on an arousal interpretation of reinforcement, we would predict that for subjects who received the bonus, arousal would move toward its characteristic level and, therefore, these subjects would be more satisfied than those who didn't receive the bonus, regardless of their performance levels. We would also predict that the performance of subjects in the second period of the study would depend on the nature of the contingency established in the first period of the study. More specifically, in the second period of the study we would expect that subjects who were rewarded appropriately during the first period would outperform those who had been rewarded inappropriately.

Cherrington, Reitz, and Scott (1971) found support for all the above predictions. Subjects who received the bonus were more satisfied in general and with their pay, fellow workers, and the task itself than subjects who did not receive the bonus, regardless of their performance levels. These findings provide support for the proposition that rewards cause satisfaction. In addition, Cherrington et al. also reported that appropriately rewarded subjects performed significantly higher in the second period of the study than did those who were inappropriately rewarded, providing support for the proposition that performance is a function of the contingency established between prior performance levels and the rewards received for that performance.

Results similar to those obtained by Cherrington, Reitz, and Scott (1971) with respect to the effects of monetary reinforcers on performance and satisfaction have also been reported in several other laboratory (Baird and Hamner, 1979; Farr, 1976) and field (Greene, 1973, Greene and Podsakoff, 1978; Jorgenson, Dunnette, and Pritchard, 1973) settings. When taken together with the generally supportive results obtained from other field studies designed to examine the relationships between leader reward and punishment behaviors and subordinates' performance and satisfaction (cf. Greene, 1976; Hunt and Schuler, 1976; Keller and Szilagyi, 1976; Podsakoff, Todor, and Skov, 1982; Podsakoff, Todor, Grover, and Huber, 1984; Reitz, 1971; Sims, 1977; and Sims and Szilagyi, 1975), these findings provide rather convincing evidence in support of the propositions of an arousal interpretation of reinforcement. Additionally, these findings suggest that organizational leaders must focus their efforts on the design of effective reinforcement contingencies if both high levels of employee performance and satisfaction are to be achieved.

SUMMARY

An arousal interpretation of reinforcement may not only help us to predict the effects that a particular environmental event will have on behavior prior to the time it is administered, but it also facilitates our understanding of a number of organizational behavioral phenomena, including accident behavior, performance decrements in repetitive tasks, and the relationship between employee satisfaction and performance. This interpretation suggests that stimulus events that serve as reinforcers do so because they elicit changes in reticular activity (arousal), which, in turn, determines whether there will be activity in either the reward structure (medial forebrain bundle) or punishment structure (periventricular system) of the brain. As the arousal-inducing properties of a stimulus event will vary, depending on their intensity, their configuration, and their relative novelty at the time of their presentation, we can expect that some events will have more reinforcing potential than others and that their reinforcing potential will wax and wane, depending on the frequency of their occurrence and the time since their last presentation to the individual. Furthermore, we can expect that any stimulus event to which the human organism is sensitive may have reinforcing potential. We are then encouraged to look for any stimulus change that occurs as a function of an individual's responses to his or her task environment that may, as a result of its scheduling (and, therefore, its relative novelty), its configuration, and its intensity, prove useful in producing desirable behavioral changes.

FIVE
VERBAL BEHAVIOR

The principles set forth in Chapters 2 and 3 have been found to apply to the human organism and most other vertebrates. Such generality should not surprise us, for all vertebrates have much in common, neurologically and otherwise. But there are also some notable structural differences between the human being and other organisms, and for that reason, among others, our account of human behavior is far from complete.

One structural difference of awesome significance is found in the human vocal musculature, which includes the diaphragm, the vocal cords, the tongue, the soft palate, and the lips. Because human infants come equipped with these structures, they are capable at birth of producing the some 50 different sounds observed in all human speech and will typically emit all of them within the first five months.

Early on, of course, the small child babbles, but in an amazingly short period of time, most young children reared in a normal social environment will acquire a fairly complex verbal repertoire. Somewhere around 18 to 24 months, for example, the child will begin to emit sequences of two and three words in an order that is judged to be grammatically correct (e.g., "Go home"; "Mommy spank"; "Daddy pet doggy"). And though the child's verbal behavior will continue to undergo refinements for nearly a lifetime, by the time the child is seven or eight, its verbal behavior has begun to take on most of the basic properties and functions of an adult verbal repertoire.[1]

It is our objective here to describe the various features and functions of a verbal repertoire and the manner in which it is shaped. We do so for a number of quite important reasons. As we trace the development of a verbal reper-

---

[1] It would be most unwise to conclude that speech is the essence of verbal behavior or that infrahuman organisms cannot acquire a verbal repertoire. Linguists have been prone to assert that the acquisition of even a rudimentary language is beyond the capacity of any living organism other than the human species. But the Gardners (1969) and Premack (1970) have shown quite conclusively that chimpanzees are altogether capable of acquiring a complex verbal repertoire. Neither the Gardners' "Washoe" nor Premack's "Sarah" acquired a vocal repertoire, presumably because their inherited musculature does not permit it. But both readily acquired operant responses that involved the eyes, limbs, and hands to produce visual stimuli. They also learned to respond appropriately to those same visual stimuli when produced by the trainer. Most interesting of all was the fact that these complex responses were obviously shaped by the application of operant conditioning procedures.

toire, it will be necessary to repeat or exemplify the basic principles. Such redundancy is not all bad. But an exemplification of behavioral principles and a description of the way in which they may be applied is not our only objective.

We believe it is also important to emphasize the dramatic advantages of a verbal repertoire, once it has developed. As we shall see, the acquisition of a verbal repertoire makes it possible to bring human behavior under the control of "instructions," thereby allowing us to behave more effectively even in relatively novel settings. It also makes it possible for us to engage in certain more complex forms of behavior often referred to as thinking and problem solving.

Perhaps the most important reason for studying the nature and functions of verbal behavior is that the practice of management, as we know it, is utterly dependent on the prior development of a sophisticated verbal repertoire. Adult human beings "get ideas," "develop technologies," "originate and modify" organizations, and "persuade" others to join them. Organizational leaders train others to behave in effective ways, not through basic shaping procedures, but by composing and providing instructions, the effects of which are to rearrange or appropriately sequence operant repertoires previously brought under control of verbal stimuli. Organizational leaders also refine the skill properties of the behavior of others and their own, attempt to evoke and sustain behavior believed to be functional, if not essential, to the success of the group of individuals that comprise an organization, and promote the development of effective forms of self-control. They also engage in concerted efforts to analyze the complex contingencies that face the group, to anticipate changes in those contingencies, and to plan otherwise for the future. None of these activities—and especially the more effective forms—could take place in the absence of well-developed verbal and receptive operant repertoires.

THE STUDY OF VERBAL BEHAVIOR

Verbal behavior has many unusual properties aside from its complexity and the speed at which it is usually acquired. First of all, it appears to be creative in the sense that children at an early age can be observed to respond appropriately to and produce combinations of words (sentences) that they have neither heard nor emitted before.

Secondly, verbal behavior can be recorded in a rather precise way. At some point in our history, it was discovered that speech could be broken down into smaller sound units, and an alphabet was invented to represent those units. This was quite an amazing invention, for it made possible the intricate art of writing or transcription. Much later, of course, the development of sound recording technology made it possible to record and reproduce samples of verbal behavior without the intervening steps of transcribing and then reading the transcription.[2]

[2] It should be emphasized that it is the speech sounds that are observed and recorded, and not the actions of the vocal musculature in producing those sounds. Possibly a more complete record

A technology that makes it possible to record and analyze samples of verbal behavior is convenient. But the practice has also been misleading, for it allows the scientist to analyze the products of speaking apart from the behavior of the speaker and apart from the circumstances in which speaking takes place. One unfortunate consequence has been that it has reinforced the erroneous assumption that verbal behavior is independent of environmental events and, therefore, calls for a different set of explanatory principles. Chomsky (1957), for example, postulated that the human species is genetically programmed to develop a set of linguistic rules that enable the individual to produce an infinite variety of sentences. Although the rules are presumed to be known only implicitly and to be extracted from the speech that surrounds the child, the manner in which they are extracted and operate to produce verbal behavior has not been specified.

Chomsky's theory fostered a number of studies of the "spontaneous" speech of young children (Brown, 1973). The focus of these studies has been on the topography or structure of the child's developing verbal repertoire. The environmental circumstances in which the verbal repertoire appears and develops have been largely ignored, in part, we believe, because environmental events were not regarded as crucial variables in Chomsky's theory. Such studies have, nevertheless, been informative. They have told us a great deal about the structure of verbal behavior, the child's as well as the adult's. The studies have also revealed serious deficiencies in linguistic theories that attribute speech to autonomous central processes. In particular, they have suggested that one cannot go far in either analyzing or understanding speech unless one observes and analyzes the environmental context in which it occurs (Brown, 1973; Segal, 1975).

The history of Soviet research shows a similar trend. At first, Soviet researchers concentrated their efforts on the conduct of naturalistic studies in which they gathered samples of spontaneous speech. Early on, however, they became interested in the relations between the structure of a verbal repertoire and the environmental conditions in which it was acquired. Possibly as a consequence of their abiding interest in thinking and other complex behavioral processes and of their early recognition of the importance of verbal behavior in thinking, Soviet psychologists, beginning with Kornilov (1922), moved away from field studies to controlled experiments. In their experimental studies either speech stimuli of varying degrees of complexity were systematically introduced and their effects on attentional and motor behaviors were noted, or various stimulus objects and tasks were introduced while noting the corresponding effects on the child's verbal behavior.

An underlying, though possibly unstated, premise of the early Russian experiments was that speech was an important class of human behavior that

---

would include some sort of recording or description of those actions, but it is not necessary for the same reasons that we need not refer to all the detailed movements of opening a door when that class of operant behavior is studied. In the treatment of speech pathology, however, it is helpful to know something about the actions of the vocal musculature.

could ultimately come to be understood as a function of environmental variables. Watson (1930), in this country, was quite explicit about the matter. He stated that speech is simply behavior that is acquired and maintained in the same manner as other classes of human behavior. It was not until several years later, however, that a comprehensive functional analysis of verbal behavior appeared (Skinner, 1957).[3]

Skinner pointed out that verbal behavior has unique properties because it is behavior that is reinforced through the mediation of others, but that it was not otherwise different from other classes of human operant behavior. He then proceeded to show that verbal behavior was within the reach of the principles described in Chapters 2 and 3.[4]

Skinner's contribution represented a bold and innovative step, one that was bound to generate a lot of steam. And it did. Chomsky (1959) published a scathing review of *Verbal Behavior*, which received more attention than the book itself, and because behaviorists, incuding Skinner, did not respond to the criticism for some eight to 10 years, it was apparently assumed that Chomsky was correct—verbal behavior requires a different causal analysis. More recently, however, there has been a rather dramatic turnaround. Wiest (1967) and MacCorquodale (1970), among others, have responded to Chomsky's critique, but more important, there is growing evidence everywhere that verbal behavior is indeed operant behavior and is shaped and maintained in the same manner as nonverbal operants. Segal (1975), for example, has noted that much of the data uncovered by psycholinguists can be accounted for by the same principles found to apply to other classes of behavior. Segal (1977) has also described a few of the "spate" of recent studies in which behavioral principles have been employed to shape and maintain syntactic (verbal) behavior.

THE DEVELOPMENT OF VERBAL BEHAVIOR

We turn now to a description of several classes of verbal operants and to a consideration of the manner in which they are shaped and maintained.[5] In the process, the important role of verbal stimuli in human affairs will be indicated.

It was earlier mentioned that human infants can be observed to babble a great deal during their first five or six months of life. It is from this crude and

---

[3]In fact, a treatment of verbal behavior, similar in many respects to Skinner's analyses, was published in 1936 (Kantor, 1936). Unfortunately, however, it received little attention from members of the scientific community.

[4]It should be clearly understood that Skinner's extension of behavioral principles to verbal behavior was "an exercise in interpretation rather than a quantitative extrapolation of experimental findings." The analysis included no references to experimental data. However, the degree to which the analysis reflects and provides a plausible account of the available experimental studies of verbal behavior is rather striking. In his preface, Skinner noted that earlier versions of the manuscript had begun to take on the character of a literature review. It thus seems obvious that his "extension" was made with full awareness of the Soviet studies as well as other experimental data.

relatively undifferentiated behavior that a verbal operant repertoire of considerable complexity is eventually shaped and maintained.

Babbling appears to occur spontaneously and in cycles, an observation that seems to suggest that parents must wait for it to occur before shaping procedures can be applied. But when it is said that it occurs spontaneously, this does not mean that babbling is necessarily independent of environmental variables or that it cannot be produced. For example, sometime after the first month, modest changes in the environment have been observed to elicit diffuse activity in the awake but relatively quiet infant. This reflex activity is comprised of uncoordinated muscular contractions, changes in respiratory and heart rate, an occasional vocalization, and nonspecific orienting responses, all of which are indicative of a corresponding increase in arousal level. After the second month, when it is usually possible to develop reasonably stable conditioned respondents, the presence and behavior of parents who have fed and otherwise cared for the infant acquire the capacity to elicit this "animation reflex" as well. It is especially important that parents "talk to" the infant while feeding or otherwise caring for it.[6] Under these circumstances, parent-produced auditory stimuli come to serve as conditioned stimuli, eliciting an intermediate level of arousal, receptor-orienting responses, and general activity including vocalizations. Parents' vocalizations will also serve as conditioned reinforcers, increasing the frequency of any infant behavior on which those vocalizations are made contingent. It is quite possibly good practice, however, to use contingent vocalizations sparingly as reinforcers. Among other things, we want to teach the infant to "hear itself," and contingent parental vocalizations may interfere with that process.

The eliciting and reinforcing properties of parental vocalizations will, of course, diminish with repeated presentations. It is, therefore, incumbent on parents to reinstate or maintain those properties by making certain that their vocalizations continue to be paired, at least, intermittently, with other reinforcing events (food, touching, holding, and the like).

When the above conditions are met, the parent has solved the practical problem of producing babbling rather than waiting for it to occur. The parent merely approaches the comfortable but awake child and proceeds to "talk to

---

[5]This is not the place to present a comprehensive program for the development of a verbal repertoire, but such programs are now available. The interested reader might wish to peruse *A Language Program for the Non-Language Child* by Burt Gray and Bruce Ryan (Champaign, Ill.: Research Press, 1973) or *The Autistic Child: Language Development Through Behavior Modification* by O. Ivar Lovaas (New York: Irvington Publishers, Inc., 1977). The latter book, despite its title, provides a wealth of useful information for parents who desire to shape their offspring's verbal repertoire effectively.

[6]It goes without saying, perhaps, that parents should not shout at the infant, handle it in a violent fashion, or introduce sudden changes into the infant's environment. Otherwise, the presence and verbal behavior of parents will come to serve as conditioned aversive stimuli eliciting high arousal, crying, and other defensive respondents that may be incompatible with the verbal operants they wish to shape. This does not mean, of course, that parents should follow the opposite caretaking practice of keeping the environment as constant as possible, for variable and mild forms of stimulation are fundamental to the neural and behavioral development of the small child.

it." When babbling occurs, the parent then reinforces the activity with smiles, hugs, and the application of mild tactile stimulation to the face or torso and also by presenting other stimulus events discovered to have reinforcing properties for the infant. The reinforcers should be applied immediately and more-or-less continuously at first. After a few trials, the frequency of babbling can be increased by momentarily withholding reinforcers until a higher rate is observed, at which time the reinforcers are again presented.

It should be noted that the above procedures establish a "self-strengthening" contingency of considerable importance to the development of a verbal repertoire. As the small child can hear the sounds it produces, behavior producing those sounds is automatically reinforced. The sounds are admittedly weak reinforcers that quickly lose their reinforcing properties with repetition. But when they are paired with more durable reinforcers, as they will be when parents consistently reinforce babbling in other ways, the babbling sounds will come to sustain the vocal operants producing them. In short, the small child will often babble to itself.

Most of the sounds characteristic of *every* human language are usually observed in early infant babbling, whatever the child's cultural heritage. It is no doubt good policy to encourage that diversity at least for a time. If the parents speak often *and of many things* while approaching, feeding, and otherwise caring for the child, a wider variety of speech sounds in the parents' language will begin to serve as conditioned reinforcers, facilitating the self-strengthening of the several operants that produce them. The range of sounds emitted by the child will naturally diminish over time, for those vocal operants that do not produce sounds paired with reinforcing stimuli will gradually extinguish. This is an important development, if not carried to extreme,[7] for the small child is then well prepared for the acquisition of the more complex verbal operants required to produce the "words" and "sentences" of a language.

ECHOIC VERBAL BEHAVIOR

An echoic response is a verbal operant that produces an auditory stimulus similar to the antecedent stimulus that serves to control the response. In symbolic form, we have the familiar $S_D:Rx \equiv Sc+ \rightarrow r$, where the S_D is the auditory stimulus "Momma" uttered by the parent; the Rx is the action of the child's vocal musculature, which produces an approximation of the sound "Momma"; the $Sc+$ is a reinforcer delivered by the parent; and the r indicates the respondents elicited by the reinforcer. We need only to remind ourselves that the sound produced by the Rx is an additional stimulus event that, when

---

[7]If, for example, the parent never talked to the infant or vocalized only sparingly in its presence and did not bother to reinforce babbling, then much of the operant behavior producing babbling may ultimately extinguish. Under these circumstances, further training of the typically casual type provided by parents may not be very successful.

paired with the reinforcer supplied by the parent, will also serve to reinforce the *Rx* automatically.

As we have noted, parents who talk to the infant rather intuitively administer the echoic shaping procedure very early in life. Their vocalizations not only begin to elicit the animation reflex but also come to serve as S_D's evoking a stream of babbling, which the parents then reinforce. With repeated applications of this procedure—and particularly when the application is systematic—the babbling begins to take on the characteristics of the parents' vocalizations. Not only will the babbling sequence be punctuated by rises and falls in pitch like the sentences and questions produced by the parents, but also the operants producing those sounds contained in the parents speech will increase in frequency.

The early echoic behavior of the infant is typically wide of the mark. To obtain a closer match between the parents' vocalizations and those produced by the small child, the alert parent must become more discriminating, withholding reinforcers until closer approximations to their speech are emitted. The experienced trainer begins with the sounds that are easiest to shape. A crude approximation of "Momma" can be produced by the accidental opening and closing of the lips while air is being expelled over the vocal passage. It is, therefore, observed to occur early in echoic babbling before systematic shaping procedures are applied, as are crude approximations to "Daddy," "Doggy," and "Ball." One naturally attempts to condition ever more close approximations to those words before attempting to shape the more complex movements of the vocal musculature required to produce such words as "table," "Phyllis," or "television."

When the small child begins to echo a few identifiable words, a curious thing happens to the speech of parents. It becomes simplified in the presence of the child. Their vocalizations are in the form of single words or, at most, two- and three-word sentences. Frequently, their word utterances are also "phonologically" simplified as in "wawa" for "water" or "potty" for "toilet." This may be an appropriate, though not often a deliberate, conditioning strategy in early shaping. Parents seem naturally to present those words that the child has emitted for purposes of maintaining or increasing their frequency. If carried to extremes, however, parental "baby talk" is likely to retard the development of an echoic repertoire both in terms of the number of different units that may be acquired and in the development of closer approximations of the words to acceptable adult speech. This is not to imply that the parents should withhold reinforcers until close matches are produced. Rather, parents should present simple words as they *should* be emitted, at first reinforcing only crude matches and then ever-closer approximations of the words presented to them.

Parents knowledgeable of the conditioning principles involved can train the small child to emit a large number of words long before they typically appear. It must be admitted, however, that if they were required to shape every verbal operant from the undifferentiated behavior called babbling, progress would be so tortuously slow that the shaping behavior of parents would no doubt extinguish. It is, therefore, fortunate that when a few echoic operants have been shaped, new echoics are acquired at a progressively faster rate. Indeed, small children sometimes acquire an echoic repertoire so rapidly that conditioning principles do not seem to be involved, but a closer examination reveals otherwise. We have previously observed that when parents effectively strengthen babbling, they have provided for the more-or-less automatic strengthening of vocal operants producing sounds contained in the parent's language and for the gradual extinction of those operants producing "foreign" sounds. Furthermore, many words in a given language have common sound components, so that the child who has been conditioned to echo "Dada" and "Doggy," for example, may quickly learn to echo "Dolly" because the movements of the vocal musculature required to produce the "dee" sound have already been acquired and brought under the control of the verbal stimulus "dee" produced by the parents. Another interesting example of this process is seen when the child who has been trained to echo the sounds "p" and "b" will quickly acquire the two vocal operants required to produce "t" and "d" and other pairs of sounds in which a common distinction is in the presence or absence of vocal cord vibration.

The first echoic operants acquired by the child are usually those that produce integrated patterns of sounds we refer to as words. At least, they are the first to be recognized as such. This is because most parents intuitively begin their conditioning treatments at that level. They will, for example, attempt to get their small child to echo "Kitty" rather than first presenting and then reinforcing approximations to "ki" before progressing on to "tee." It is probable, however, that smaller echoic units, at the level of the phoneme[8] or even smaller," are developed during the latter babbling stages, and, in any event, smaller echoic operants seem to develop naturally when echoic operants at the word level are conditioned. Having acquired a few echoic responses beginning with "M" (e.g., "momma," "milk," and "mum"), the small child is likely to reproduce correctly the first part of the verbal stimulus "Myrtle" when it is first presented by the parent, though it is not likely to echo correctly the complete word until several conditioning trails have been applied. (The child is likely to say "Mu" or "Mutta.")

It is best not to leave the development of minimal echoic units to chance. The wise parent, in attempting to shape more complex echoic responses, will break the word into its constituent speech sounds and present, then reinforce, closer approximations to each sound in serial order. Later on, when at the zoo, for example, the parent who fails to evoke the echoic operant "kangaroo" when it is first presented will then present "ku" or "kang," then "ah," then "roo." (The child at this stage, perhaps 18 to 36 months of age, is not likely to

---

[8] It has become standard practice to distinguish between *phonemes*, which are a group of distinctive sounds that "comprise the words of a language," and smaller units called *allophones*, which are discriminable variations of a given phoneme. The *p* and *b* in *pit* and *bit* are different phonemes. The *p* in *pit* and the *p* in *ship* are the same phoneme but different allophones because there are subtle differences in the two sounds and, of course, in the configuration of the vocal musculature.

have difficulty echoing the first and second syllables, for it has already acquired such echoic units as the "ku" in *kitty* or *candy* and the "ang" in *bang*, but several trials may be required before "roo" is correctly echoed). In addition to the training provided by parents, formal education treatments in which the child is taught to echo small speech sounds (as in phonetics) will further contribute to the development of a fine-grained echoic repertoire.

Large echoic units in the form of sentences may also be acquired as a consequence of both casual and systematic shaping efforts. There are, however, definite limits to this process. Small children and many adults cannot successfully echo a long-drawn-out sentence, in part because the first words in the sentence are no longer present to serve as effective S_D's or because there are many competing S_D's present at the same time.

Self-echoic responses are also likely to develop as a matter of course when the child is exposed to extensive shaping efforts. Although we have alluded to this process before, it needs to be emphasized that verbal stimuli produced by the child itself can come to control other operants in the child's repertoire just as verbal stimuli produced by others can. As a consequence, we should not be surprised to find young children echoing themselves, producing what appears to be a "meaningless repetition of words." Self-echoic responses appear in adult speech as well, and sometimes in rather unusual forms as in the frequent occurrence of pairs of words and phrases like *"wear* and *tear"* and *"Haste* makes *waste."* Self-echoic tendencies may also be responsible, in part, for *alliteration* (several words beginning with the same consonant sounds) and *assonance* (words containing the same vowel sounds) in poetry. In extreme forms, self-echoic behavior is called *echolalia.*

Echoic behavior—and especially self-echoic behavior—is likely to prove aversive to parents. Consequently, they may come to ignore or even punish the more protracted forms. However, the control exerted by auditory stimuli over vocal operants that reproduce them is often so strong that when the echoic response is punished, it merely becomes *covert.* That is to say, the echoic response continues to be evoked, but it occurs at such a reduced level that it cannot be readily detected by parents or other observers. In the verbal case, neither lip movement nor audible sounds can be seen or overheard though one might be able to detect movement of the vocal musculature by placing the fingers against the throat.

Covert Verbal Behavior

Covert verbal behavior is difficult to analyze simply because it cannot be readily observed. But it figures so importantly in human affairs that it is well to devote some time to it here.[9]

---

[9]We hasten to add that we are *not* proposing that parents systematically punish overt echoics in order to develop important covert forms, for such a procedure might retard the development of *all* forms. If the parents find the child's protracted echoic behavior aversive, we suggest that they first try "changing the subject." They can do so by introducing a new word or toy that will serve to evoke operant behavior incompatible with the echoic responses.

Contingent punishment is not the only reason why overt behavior becomes covert. Operant behavior in *all* its variegated forms normally declines in magnitude unless vigorous forms are differentially reinforced, and it will continue to do so until reinforcing events no longer occur. Verbal operant behavior, whether it be echoic or some other form yet to be analyzed, is especially likely to drop to the covert level because private stimulation accompanying or produced by covert verbal operants can easily serve to reinforce verbal operants at the covert level.

The structure or topography of covert verbal behavior often appears very similar to its overt counterpart except for differences in amplitude. In describing verbal behavior in terms of "descending order of energy," Skinner (1957, p. 438) noted that the range in amplitude is roughly suggested by shouting, loud talking, quiet talking, whispering, muttering under one's breath, subaudible speech with detectable muscular action, subaudible speech of unclear dimensions, and possibly the "unconscious thinking" sometimes inferred in instances of problem solving.

Differences between talking and whispering in Skinner's example are not easily distinguished except in terms of vigor or amplitude. However, there is a point along the continuum at which the behavior becomes covert, and we cannot assume that covert behavior is always executed by the same musculature involved in the overt form. Readers can demonstrate some apparent structural differences to themselves by reciting a series of numbers, first whispering each number and then saying it silently. To be sure, some similarities may be observed if one repeats the exercise, but now holding the mouth wide open when saying the number silently. With practice, however, many adults can do this without producing tongue movement, which they can readily detect, or the sounds they heard on the first few trials (i.e., air rushing over the vocal passages). Thus, it is clear that the vocal musculature involved in the execution of overt verbal behavior is not always identical with that involved in the execution of covert forms. But it seems equally clear that *some* features of the body involved in the execution of overt behavior are also involved in the covert case.

Stimuli generated by or accompanying covert verbal behavior may also serve as S_D's controlling other responses, overt or covert, verbal or nonverbal. To return to echoic verbal operants, for example, the small child might echo the parent covertly, thereby producing the same stimulus (except for magnitude) as that produced by the parent. That stimulus may evoke a second echoic response, which may occur at either the covert or overt level. Later on, a simple instruction by the parent to "find your blanket" may evoke a covert echoic response, which then evokes another in a chain until the blanket is found. In this case, however, the covert echoic may become fragmentary in the sense that only the word "blanket" or a partial form of it is self-echoed.

Covert verbal behavior is often involved in the development and maintenance of other classes of operant behavior, verbal and otherwise. Consequently, we will, on occasion, refer back to our analysis and elaborate upon it.

The Importance of an Echoic Repertoire

The development of an extensive echoic repertoire is more important than we may realize. The adult who was fortunate enough to have been exposed to successful tutoring efforts will echo verbal stimuli in relatively novel patterns when these are first presented. An effective adult listener echoes the response of an instructor so that they will be emitted at a later time, thus evoking other operants described in the instruction. An earlier echoic response emitted under different circumstances is no longer an echoic operant because the S_D evoking it is not the auditory stimuli produced by the instructor. However, it is not likely to be evoked in other circumstances unless it was earlier emitted as echoic, fragmentary or otherwise.

In the shaping of an echoic repertoire, the small child's verbal behavior is brought under the control of verbal stimuli for the first time. It may also be an important early occasion for the development of a rudimentary type of self-control wherein we are conditioned to behave verbally so as to produce stimuli that evoke other operants of the same or a different form.

Most important, the development of an echoic repertoire facilitates the development of a wide variety of other verbal operants, which remain to be discussed. But first, one more important digression.

THE DEVELOPMENT OF A "RECEPTIVE" OPERANT REPERTOIRE

Though we may be amazed at the rate at which the small child's verbal repertoire develops, a variety of nonverbal operants are acquired at an even faster rate. Before the child has learned to speak, it has learned to track moving objects visually; to reach for, grasp, and manipulate objects; and to crawl toward, away from, and around things in its environment. The reinforcement contingencies prevailing in the inanimate environment are such that behavior with respect to it is usually followed by immediate reinforcing consequences. On the other hand, the reinforcement contingencies responsible for the development of verbal behavior are mediated by other human beings and their behavior in presenting reinforcers is frequently inconsistent and delayed.

Even so, it is especially reinforcing for parents to be able to control the behavior of the young child easily and reliably. (Indeed, it becomes a necessity when the child becomes ambulatory, for it might not otherwise survive!) Consequently, parents begin quite early to shape a *receptive operant repertoire* wherein some portion of the child's nonverbal behavior is brought under the control of verbal stimuli produced by the parent. The process is exemplified by a procedure that may well be universal in households that include the male parent. Having entered the room and while the child is looking at him, the father says, "Come to Daddy!" and then reinforces the small child with hugs or possibly a new toy when it crawls to him. Many conditioning trials will be required before the control of the child's behavior by verbal stimuli becomes reliable. The small child may not crawl to its father on command when it is occupied by something else, and it may crawl to the male parent in the absence of "Come to Daddy!" The conditioning trials must also, of course, incorporate the differential reinforcement procedure. In other words, the male parent should consistently reinforce the small child when it crawls to him after "Come to Daddy!" and ignore the child or leave the room when it crawls to him in the absence of the command. Parents will not be consistent in their application of this procedure for obvious reasons, but there is *some* consistency, for many children are observed to respond appropriately to verbal stimuli as they approach their twelfth month. Certain words or phrases such as "Kiss Mommy," "Pet doggy," "No, no!" and later "Turn around," "Give me your hand," "Look!" and "Listen!" will evoke an orienting response and simple but appropriate nonverbal operants. With repeated application of the differential procedure, the controlling function of those stimuli will be sharpened in the sense that the verbal stimulus, rather than other features of the environment, will evoke the response. The control, however, remains relatively crude, much like that observed in the behavior of the family pet in the presence of such commands as "Heel!" "Roll over!" and "Shake." If the verbal stimulus is presented by a different person or with different pitch or intonational properties or in settings in which the behavior has not been conditioned, the controlling effect may not be seen. The more sophisticated control over nonverbal operants by verbal stimuli begins to develop only after the child has become a reasonably accomplished speaker. And that brings us to other important processes.

Skinner (1957, p. 195) has noted that, in acquiring a receptive repertoire, one does not necessarily or automatically acquire a verbal repertoire and vice versa. The truth of Skinner's hypothesis (or assertion) seems apparent in the case of the family pet, and we believe that it is no less true in the human case. However, we need to explain the "transfer" effect frequently observed in the behavior of children approaching their eighteenth month. The effect is seen when the behavior of petting the family dog is brought under the control of the parental command (or suggestion, if one prefers) to "Pet doggy," and the small child suddenly begins to say "Pet doggy" while it is petting the dog. The appearance of the child's verbal response seems a bit magical if parents have not attempted to shape it. On the other hand, if earlier echoic training has been applied in a reasonably consistent manner, the child's response "pet doggy" is likely to appear as an echoic response at the same time that its behavior of petting the dog in the presence of the parental command is being shaped. Both classes of operants are reinforced by the tactile stimulation from petting the dog and ordinarily by the parents who supply reinforcers when the child pets the dog. This conditioning process is quite important for several reasons. First, the echoic repertoire continues to be refined and strengthened. Secondly, once an extensive echoic repertoire has been strengthened, various parts of it can easily be brought under the control of nonverbal stimuli. In our example, parents can readily bring the child's "Pet doggy" under the control of its own behavior of petting the dog and can further reinforce the response when it is emitted in the presence of someone else petting the dog. Even further, parents may reinforce the child's verbal response in the mere presence of the dog by petting the dog. Finally, the conditioning process is important because it sets the stage for the development of verbal thinking, problem solving, and other forms of *self-control*, in which the child learns first to respond verbally, thereby producing S_D's controlling other parts of its operant repertoire.

Verbal stimulus control of the child's attentional, manipulatory, and locomotor operant repertoire is expanded and strengthened when those behaviors are consistently reinforced in the presence of such stimuli as "See," "Look," "Listen," "Hear," "Walk," "Run," "Go outside," "Make truck go," and "Get your coat." This type of control is further promoted as the child's echoic repertoire is extended and strengthened, for the nonverbal operants then have at least two sources of strength—the verbal S_D's produced by parents and others and those produced by the child itself. With appropriate training, the child's nonverbal repertoire can be brought under a form of control in which reasonably complex instructions, heard earlier, are later reproduced by the child in a different setting, thereby evoking effective, nonverbal behavior in that setting. By the age of 36 months or earlier, the child instructed to "Look both ways before crossing the street" may be observed to behave in that manner when later approaching a curb, possibly for the first time.

OTHER VERBAL OPERANTS UNDER THE CONTROL OF VERBAL STIMULI

In addition to echoic operants, there are other classes of verbal behavior under the control of verbal stimuli. We take them up here, if only briefly, before our analysis of important classes of verbal operants that are brought under the control of nonverbal stimuli.

Intraverbal Operants

In echoic behavior, there is a close relation between the auditory stimulus that evokes the response and the stimulus that the echoic response produces. When an auditory stimulus evokes behavior producing a *different* auditory pattern, the behavior is classified as an *intraverbal operant*. An example is the response "Fork" to the auditory stimulus "Knife," produced by someone else.

The origins of intraverbal operants are found in early echoic behavior where *any* vocal response evoked by parent-produced verbal stimuli is reinforced by the parent. As we have seen, the range of verbal behavior then typically narrows, becoming more precisely echoic in form, but recognizable intraverbals usually appear as a matter of course as parental shaping efforts continue.

Literally thousands of different intraverbal operants may be found in the adult repertoire as our word association studies have shown. Many are relatively trivial. Presented with the verbal stimulus "pink," one adult may respond with "panther"; another, with "blue"; and another, with "Pink sky at night is a sailor's delight." Not all intraverbal operants are either unpredictable or trivial, however. Presented with the verbal stimulus "I pledge allegiance," most of us reared in the United States are likely to rattle off the remainder of the pledge of allegiance without a hitch. When presented with the verbal stimulus "two times three," all of us are likely to respond, "Six," and it is usually important that we do so. Intraverbal operants may be quite large, as in reciting the Gettysburg Address or very small, as in the response "b" to the auditory stimulus "a." Finally, intraverbal operants may be evoked by self-produced verbal stimuli, and either or both the operant producing the verbal stimulus and the evoked intraverbal behavior may be covert.

Textual Behavior

Another class of verbal operant behavior under the control of verbal stimuli is called *textual* behavior (Skinner, 1957, p. 65). The verbal stimulus is visual rather than auditory, and the one whose behavior is thus controlled is typically called a reader. It might be possible to bring verbal behavior under the control of textual stimuli at the time the former is being shaped. But the process would be tortuously slow and no doubt dysfunctional for the child and the trainer as well. The problem is resolved when an extensive echoic repertoire has already been developed, for it is then a matter of "transferring" the control of that repertoire to visual stimuli. Bringing operant behavior, whatever its form, under discriminative stimulus control is a different and much more rapid process than shaping and strengthening it in the first place. In the present case, the trainer evokes an echoic operant, for example, "cat," in the presence of the printed word CAT. Then the trainer gradually withdraws or "fades" the auditory stimulus while continuing to reinforce each instance of the child's vocal operant, "cat." When it is being reliably evoked by the printed word alone, one proceeds to another printed word, for example, *DOG*, and repeats the procedure. Introducing the auditory stimulus "dog" will tend to ensure that the child will now say, "Dog" rather than "Cat," but there will be "mistakes," and it is essential that the trainer correct them by saying, "No" or "That's not right," and then generously reinforcing the child by saying, "Good!" or by applying a tactile reinforcer where the correct response occurs. (This is, of course, an application of the differential reinforcement procedure, so important to the development of effective stimulus control. But it is more than simply reinforcing the operant in the presence of an appropriate S_D and extinguishing the response in the absence of that S_D or in the presence of an inappropriate S_D. When one says, "No" or "That's not right," one is *applying* a stimulus, and that constitutes a punishment procedure. The trainer is at the same time withholding positive reinforcers when the response is emitted in the presence of the wrong S_D. This combined extinction–punishment procedure is nearly universal in human affairs and is generally more effective then simply withholding positive reinforcers.) Trainers can, and should, check the effectiveness of their conditioning procedures by presenting first one, then another, printed word while noting the small child's response. This provides additional opportunities to apply the differential reinforcement procedure, thus further strengthening effective stimulus control.

As discrimination training proceeds, textual stimulus control develops rather quickly, for the child is also learning to orient its visual receptors to materials presented by the instructor, to respond appropriately to pointing, and to respond appropriately in the presence of simple instructions. We might say, in the language of an adult, that the child is learning that when it responds as the trainer does in the presence of those little marks and then responds in the presence of the marks alone, it will be reinforced.

Textual behavior, like other classes of verbal operants, may occur at the covert level. In fact, silent reading is far more common than reading aloud in the case of the human adult though, interestingly enough, covert textual behavior did not apparently become prevalent until the Middle Ages (Skinner, 1957, p. 141).

Textual operants continue to be emitted at a high rate long after the contingencies responsible for their acquisition have been withdrawn. Indeed, human adults will often find themselves reading advertisements in display windows, billboards, and the labels on a milk carton as well as newspapers, magazines, and books. The reasons are to be found in the reinforcement contingencies that prevail in daily life. In consulting a dictionary or in reading the definition of a term in a text, one may acquire a new intraverbal operant. When the term is subsequently heard or seen, it will evoke other words having the same meaning (the definition). When one travels in strange territory, the reading of signs produces S_D's evoking behavior effective in arriving at one's destination. We should note here that some street or highway signs are encountered so often that nonverbal behavior comes to be evoked directly by the visual stimulus in the absence of an intervening textual response, overt or covert. In this case, the behavior of the most sophisticated human adult resembles that of the lowly rat who has been conditioned to turn left in the presence of the printed word *LEFT*. On the other hand, when nonverbal behavior is complex or must, for any reason, be delayed, there is intervening textual behavior that, when later repeated in a different setting, serves to evoke nonverbal operants effective in that setting. This behavioral process could not occur in the absence of a well-developed receptive repertoire, but when that condition is met, the reinforcers contingent on the effective nonverbal operants also serve to reinforce the prior textual behavior.

Transcriptive Operants

Another class of verbal behavior under the control of verbal stimuli is called *transcription* (Skinner, 1957, p. 69). Up to this point, we have only discussed *vocal* operant behavior; that is, behavior involving the vocal musculature and resulting in auditory stimulation. In the class of verbal behavior considered here, the operant responses are of a different topography and result in the production of verbal stimuli in visual form.

The early shaping of transcriptive operants (writing) is usually begun by presenting visual stimuli—either letters of the alphabet in upper and lower cases or combinations of several letters—and requiring the child to copy them. When the behavior producing ever closer approximations to the final forms is systematically reinforced, it develops rather quickly. Visual stimuli may be presented without accompanying auditory stimuli, or trainers may present both a visual stimulus *and* an auditory stimulus, requiring echoic as well as transcriptive operants before reinforcers are applied. Both procedures require skill in their initial application because the trainer must closely monitor the child's behavior and respond quickly and appropriately to very subtle changes in it. For that reason, the latter, more complicated procedure may prove to be dysfunctional if applied too early in the shaping program. If, for example, a closer approximation of the required sound is produced on a given trial, but there is regression in the behavior producing the visual stimulus, the application of reinforcers will appropriately strengthen the echoic operant and inappropriately strengthen a transcriptive operant of a less effective form. If the reinforcers are withheld altogether, an effective textual operant is weakened. It, therefore, appears to be a better strategy to shape first one, then the other class of verbal behavior, maintaining some degree of independence in the programs. As we will note, however, it will be important to combine programs as a basic repertoire of each class is effectively shaped.

In shaping transcriptive operants, trainers have recourse to a procedure that is impossible to apply in the development of vocal operant behavior. They can grasp the child's wrist and fingers and literally guide or mold the operant response. This sort of conditioning support should be provided sparingly and withdrawn as quickly as possible, but it can be applied to hasten the development of transcriptive operants early in the shaping process.

As the child acquires a basic, transcriptive verbal repertoire to the point that it can reproduce the letters of the alphabet and simple words, other important conditioning procedures can be introduced. For example, the verbal stimuli can be presented in auditory form, and the child "writes them down" and is reinforced (or corrected, then reinforced). This is, of course, a spelling lesson, which not only hastens the acquisition of transcriptive operants but also promotes the development of other behavioral processes. The auditory stimulus may be presented with the requirement that it be correctly echoed before it is produced in visual form. In this case, at least two conditioning procedures are involved. First, the transcriptive operant begins to come under the control of the auditory stimulus produced by the child's echoic operant, whether covert or overt. Thus, the stage is set for the development and refinement of behavior called *editing* and *composition*, to be described later. Secondly, when an auditory stimulus, whether self-produced or otherwise, consistently precedes a stimulus in visual form, the auditory stimulus comes to evoke conditioned seeing. That is to say, the child will be able to see the visual stimulus or portions of it even though it is not present. (The reader may discover the importance of the behavior of seeing something in its absence and also the degree to which it has been strengthened by attempting to describe the route to be taken from his or her present location to a familiar point several miles away. The reader will discover that he or she is seeing, but possibly not very "clearly," portions of the route to be taken. Readers may also find themselves "driving their automobile." In either case, one is seeing again or driving again as one has seen or driven before.)

Transcriptive verbal behavior is maintained by a wide variety of reinforcement contingencies long after it has been acquired. The ubiquitous note-taking student is but one of hundreds of examples in which transcriptive operants under the control of verbal stimuli produced by the professor and the student result in verbal stimuli in the form of "notes." Later, the notes serve to evoke textual operants, thus reproducing some of the verbal behavior of the professor. If the professor has said something important, as in describing nonverbal operants effective in a given setting, and if the notes are sufficiently comprehensive, a subsequent "re-view of the notes (responding textually), produces S_D's evoking the operant behavior described. If the behavior proves to be effective, the reinforcing consequences may serve to strengthen the listening, transcriptive, and textual operants as well as the nonverbal operants originally described by the professor. In the usual case, however, the reinforcers contingent on the latter are so long delayed that they have little effect on the preceding verbal operants. The professor is, therefore, required to introduce intermediate shaping and strengthening procedures. For example, students are required to review their notes and then reproduce portions of the professor's verbal behavior in an examination. A host of behavioral processes are implicated in these intermediate conditioning procedures, but to mention only a few, the resulting examination paper allows the professor (1) to shape and strengthen comprehensive note-taking; (2) to reinforce the student's vocal (textual) behavior under the control of the notes; (3) to strengthen transcriptive behavior (writing the exam) under the control of stimuli produced by the student's covert vocal operants, which are the same vocal operants evoked by the notes; and (4) to check the degree to which the verbal instruction and/or the behavior described is likely to be evoked by appropriate features of the setting in which the instruction is presumably applicable. The latter process is, without doubt, the most complicated of the four behavioral processes, quite possibly the most important, and, almost certainly, the least understood. We will do little to clarify it here except to note that if the student accurately reproduces the instructions (descriptions of effective operant behavior and the environmental circumstances under which the behavior should occur), there is an increment in the probability that the instructions or the behavior described or both will occur in that setting, but the appearance of either or both in that setting is far from guaranteed.

In a similar fashion, we may write down what we find ourselves saying in order to "clarify our thoughts" or to control our behavior, verbal or nonverbal, at a later date. The process serves to emphasize that auditory stimuli are fleeting whereas a note or a text is more or less permanent. Notes and texts are, therefore, important in human affairs in that they can be viewed and reviewed, repeatedly evoking the same vocal operants. They can be trotted out at any time thus serving to evoke directly operant behavior of a different form or to evoke intervening textual behavior and then effective nonverbal operants.

VERBAL OPERANTS UNDER THE CONTROL
OF NONVERBAL STIMULI

The classes of verbal operants thus far examined are under the control of verbal S_D's, both auditory and visual. We now turn to important classes of verbal operants that come under the control of various features of our nonverbal environment. Skinner (1957) coined the terms *mand* and *tact* for the classes of verbal operants to be discussed here, and we will adopt his terminology though our analysis differs in some respects from his.

Mands

The verbal operant called a *mand* is typically reinforced by a very limited set of stimulus consequences. We might say that the mand specifies the reinforcing event whether it be an object to be supplied by a mediator, as in "water," or the behavior of another person, as in "Come here," or both, as in "Please pass the bread." The mand, as Skinner (1957 p. 36) has noted, works primarily for the benefit of the speaker.

According to Skinner (1957, p. 35), the mand is under the control of "relevant conditions of deprivation or aversive stimulation" but otherwise has no specified relation to a prior stimulus (an S_D). He later qualifies his definition (1957, p. 36) somewhat, but the position needs to be stated unequivocally. *All* verbal operants, including mands, are under the control of antecedent stimuli. The S_D's controlling mands may be difficult to identify because a given mand is typically reinforced in a variety of settings and because stimulus events taking place beneath the skin may come to serve as controlling S_D's. However, the verbal operants classified as mands have specifiable relations to antecedent stimuli that evoke them, and the controlling S_D's are most obvious in the early shaping of mands.

The conditioning procedures that shape mands are quite similar to those that shape textual operants. Once the child has begun to acquire echoic operants, these can be "transferred" to nonverbal stimuli. The parent usually begins the process with stimulus objects that have been identified as having reinforcing properties for the child. A bottle of milk will do if the child has not been recently fed. While holding the bottle in front of the child, the parent produces the auditory stimulus "milk." When the child echoes, however crudely (e.g., "muk"), the parent reinforces the verbal response by giving the bottle of milk to the child. Then the parent gradually fades the auditory stimulus on subsequent trials so that the bottle of milk, by itself, begins to evoke the verbal response. Early in the shaping process, parents will find it necessary to reinstate the auditory stimulus "milk," and when they do, the word should be pronounced in its most acceptable form. Under those circumstances, they can proceed to shape a more precise operant (the child's response more closely approximates "milk") while continuing to bring the response more and more under the control of the bottle alone. Needless to say, parents should not be too stringent in their response requirements before delivering the reinforcer, for they may thereby extinguish the child's verbal responses and elicit crying as well. Nor will parents be effective if they wait until the child is "crying from hunger" before they initiate a conditioning trail.

The conditioning of mands, once begun, usually proceeds quite rapidly. With the deliberate application of the above procedures, the small child soon comes to emit "Cookie," "Doll," "Ball," "Horsey," and so on in the presence of those reinforcing objects and the parents and in the absence of the echoic stimulus provided by them.

When the small child has acquired even a minimal repertoire of mands, it can obtain a variety of reinforcing events faster and with far less effort than heretofore possible. As the child's control over its environment is thus extended, the further development of verbal operants in the form of mands becomes easier yet. When encountering an object that has reinforcing properties, the small child may at first simply point to it when the parent is present (or fetch the parent to the location of the reinforcer and then point). The parent may then take this opportunity to shape a new mand, first supplying an echoic stimulus and then requiring an approximation to it before making the reinforcing object available to the child. (If the parent, for any reason, prefers not to make it available, the small child can be ignored, or, better yet, the parent may hold up another reinforcing stimulus and proceed accordingly.) When the small child has acquired the mand "What that?" and has also learned to respond to the parents' "Can you say ——?" only one trial may be required. The conditioning procedure quickly becomes, for the child, a game of which many parents soon tire. But it is an important game, nevertheless, for it not only extends the child's control over its environment but also promotes and facilitates the development of other more complex verbal operants. Before we turn to those, however, it is necessary to consider the subtleties of the stimulus control of mands.

During the initial conditioning of mands, the stimuli that come to serve as S_D's controlling the mands are usually obvious. Both the presence of the parent-donor and the reinforcing event set the occasion for mands and, therefore, serve to control them. However, other stimuli in a setting will typically gain some measure of control. When the mand "Cookie," emitted in the presence of a chocolate cookie, is reinforced by the presentation of that object, the mand will come to be evoked by the presence of chocolate cookies *and other cookies similar in shape and color*. This type of stimulus generalization is acceptable, of course, and parents typically promote it by reinforcing the mand "Cookie" in the presence of a wide variety of stimulus objects we call cookies. However, a small round tinker toy resembling a cookie may also evoke the verbal response "Cookie," and, in these cases, the parents' reinforcing practices may be inconsistent. The most appropriate response is to ignore the child or to deliver a "No, no" and then proceed to evoke a more appropriate verbal response in the presence of the tinker toy. On the other hand, if the child has not been recently fed, they may reinforce the mand "Cookie" by providing a cookie even though the response has been evoked by a stimulus object that is obviously not a cookie. Indeed, some parents may supply a cookie, though the child has recently been fed, on the premise that small children should always be surrounded by tender, loving care no matter how inappropriate their behavior or on the premise that fat children are healthy children.

The stimulus control of mands may also be extended to those objects and events frequently *associated* with the object manded. For example, the mand "Cookie" may come to be evoked by a cookie jar, a cellophane wrapper, the oven door, and odors that emanate from the baking of pastries. Here again, the parents' reinforcing practices may be inconsistent. If they supply the child with a cookie, the control of the mand by associated stimuli is effectively strengthened. If, on the other hand, they are conservative about between-meal snacks, they may not deliver the cookie, in which case, this type of stimulus generalization is checked. However, the parents are most likely to reinforce the mand "Cookie" when it has been evoked by stimuli frequently associated with cookies *and* when the child has *not* recently been fed. This rather common reinforcing practice serves to introduce a third class of stimuli that come to serve as S_D's for mands.

All the controlling stimuli discussed thus far are external or "public" events. But as we have noted, it is possible, indeed highly probable, that the control of mands will be extended to private events taking place beneath the skin. For example, with the passage of time since the last feeding, a number of physiological changes occur in the active, growing child. The liver, in particular, begins to manufacture glucose and other utilizable fuels from substances coming to it from adipose (fatty) tissue and from substances stored in the liver itself (Friedman and Stricker, 1976). Concomitant neural activity arising in the liver and associated increases in activation level are, therefore, always present as stimuli when the child's suppy of utilizeable fuels is diminished. Parents cannot and do not, of course, observe these stimulus events when they reinforce a mand. However, when they reinforce mands for foodstuffs only when the child has not been recently fed, those internal stimulus events will always accompany the public events in the presence of which those mands are reinforced. The result of this process is that mands for certain classes of reinforcing events may appear to be independent of environmental control, arising, so to speak, out of nowhere. But they have simply been brought under the predominant control of internal or private stimulus events. We hasten to add, however, that private stimuli are rarely, if ever, the only stimuli serving as S_D's for mands.

Mands are typically controlled by a variety of S_D's, each of which contributes to the strength or probability of the verbal response. Given the usual reinforcing practices of parents, we may suppose that the mand "Cookie" is least likely to be emitted when the child has just been fed, when there are no human adults present, and when no stimuli resembling or commonly associated with cookies are present (Case I). The mand is more likely to be evoked if a parent who has reinforced the child in the past comes into view (Case II), and it is more likely still in the presence of the parent and private stimuli arising from food deprivation (Case III).[10] The mand is quite likely to be evoked by that combination of stimuli that includes the presence of a parent, internal stimuli arising from food deprivation, and stimuli resembling, or commonly associated with, cookies (Case IV). The mand is virtually guaranteed when the cookie itself, the parent, and private stimuli arising from food deprivation are present (Case V).

Tacts

Unlike mands, the verbal operants classified as tacts (Skinner, 1957, p. 81) are typically brought under the control of one or a sharply limited set of S_D's. Another contrast is seen in the reinforcing consequences of mands and tacts. As we have seen, the mand usually specifies the reinforcing event whether it be an object to be supplied by a listener or the behavior of the listener or both. The tact, on the other hand, is shaped and maintained by a variety of reinforcing events, including generalized reinforcers. One might say that the mand specifies the reinforcing stimulus but leaves the S_D vague whereas the tact specifies the controlling S_D but leaves the reinforcing consequences vague.

The development of tacts usually follows on, and is facilitated by, the prior acquisition of an echoic repertoire and a few simple mands. It is an extension of the game that began with parental efforts to shape mands, and like the shaping of mands, it can proceed quite rapidly once a few tacts have been acquired and strengthened.

Parents who set out to develop tacts often start with a stimulus object that was originally manded. For example, when "Cookie" is evoked by the presence of a cookie when the child has recently been fed, the parent might reinforce the child *not* by providing a cookie, but with hugs, smiles, and such verbal expressions as "Good girl!" or "That's right!" or "Yes!" and so on. Other, quite accidental applications of the procedure may occur when parents converse a great deal in the presence of the child and have also gone to some lengths to shape and strengthen echoic operants. For example, in discussing the various features of a new chair and in deciding where to place it, the parents may be surprised to hear the small child emit, "Chair" while touching

---

[10]During the early shaping of mands, parents may find the mand "Cookie" to be quite strong (occurring frequently) under the conditions described in Cases II and III. In fact, once a single mand has been acquired, it may be evoked by *any* reinforcing stimulus because stimulus generalization is most common when no other response is available. In the vernacular, we might say that the child says, "Cookie" when it means orange juice. Needless to say, these are very important opportunities for the development of additional mands.

or attempting to climb into it. The child's response is not easily classified at this point. It may be simply echoic, a mand to be placed in the chair or for parental attention, an early tact, or possibly a combination of all three. Thoughtful parents may, however, take this opportunity to strengthen the response as a tact by attending to the child and providing supplementary stimulation such as "What is that?" or "Chair?" in order to evoke the child's response once more. When the child again emits the word "Chair," parents may then strengthen the tact with the generalized reinforcers mentioned earlier.

A more deliberate conditioning procedure is applied when the male parent, observing that his child is looking at his watch, supplies the verbal stimulus "Watch" or, more likely, "Tick-tock." When the child echoes the response or some variation of it, the father applies generalized reinforcers. A few more trials may be needed to strengthen and refine the response in the presence of the time piece and in the absence of the parent's echoic stimulus, "Tick-tock."

The differential reinforcement procedure is not completed by merely reinforcing the response in the presence of an appropriate stimulus, for tacts will extend to other stimulus objects in much the same way that mands do. A classic case of the extension of this tact has been reported by Clark (1973). A small child who had acquired the tact "Tick-tock" in the presence of her father's wristwatch, was then observed to emit the tact in the presence of other clocks in the house *and* in the presence of a gas meter, a bathroom scale with a round dial, and a fire hose wound around a spool. This rather amusing example shows that stimulus generalization is at work in the case of tacts as it is in the case of mands and all other operants. It also points up the necessity of curbing stimulus generalization, particularly in the case of tacts, where precise stimulus control is very important. One does this, of course, by applying an extinction procedure (ignoring the child) or a mild punishment procedure ("No, that isn't a tick-tock") when the verbal operant is emitted in the presence of an inappropriate stimulus object. In the early and more deliberate applications of the procedures, however, the *alternate* objects should be quite dissimilar to clocks. The reason for this is that the tact "Tick-tock," is likely to be evoked by objects similar to clocks (e.g., the bathroom scales) and will, therefore, need to be extinguished. As a consequence, the response is less likely to be emitted in the presence of those objects *and in the presence of clocks as well.*

The fact that the little girl also emitted "Tick-tock" in the presence of clocks other than her father's wristwatch reminds us that not all instances of stimulus generalization are inappropriate. When an acceptable extension of a tact occurs because a new stimulus object has properties in common with the original, the extended tact should, of course, be reinforced.

It is not necessary to wait for "spontaneous" generalization to occur. The parents of the little girl for example, could have proceeded to introduce a variety of timepieces to her and reinforced "Tick-tock" (or "Clock") in the presence of each while continuing to extinguish the response in the presence of nonclocks when deliberately attempting to extend the tact. However, one should initially select clocks that are similar to the one in the presence of which the response was originally reinforced. A clock of quite different properties (e.g., a digital clock) is less likely to evoke the tact and may, in fact, evoke a different response. In either case, an opportunity to strengthen the appropriate tact is lost.

Tacts under the control of various objects in the child's environment are ordinarily classified as nouns and are typically the first to be acquired. However, the acquisition of tacts that we call verbs follows very quickly because the *actions* of persons and things are also important features of the small child's environment.

The behavior of others, like any stimulating event, can come to serve as an S_D when one is exposed to applications of the differential reinforcement procedures. Furthermore, the small child can learn to respond differentially to its own behavior, and it is important that it be conditioned to do so. Parents usually begin by shaping verbal responses descriptive of the child's current or ongoing behavior. The child is well prepared for this task if parents have previously taken pains to shape a receptive repertoire and an extensive echoic repertoire. As we have seen, when the child has been conditioned to respond appropriately to the verbal stimulus "Pet doggy" and has also learned to echo, the echoic response can be readily transferred to (brought under the control of) the child's own behavior of petting the dog. In the same manner, such tacts as "Play," "Go," "Potty," "Cry," "Eat," "Fall down," "Run," and "Sleep," will come to be emitted in the presence of those behaviors whether they are being displayed by the child or others. The acquisition of verbs is further accelerated, of course, when the parents provide running commentaries on the child's activities while reinforcing the child's approximations of those tacts and when they have also taught the child to respond appropriately to "What are you doing?"

When parents are shaping tacts descriptive of the child's own behavior, the features of the child's nonverbal behavior controlling the parents' verbalizations are visual. However, the child cannot always see its own behavior, and in no case does the child see it from the same vantage point as the parent-observer. As a consequence, the stimuli controlling the child's tacts of its own nonverbal operants are rarely identical with those that control the parents' behavior when shaping those tacts. In fact, the process of stimulus induction gives rise to the possibility that the child's self-descriptive tacts will come under the control of proprioceptive and other covert responses that are generated by, or accompany, its nonverbal operants.

THE FURTHER DEVELOPMENT OF A VERBAL REPERTOIRE

Longitudinal studies of the acquisition of verbal operants have revealed that they are acquired in a sequence that is remarkably consistent across children. A high rate of babbling precedes simple echoic operants, which, in turn, precede the acquisition of one-word mands and tacts. After a number of one-word mands and tacts have been shaped and strengthened, slightly more complex operants in the form of multiword utterances begin to appear. The latter are comprised of strings of nouns and verbs plus a few adjectives and are often emitted in an order judged to be correct (e.g., "Daddy fix," "Hit ball"). However, the verbal operants at this stage have been called "telegraphic speech" because such grammatical elements as verb inflections, case endings on nouns, definite and indefinite articles, and prepositions are notably absent (Brown, 1973). For example, the small child somewhere around the twenty-fourth month might say, "Daddy sit chair" rather than "Daddy is sitting in the chair." The grammatical refinements (*is, ing, in, the*), which Brown (1973) calls obligatory morphemes, begin to appear after the child's speech has become telegraphic and are themselves acquired in an orderly sequence.

Grammatical Refinements

In order to provide for the acquisition of more complex verbal operants, parents might be simply advised to talk to the child a lot. That advice has some merit, but we hasten to add that mere exposure is not enough. Moskowitz (1978) has described the case of a small boy who was provided extensive exposure to television because he had not acquired a vocal operant repertoire. (He was both asthmatic and the son of deaf parents). Although he had normal hearing and became fluent in the American Sign Language of his parents by the age of three, he neither spoke nor responded appropriately to the vocal operant behavior of others as a consequence of his exposure to television. There is other evidence that mere exposure to speech is not enough. Teachers at all levels all too frequently encounter children *and* adults whose verbal repertoire is painfully deficient though at least some of them have been exposed to effective speech in the home and elsewhere.

Brown (1973) has observed that parents frequently understand (and therefore reinforce) the telegraphic speech of their children. He concludes that if "selection pressures to impel children to bring their speech into line with adult models" operate at all, they must operate outside the home. No doubt they do, but Segal (1975) has pointed out that parents may reinforce fewer of the child's primitive utterances in the home than Brown assumes. Suppose for example, that the child's "Daddy sit chair" was not a tact but a mand to be placed in her high chair by the male parent. If her verbal operant is glossed (interpreted) by the parent as "Daddy is sitting in the chair," the child's mand in the form emitted is not reinforced. If the child repeats the mand, possibly while approaching and pointing to her high chair, and the male parent then places her in it, then Brown is correct. There has been no "selection pressure" for a more advanced form. If, on the other hand, the child's mother intervened by providing the verbal stimulus "Daddy sit Kimmy in chair?" delaying the reinforcement slightly until Kimberly echoed all or some portion of the expanded form, an effective differential reinforcement procedure has obviously been applied.

As we have noted, parental speech frequently becomes simplified in the presence of the child. In the exchange between Kimberly and her parents, for example, the mother did not say, nor did she require Kimberly to say, "Daddy would you place me in the high chair, please?" Nevertheless, a conditioning trial had been applied. Baldwin and Baldwin (1973) found that the verbal behavior of mothers, though simplified in the presence of their children, was always more advanced than the child's and remained that way even as the child's verbal repertoire expanded. If such practices are common, then reasonably effective conditioning trials must be occurring daily in the lives of many small children.

Our studies of parental conditioning practices, limited though they may be, lend emphasis to the principle that the behavior of effective trainers must be under the discriminative control of the behavior of the trainee. If the shaping of an echoic repertoire is to proceed, the parent must first provide a verbal stimulus and then reinforce the child's first crude imitation of the response. When that response has been strengthened, the parent must then withhold reinforcers until a closer approximation of the final form is emitted. Reinforcers are again applied without delay. The process must be carefully repeated, possibly many times. The successful application of this very basic shaping procedure obviously requires that the parents' reinforcing behavior be under the precise control of very subtle advancements in the child's verbal responses. The same may be said when the child's speech has advanced to the telegraphic stage. It may well be good practice to reinforce telegraphic speech until it is occurring at a sustained rate, as the parents in Brown's studies seemed to do. If, however, the child's verbal repertoire is to advance beyond the telegraphic stage, it is also good practice gradually to add and then reinforce the more complex verbal operants that characterize effective speech.

The Development of Obligatory Morphemes

Important clues as to how to proceed come from several sources. On the negative side, the results of a study by Cazden (1965) suggest that parents should *not* attempt to expand the child's verbal repertoire all at once or in all possible ways. Rather, they should proceed in orderly steps, first concentrating on the shaping of the less complex obligatory morphemes before progressing to those that are more difficult to shape.

The studies by Brown (1973) and the DeVilliers (DeVilliers and DeVilliers, 1973) have provided us with an approximate order in which obligatory morphemes are acquired (and, therefore, an estimate of their relative grammatical complexity). They have found, for example, the present progressive *ing* on verbs is among the first of the obligatory morphemes to appear.[11] Therefore,

---

[11] This may be partially accounted for by the fact that parents most often talk to their small children about the here and now. There are, however, other more important considerations. First, the present progressive form is *always* formed by adding "ing" to the present tense verb. Secondly, there is little or no variation in the pronunciation of "ing." Finally, it is much easier to bring a verbal operant under the control of a stimulus event (in this case, ongoing behavior) that continues to be present.

parents might first concentrate on the development of *ing* forms before attempting to shape the more complex obligatory morphemes.

Present Progressive Verbs

The shaping and strengthening of present progressive verbs should begin when the child has begun to speak in two-word sentences. When, for example, the child tacts the ongoing behavior of others, including the family pet, the parent might at first simply add the "ing" to the child's tact and reinforce the child's response when it occurs ("doggie slee*ping*," "Julie cry*ing*," "Cindy read*ing*," etc.). This informal training can be supplemented by deliberately engaging in some activity while the child is attending to the parent, supplying the appropriate tact (Daddy jump*ing*), and reinforcing the child's approximations of it. Once present progressive forms have begun to appear, parents can add the mand "What am I doing?" prompting only as necessary and reinforcing the child's tacts when the present progressive form is included. This game can be played whenever the opportunity presents itself, and when the child is responding consistently, the parent can then teach the child to tact its own ongoing activities. This can be accomplished by posing the question, "What are you doing?" whenever the child is engaging in some activity and subsequently prompting and reinforcing the child's reply (Cindy walk*ing*, play*ing*, sing*ing*, and so on). To carry the game further, the parent can begin to command the child to engage in various activities that it has already learned to tact and then pose the question, "What are you doing?"

As always, when parents set out to shape and strengthen one form of verbal operant, they initiate the development of many other important operants, both verbal and nonverbal. However, they should concentrate on the shaping of one form at a time. It may be noted that the parent's prompts and mands will include appropriate forms of the verb *to be* ("What *am* I doing" and "Kimmy *is* playing" and "What *are* you doing?") and other obligatory morphemes such as pronouns and articles. On the other hand, these will not often be included in the child's verbal operants, and the parent should neither add nor require them before reinforcing the child. At this stage, the major and perhaps only requirement for reinforcement is the appearance of the verb in its present progressive form.

Prepositions

Brown and the DeVilliers found that a limited set of prepositions begin to appear after the present progressive verb forms. The next obligatory morphemes to appear in the order of their appearance are the plural *s* inflections on nouns, a limited number of past irregular verb inflections (*did, went, came,* etc.), followed somewhat later by the past regular *ed* inflection on verbs.

Lovaas (1977) has developed programs for the shaping of a number of these obligatory morphemes. As their basic features are both interesting and instructive, we describe a few of them, beginning with the program that has been successful in the shaping of prepositions.

Parents will have to resolve the question of when to provide this training. McCarthy's review of the literature (McCarthy, 1954) indicates that many children will be ready for the training somewhere around the twenty-fourth month. However, small children vary enormously in the rate of acquiring verbal operants, so age is not a fundamental criterion and may be a misleading one. A more important consideration is whether or not the child has begun to speak in multiword utterances. If the child's verbal operants are commonly in the form of two- or three-word utterances and, further, if its tacts of ongoing activities now typically include the present progressive *ing* form, then it is likely that the child will readily acquire the verbal operants known as prepositions.

The parent-trainer, like all effective trainers, will have to prepare for the shaping of prepositions. In particular, he or she will need to have at hand a number of training objects that can be placed *on, in, under, behind,* and *in front of* each other. Coins, cups, a small box, blocks, and other small objects familiar to the child will do. The next important step is to select a familiar setting (such as the kitchen table) so that potentially competing behavior is not likely to be evoked or elicited. Then, when the child seems to be "looking for something to do" or, better yet, when the child mands play activities, the training can be initiated.

Lovaas (1977) has found that the acquisition of a preposition is facilitated by first shaping (or strengthening) *receptive* operants in the presence of parental mands that contain the preposition. Therefore, when seated at the table with two of the objects (e.g., a penny and a cup) in sight, the parent first instructs the child to put the penny in the cup. The parent might simply say, "In" or "Put the penny *in* the cup," vocally emphasizing "in." The appropriate response may be prompted, if necessary, by taking the child's hand, placing the penny in it, then guiding the child's hand toward the cup and releasing the penny into it, always generously reinforcing the child at the completion of this sequence. The parental prompts are then gradually faded until the child is consistently, though not inevitably, placing the penny in the cup on request. At this point, the parent exchanges the cup for the small box, introduces the mand "Put the penny *under* the box," and proceeds to shape the nonverbal operant of placing the penny *under* the box in the same manner as above.[12] The receptive operant is prompted as necessary, and then the prompt is faded, all the while generously reinforcing the child at the completion of each sequence. Then the parent should return to the "in" response for a few trials and return back to the "under" response until the child consistently places the penny in the cup or under the box. Finally, the parent gradually removes the

[12]We have not indicated what the parent should do when the child "makes a mistake." There are three procedures that may be implemented. (1) The parent may gently say, "No, no" or (2) simply do nothing for five to 10 seconds and possibly turn away from the child or (3) repeat the request and return to an earlier and more complete prompting procedure. Typically some combination of, or all, the above procedures is most effective.

cup so that it is now more convenient for the child to place the penny in the box or under it.

When the child is responding correctly to "in" and "under," the parent may then switch containers and articles and repeat the commands to put article X *in* or *under* container Y. Needless to say, the parent should not continue the training sessions if the child seems to become tired of the game or regresses. This typically indicates that the materials used as well as the parent's extrinsic reinforcers have lost much of their reinforcing potential for the moment. The training sessions may be continued at a later time, and responses to new prepositions such as "on" ("put the cup *on* the saucer") may then be added, using the same procedures described above.

After three or four receptive operants have been shaped and strengthened, the explicit shaping of verbal operants (prepositions) may begin. It may be noted that when parents have taken steps to shape and strengthen an echoic repertoire, the child is quite likely to have been echoing, though perhaps covertly, all or some parts of the parent's verbal requests during the receptive operant training. For example, when the parent says, "Put the penny *in* the cup," vocally emphasizing "in," the child may be echoing "in" and other parts of the request. Consequently, the parent's reinforcement, contingent on the receptive operant, will strengthen the echoic operant as well, and the latter may already be under the partial control of the penny *in* the cup. The parent should not, therefore, be surprised if the child occasionally emits the verbal operant "in the X" in the presence of an object *in* a container. But it is necessary specifically to strengthen the verbal operant under the control of the appropriate S_D. This is accomplished as follows: The parent places the object *in* the container (or instructs the child to do so) and then asks, "Where is the penny?" If the child does not respond, an echoic prompt should be supplied and then gradually faded. Any of a wide variety of the child's verbal responses, so long as they contain the verbal operant "in," should be generously reinforced. When the child is consistently responding (e.g., four out of five times or eight out of ten) "Penny in the cup," "In cup," or merely, "In," the parent may proceed to other prepositions such as *under* or *on*, using the same procedures. Finally, additional containers and objects should be presented along with the same question, "Where is it?"

After the simpler prepositions are shaped and strengthened, the parent can proceed with the development of the more difficult ones such as *behind, in front of*, and so on, using the same training procedures.

It is reasonable to expect some difficulties as one proceeds to shape prepositional speech. We have already mentioned one problem—the reinforcers, both extrinsic and those intrinsic to the training, momentarily lose their reinforcing properties. Another problem is commonly found in the fading of echoic prompts. The child may respond to very minimal prompts and not respond at all when the prompt is completely withheld. It is possible that parents are inclined to prompt too often. Lovaas (1977, p. 20) provides some suggestions, including the general rule of providing the minimal number of prompts necessary to evoke the appropriate verbal operant when the operant has previously occurred in the absence of the prompt. In other words, if the verbal operant does not occur, turn away from the child for five to 10 seconds and then repeat the question, "Where is the penny?" Another problem that may be encountered is the apparent loss of previously learned prepositions as new ones are acquired. This is why the parent-trainers should occasionally return to the shaping and strengthening of earlier prepositions as they proceed to develop new ones.

As in the case of shaping most verbal operants, it will be necessary to extend the control of the preposition to other objects (or, more specifically, to the spatial relation between them). The formal process of extending stimulus control is included in the above training procedures, and, of course, it will occur naturally. But it is necessary to promote further extensions of appropriate stimulus control, and this is best accomplished as the opportunities present themselves in the child's everyday life. For example, the parent might ask where a given object (her doll, the dog, etc.) is, prompt the answer (on the bed, in his box, etc.), reinforce the child's response, and then repeat the question without the prompt. Discrimination trials of this sort could be implemented almost daily and will serve to refine and strengthen this class of verbal operants.

It should be noted that the controlling S_D's for the above prepositions are spatial relations between objects *external* to the child. Once these can be reliably evoked by a "where" question and the controlling relation or merely by the controlling relation itself, it is time to bring the verbal operants we call prepositions under the control of the spatial relationship between *the child* and various features of its world. This can be accomplished by getting in, on, under, or beside an object and then asking, "Where am I?" and providing prompts as necessary ("on the floor," "under the table," "beside the chair," and so on) and reinforcing the child's verbal response if appropriate. Then, the parent commands the child to place itself in the same manner (e.g., "Sit on the floor"), shaping and strengthening the receptive operant as necessary. While the child is *on* the floor, *in* the box, *under* the table, or *beside* a chair, the parent poses the question, "Where are you?" and shapes the appropriate verbal operant, utilizing the discrimination training procedures previously described.

Plurals

Once the above training program has been successfully implemented (one should not demand or wait for perfection), a program for the explicit development of plurals can be initiated. The objective is to teach the child to add an appropriate tag to verbal operants (tacts) when there is more than one object of the same class to be tacted. In this case, receptive operant shaping is not called for. However, one does begin with objects that have already come to control appropriate tacts in singular form. It is also important to begin with objects that require the "regular" form (i.e., the addition of "s" to the singular tact). The parent gets ready for the training sessions as before, this time selecting multiples of objects that the child can tact (blocks, coins, pencils, sticks, balls, spoons, etc.). The parent then places two objects (e.g., two pennies) in front of the child, picks up one of them, and says, "Here is one penny." Holding the penny in one hand, the parent then picks up the second and says, "Here are two ————" and waits for the child to say, "Pennies" and reinforces the child if the operant "pennies" is approximated. The shaping trials are repeated in the same manner until the child utters the differential response (penny or pennies) without prompting. Then the parent selects a new set of items (pencil, pencils) and shapes and strengthens the appropriate response to the singular and plural examples, occasionally returning to the pennies.

After the child has acquired eight or ten plurals, the parent may introduce several examples of an object and say, "Here are these . . ." or "Here are some (or many) . . . ," providing an echoic prompt only when necessary and, of course, generously reinforcing the appropriate response.

The above program includes training in stimulus generalization, but the child will also be observed to emit the plural form (e.g., "doggies" or "trees") in the presence of two or more of those objects without specific training. This is the familiar stimulus induction process working, and the parents should reinforce appropriate forms. However, it is quite likely that inappropriate forms will also occur (e.g., "foots or footsez," "mans," "boysez," etc.). It is best to ignore this form of stimulus induction until the child is consistently pluralizing without prompts. Then the parent can begin to shape and strengthen irregular plurals in the same manner as above, returning to regular forms previously acquired every five of six trials.

Past Tense Verbs

As Brown (1973) has noted, one of the last obligatory morphemes to be acquired is the past *ed* inflection on verbs. It is, therefore, suggested that parents not attempt to shape this class of verbal operants until after the child has acquired some of the less complex forms that we have already described. Lovaas (1977, p. 164) indicates that the parent should prepare for the training by selecting from 12 to 15 common activities that require the regular *ed* inflection (walk*ed*, play*ed*, jump*ed*, clapp*ed*, clos*ed*, touch*ed*, etc.). Then, while the child is attending to the parent-trainer, the parent engages in one of the activities (e.g., walking) and asks, "What am I doing?" The parental prompt, "Mother is walking," may be provided if necessary and quickly faded. As this procedure is merely an extension of the earlier program for shaping the present progressive *ing* form, the child should be tacting the parent's activity, "You are (or Mommy's) walking" in short order. The next step is to engage in the activity, stop, pose the question, "What did I just do?" and prompt the child to say, "You (or Mommy) walk*ed*," vocally emphasizing "walked." This procedure is repeated until the child correctly answers the question without prompting.[13] Then the parent engages in another activity (e.g., clapping the hands) and repeats the entire procedure. Other activities are then introduced in the same manner, returning to the earlier ones from time to time.

Once the child is appropriately tacting 10 to 12 behaviors that have just occurred, the parent should then ask the child to engage in those activities. As the child performs each one, the parent asks, "What are you doing?" When the child stops or is told to stop, the parent asks, "What did you just do?" and prompts the appropriate tact (e.g., I clapped my hands) and reinforces the child's response when it includes the past tense form. When the child is appropriately tacting the original set of activities in the past tense without prompting, the parent may introduce a new set of activities and repeat the procedure.

Stimulus induction accounts for the fact that the child will appropriately tact other behaviors that it has completed, and the parent should, of course, generously reinforce the child when it does so. However, stimulus induction also accounts for the mistakes the child will make (e.g., "I goed," "I eated," "I runned"). These may be ignored until the child is consistently tacting the just-completed activities that were incorporated in the training. Then training on *irregular* past tense verbs can be initiated. The procedures utilized for the shaping of regular past tense verbs can be used for this purpose as well. Parents should again be cautioned not to expect or demand perfection because the acquisition of irregular past tense verbs, in particular, will require many discrimination trials.

Self-controlling Operants

As always, when parents set out to shape a given class of verbal operants, the child acquires much more. The acquisition of past tense verbs is no exception. Not only is the child's verbal and receptive operant repertoire being refined and expanded, training in self-awareness, which began when the child learned to tact its ongoing behavior, is also continued. But tacting ongoing behavior, whether one's own or that of another person, and tacting it after the fact are quite different processes. When, for example, parents train the child to respond to the question, "What did you *just* do?" the response cannot be said to be under the control of the child's past behavior because it is no longer present. Rather, as Skinner (1957, p. 143) has pointed out, the child's

---

[13]Perhaps it goes without saying that the child whose echoic operant repertoire has been well developed may be repeating the parental prompt or parts of it. Thus, the child's tact of a previous behavior may be, in part, self-echoic. That is to say, it may be under the control of the parental prompt *and* the stimulation from the child's covert echo of the prompt. This is troublesome, of course, and one therefore fades the parental prompt as quickly as possible. However, the strong probability that the child will covertly echo the prompt is an important precedent for the development of self-control wherein the child emits behavior, verbal or otherwise, that produces S_D's evoking other operants, whether they be echoic, intraverbal, or non-verbal in character.

verbal operant must be understood as a response to *current* stimuli, *including events within the child itself*, generated by the question. Therefore, in the shaping of the verbal operants known as past tense verbs, an additional behavioral process is being systematically developed, possibly for the first time. This all-important behavioral process is usually referred to as problem solving, thinking, or, more generally, self-control, and we shall have more to say about it in the next chapter. In the meantime, however, an analysis of Lovaas' programs for the development of past tense verbs and *"recall"* will help clarify it.

Initially, the child's response to the question, "What did you just do?" is probably little more than an echoic or self-echoic response, for the parent prompts the correct past tense response. As the parental prompt is faded, however, the response gradually comes under the control of the question and other S_D's generated by the child itself, as Skinner noted. In other words, *the child is required to behave so as to produce additional stimuli serving to evoke the final response* (e.g., "I closed the door"). The subsequent reinforcement from the parent strengthens the final response *and* any precurrent operants that produced the additional discriminative stimuli. Much remains to be learned about the topography of these precurrent self-controlling operants because both the operants themselves and the resulting S_D's often occur at the covert level. Perhaps for that reason, neither Lovaas nor anyone else to our knowledge has attempted to shape them directly for the child and to reinforce the "solution" response when it occurs. For example, in developing recall, Lovaas (1977, p. 167) instructs the child to perform a simple activity that it has already learned to tact and then asks the child what he or she just did. When the child appropriately tacts a half dozen activities after the fact, the child is instructed to engage in two activities before tacting both, then three activities, and so on. Finally, the child is asked to tact behaviors that had been emitted several minutes prior to the request and, finally, those that had occurred hours or days ago. When the trainer reinforces the child in the absence of prompts, one operant that is required for reinforcement can be unambiguously described, and that is the tact itself. What remains obscure is the nature of the child's self-controlling operants that served to produce additional S_D's evoking the tact. However, some hints regarding the properties of this behavior are contained in the training programs described by Lovaas (1977, pp. 164–170).

The first clue comes from Lovaas' recommendations that in the first stages of recall training, it is useful to have the child tact its behavior while it is occurring. The procedure is helpful, no doubt, because it strengthens verbal behavior that the child can then turn on itself when later faced with the problem of describing his or her behavior some time after the fact. Early on, the tact may at times be little more than self-echoic, partially under the control of the parental question, "What did you do?" and the stimulation from the child's covert or overt response, "I closed the door." A similar process of self-control may sometimes be observed in adults who locate a phone number in the directory and keep repeating it (either covertly or overtly) until they reach the phone to dial the number. However, this form of self-control is certainly not very efficient and becomes impossible as the child is required to tact *several* activities hours or days after the fact. It is, therefore, not likely to be strengthened to any degree or, if so, is soon replaced by more effective forms of self-control as training in recall progresses.

The more effective self-controlling operants could be verbal operants in minimal form. In fading the prompt, Lovaas suggests that the parent proceed from the complete statement of the child's desired tact of past activities to partial prompts such as "I closed the . . ." or, "I closed the door, and then . . ." before fading the prompt altogether. It is further suggested that, in the early phases of training, the parent should select activities that have concrete objects associated with them (e.g., ball, door) and then pose the question, "What did you just do?" in the presence of those objects. Under these circumstances, the child's response in the absence of the parental prompt is probably under the control of the question *and* the child's tacts of the objects, both serving as or producing S_D's that evoke the complete answer (e.g., "I closed the door, and then I played with the ball," and so on). This procedure seems to initiate the development of more effective forms of self-controlling operants by teaching the child to emit tacts not of the entire activity but of an object associated with each activity. It is a more efficient form because it requires less behavior at the time and also later, when the child is faced with the question. At that time, the child's covert reproduction of the tact or a fragment of it may result in self-stimulation sufficient to evoke the entire answer to the parent's question. Because tacts of objects are usually the strongest operants in a given setting and, therefore, the first to be evoked in that setting, the child is not required to repeat them over and over again until the question is posed. (However, the child may be required to put together a string of tacts [e.g., "door, then ball, and then box"] and rehearse the string a few times as the activities are completed.)

The training procedure for recall may also develop nonverbal forms of self-controlling operants. As the objects associated with the child's behavior serve as S_D's at the time the behavior is emitted, the objects will continue to serve that function when they are later presented though they are likely to evoke only fragments of the earlier behavior. Consequently, in the early stages of recall training when the parent asks, "What did you do?" in the presence of those objects, it is possible that incomplete or inchoate forms of the earlier behavior will be evoked, perhaps at a covert level. The child's response such as "I closed the door" can then be understood as being under the control of the parental question *and* stimulation from the incomplete forms of the earlier nonverbal behavior. The stage was set for the development of this behavioral process in early conditioning programs when the child was taught to describe ongoing and complete forms of its behavior (present progressive verbal operants). In later stages, when the question is posed in settings that do not contain the objects, a *combination* of self-controlling operants might be required to produce S_D's sufficient to evoke the answer. For example, the parental question might evoke covert verbal operants such as "door," "ball," which in turn evoke inchoate forms of closing the door and playing with the ball, all of which might serve as S_D's that, in conjunction with the question, evoke the answer.

There is at least one other form of self-controlling operant that may develop in recall training. In teaching the child to report behavior that took place in the past, the parent is also teaching it to observe or attend to its own behavior. In addition, the parent may be teaching the child to "look at" its behavior and other events in a manner such that these can be seen again in their absence. When the parent poses the question, the self-controlling operant of seeing again some feature or features of its prior behavior is evoked, and the resultant self-stimulation serves to evoke the answer. When the parent reinforces the verbal response, he or she reinforces the child's precurrent behavior of seeing again as well as the attentional operants that made it possible. The behavior of seeing again, sometimes referred to as visual imagery, is obviously difficult to study. Moreover, traditional formulations, in which it is postulated that copies of the external world are somehow imprinted on the occipital cortex and later retrieved to be "looked at" and reported, have stood in the way of a more fruitful analysis. For these reasons, we have not learned very much about the behavior of seeing objects and events in their absence though, as we all know, most of us are capable of doing so in varying degrees. Nor can we say very much about those attentional operants that make visual imagery possible. It seems clear that there are effective ways of looking at things so that they can be more readily seen in their absence. However, until those operants have been analyzed and described, trainers will have to depend on the age-old method of posing problems of increasing difficulty and reinforcing the final verbal operant. This procedure will also strengthen the precurrent operant of seeing again that helped to evoke the verbal operant and those attentional operants that made seeing again more probable. But, of course, the latter are not likely to be the most effective forms, and they may not occur at all.

Because self-controlling operants are conditioned only indirectly, it is not easy to specify which form or what combination of forms will develop. Nor are we yet in a position to prescribe the most effective forms. Does this mean that parents should wait until this very promising field of study has produced an unequivocal description of the most effective forms of problem solving? Not by any means. In the first place, we believe it is of utmost importance to develop the basic process of self-control whatever its form. Secondly, it is clear that verbal operants will always be included in any list of effective forms of self-control. Verbal behavior does not require environmental support for its execution and can, therefore, be emitted anywhere. It automatically generates stimuli, both public and private, which may serve as S_D's for those whose receptive operant repertoires have also been developed. Moreover, the controlling verbal operants can often be covert, abbreviated, or otherwise emitted in fragmentary form and still remain effective in producing stimuli serving to evoke other operants that may satisfy the prevailing contingencies. For all these reasons—and there are perhaps others—verbal operants are among the most common forms of self-controlling or problem-solving operants and may well be the most effective forms in a wide variety of problematic settings

Further training in grammar and syntax can be provided more or less informally by engaging the child in conversations about those activities and events in its everyday life that are obviously reinforcing (new games, new toys, a trip to the zoo, and so on). When the child's tacts of those activities and events are emitted in grammatically correct form, the parent should provide generous reinforcement. If they are not, the parent may occasionally repeat the tacts in the appropriate form and then reinforce the child if the tact is a closer approximation of the acceptable form. If the child does not repeat the tact or repeats it again as before, the parent may turn to other matters and later engage the child in conversation in a different setting or as new activities and events crop up. Repetitions of this procedure will enable the parent to determine those forms of speech that are missing or incorrect and to return to an earlier program for more shaping.

COMPOSITION

As the child is exposed to the various shaping procedures we have described, its verbal repertoire loses much of its "telegraphic" character and begins to be emitted in a form that we regard as grammatically correct. The child's utterances, now in reasonably complete sentence form, include articles, prepositions, plurals, verb inflections, and so on, and are emitted in an appropriate order. Moreover, the foundation has been laid for the further development of the rather complex behavioral processes underlying composition. As we have seen, the verbal repertoire of the small child as well as of the adult does not remain under the simple control of the stimulus events that comprise a given setting. When faced with problems, the child can be taught to behave so as to produce additional and often private stimuli that evoke other operants. It may also acquire the behavior involved in creating, ordering, or otherwise "putting together" a combination of verbal operants. We need to discuss the manner in which this is accomplished and why it must be done.

As parental training advances, the number of functional units comprising the child's verbal repertoire becomes very large. Some of the units are quite small as, for example, the minimal echoic units "kang," "t," and "d." Some, whether large or small, may come under precise and exclusive stimulus control as in the case of "clock" or "tick-tock." Others will come under multiple stimulus control through induction and the reinforcement practices of parents and peers. An extensive repertoire of this sort ensures that a wide variety of verbal operants will be evoked in natural settings. But difficulties may arise when several S_D's occur together in a given setting, especially for the first time. An example of the difficulties can be noted in the effects of a multiple audience.

Because verbal behavior is typically reinforced in the presence of listeners, their presence, behavior, and special properties constitute an important class of S_D's for verbal operants. But a given audience characteristically reinforces only certain classes of verbal operants and may, by ignoring the speaker, extinguish and even punish other classes. Playmates, for example, may pay little attention to, or make fun of, the more sophisticated speech that parents consistently reinforce, but they may reinforce strings of "silly" intraverbals or obscene responses or both, which parents are likely to punish. When the two audiences come together and the verbal repertoires evoked by the two audiences are equally strong, a number of interesting effects may be noted. There may be a significant reduction in speech of any form—the child becomes silent. Or the child's speech may oscillate between incomplete forms, producing an effect we call stuttering and stammering. In either case, there is a problem because neither audience is likely to reinforce the child and both may punish by ridicule. Under these circumstances, the child might attempt to resolve the problem by moving closer to one of the audiences so that it might whisper to one audience while out of the range of the other. Or there may be an attempt to separate the two audiences physically as exemplified by the child's suggestion that "we go outside and play." But the advanced child might resolve the problem by composing verbal behavior that is more likely to be reinforced by both audiences.

Composition typically involves the dual processes of self-strengthening and self-editing (Skinner, 1957, Chapters 15 and 17). Self-strengthening refers to the type of self-control that was analyzed in our discussion of recall training. Self-editing refers to an additional and rather complex behavioral process that remains to be analyzed. In self-strengthening, the child learns to behave so as to produce additional S_D's that may evoke verbal operants acceptable to both audiences. In our example, the child might listen more carefully to a conversation between playmates and parents, thus producing S_D's evoking "safe" verbal behavior. The child joins in the conversation. Other forms of self-strengthening include a visual scan of the setting in order to produce S_D's that might evoke acceptable verbal behavior. The child thereby "fills the silence" or changes the conversation. However, the additional behavior thus produced may also be unsuccessful in the sense that it, too, fails to gain the attention of either audience or continues to be punished by one or both. Such consequences may lead to the development of self-editing, a process in which the child learns to examine its verbal behavior for its effects on prospective listeners and then either rejects it or emits it. The verbal behavior examined may be that which is evoked by features of the setting or behavior that is evoked through self-strengthening or both.

The most obvious examples of self-editing are found in the adult's transcriptive operants. When composing a letter or a chapter for a book, a word, a phrase, or a sentence is evoked and then erased or crossed out. Evidence of self-editing can also be found in the vocal behavior of adults and advanced children when they quickly add, "I'm sorry. I don't know why I said that" or "I meant to say . . ." The small child might clap its hand over its mouth to interrupt or prevent vocal behavior that is strong but that, because it has also been punished, produces aversive effects.

All the above forms of self-editing can be readily observed. Apparently, however, many, if not most, forms of self-editing occur at the covert level. To carry our multiple audience example a bit further, we might suppose that when the child was punished by one or both audiences, the child then behaves so as to produce S_D's evoking additional verbal behavior but first emits it covertly to note its effects. If it produces emotional responses of the type elicited by conditioned aversive stimuli, it, too, is revoked or withheld, and the compositional process continues. If it does not, the verbal behavior is released or emitted overtly. This is obviously a very lengthy and complex form of self-editing. We must, therefore, assume that whereas this more deliberate form of self-editing can be shaped and is occasionally evoked, its development is preceded by a simpler behavioral process. When, for example, the child has been punished for speaking in a given manner, the auditory stimuli produced by the verbal operants become conditioned aversive stimuli. Consequently, the operant responses will simply and automatically be interrupted at an early and possibly covert stage. No behavior crudely described as withholding, reviewing, revoking, or releasing the verbal operants can be said to occur. If unedited verbal behavior continues to be punished, however, self-editing is likely to develop. The child learns to "talk to itself" and to attend to the effects produced by the covert responses. If stimuli associated with the covert behavior do not produce aversive effects, it is released or simply "tumbles out." If they do produce aversive effects, the verbal operants are simply interrupted or withheld and possibly replaced by other verbal responses that are strong in that setting.

The full-blown process of composition is most likely to occur in instruction wherein the speaker is faced with the problem of tacting a complex setting so that a listener might behave effectively in that setting. Self-strengthening and self-editing may also be necessary in relatively novel settings or when the contingencies for appropriate grammar and syntax are fairly demanding. Composition only rarely occurs in casual conversation, and even then it is typically short-circuited, as it may be in instruction.

It is easy to overestimate the frequency with which compositional behavior precedes effective speech. Familiar settings, especially, are likely to evoke many different verbal operants among children who have been exposed to the developmental procedures we have described. Thus, self-strengthening is unnecessary to increase the supply of verbal behavior to be edited. The verbal responses that are evoked may often meet the requirements of the prevailing contingencies, in which case self-editing also does not occur. When the first responses to be evoked produce aversive self-stimulation, they may be interrupted in their early stages and replaced with other verbal behavior that is also strong and that is also positively reinforced. Therefore, even the self-editing process is typically short-circuited if it occurs at all.

Composition is, nevertheless, of obvious importance, and parents would do well to promote its development. They will have, of course, already begun the process in providing the training programs described thus far. However, composition may be further promoted each time a parent asks the child to tact its earlier activities outside the setting in which those activities took place or to tell a story about an animal or person in the picture on the wall or to play a game of "make-believe" in which the child is required to tell the parent what to do or how to do something. The prompts the parent supplies and then gradually fades will be taken over by the child to increase the supply of its own verbal behavior. The corrections that the parent introduces after the child has warmed to the game are likely to shape and strengthen the self-editing process. Such exercises will provide a solid foundation for the further development of composition, which will, one hopes, continue throughout a lifetime, formally, as in courses in English composition and logic, and informally when the advanced child or the adult speaks in ways that make no sense to listeners or that are regarded as "illogical" by them.

SUMMARY

Our goal in providing this rather extensive treatment of verbal behavior was not merely to exemplify further the principles of behavior or to demonstrate their application and fundamental role in the development of verbal behavior. It was also provided in order to emphasize the dramatic advantages of a verbal repertoire once developed. From the time small children begin to acquire echoic operants to the time compositional operants are shaped, they gain a measure of control over their environment and themselves that is greater than in the lives of infrahuman organisms. A basic repertoire of mands, for example, enables the small child to produce reinforcing events and to escape aversive stimulation far more quickly and easily than it could if those operants had not been shaped and strengthened. Not only does a repertoire of tacts enable the child to describe objects and events for the benefit of others, but the child also begins to observe and respond effectively to important features of the world that it would otherwise neither see nor respond to. When the child has been conditioned both as a speaker and a listener, it is prepared for further instruction, which will enable it to respond effectively to those aspects of the world to which it has been exposed only briefly, if at all. It is also prepared to instruct others and to reason, solve problems, and otherwise control itself in ways that would be impossible in the absence of a well-developed verbal and receptive operant repertoire. We now turn to these "higher order" forms of operant behavior.

SIX
THINKING, PROBLEM SOLVING, AND DECISION MAKING

In this chapter, we take up the topic of human problem-solving and decision-making behavior. First, we will discuss the importance of problem solving in human affairs in general and particularly in the practice of management. Next we will identify those environmental conditions or situations under which these complex forms of human behavior are expected to occur. Then we will attempt to describe some of the more important classes of operant behavior typically described as problem solving, decision making, and thinking. In the final portion of this chapter, we will take up the topic of how problem-solving behaviors are reinforced and sustained.

There is a tendency to overemphasize the function of problem-solving behavior in human affairs. Some social scientists, for example, have suggested that "complex cognitive processes" inevitably precede instrumental behavior. Translated by us, this means that reasonably complex forms of behavior, usually occurring at the covert level, reliably precede more easily observed operants that satisfy the prevailing contingencies. But whatever one's interpretation, we should neither underemphasize nor overemphasize problem-solving and decision-making processes in human behavior. Much of the behavior of the adult human being may occur in the absence of behavior described as "consciously searching for alternatives" or as "making rational choices." However, rudimentary forms of precurrent behavior, referred to as problem-solving routines, may often precede solution operants, and more complex operants described as "decision making" and "thinking," though not frequently required, are an important feature of the behavior of organizational leaders.

It should be stated at the outset that an analysis of those operants that are included under the rubric of problem solving and decision making is far from complete. Because the behavioral processes in question are among the most complex phenomena ever subjected to scientific scrutiny, much remains to be learned. But it is also clear that some progress has been made and that we can expect even more significant developments in the years ahead.

Because problem-solving behavior is often covert, it will be necessary to refer to events known or presumed to be taking place beneath the skin. For that reason, among others, the reader is likely to spot a behaviorist's translation of a number of processes with which cognitive theorists have been principally concerned. However, it should be understood that, in no case, will there be reference to nonphysical inner causes. Some of the events in question may indeed be private in the sense that they are not, for the moment, readily observed by others, but they are in principle observable.

A DEFINITION OF PROBLEM-SOLVING BEHAVIOR

Traditional definitions of problem solving (e.g., Dewey, 1933; Osborn, 1963; Wallas, 1926) have stressed the importance of several processes that are assumed to take place while the individual deliberates over the problem. Each of these definitions differ slightly in its details. In general, however, all of them suggest that the individual must "identify the problem," "search for alternative solutions," "choose the most appropriate alternative," and "verify his [or her] choice" after it has been made. Though these traditional definitions of problem solving are somewhat descriptive of the processes that are presumed to occur, they are admittedly crude and do not describe the behaviors involved in problem solving very well.

From our perspective, a "problem" exists in any situation where an individual has no response immediately available that will satisfy the prevailing environmental contingencies. The behavior may not be available either because it is not of sufficient strength to be emitted or because competing operant responses evoked by multiple S_D's in the setting interfere with each other, thus precluding the occurrence of the solution response. Thus, the two-year-old child who wants to get a cookie from the cookie jar, which is out of reach, has a "problem" because there is no behavior readily available that brings the child within reach of the jar. Arriving at the correct answer on a test presents a "problem" for the student who wants to get a good grade but cannot recall the material very well. Deciding which of three prospective applicants should be offered a job presents a problem to a new personnel manager if he or she feels they are all equally well qualified. Similarly, the manager who is at a "loss for words" when asked by his or her boss the status of a particular contract faces a problem, as does the manager who is faced with a novel or complex situation in which he or she does not know how to behave. In each of the above cases, the individual is faced with a situation in which he or she has no readily available response that is likely to produce reinforcement or remove the aversive stimulation present in the situation.

Within the above context, problem-solving behavior may be defined as *any behavior on the part of the individual that changes the situation so that a response (a "solution" operant) can be emitted*. Such behavior may be overt in nature although in most managerial contexts it also includes those more complex behavioral processes referred to as "thinking."

By "thinking" we do not here refer to some inner agent or some obscure "cognitive process" that goes on in a person's head and assumes the use of rational powers. Rather, we are referring to various forms of precurrent behavior (usually verbal and covert) that result in the evocation of other forms of behavior that prove to be effective in satisfying the prevailing contingencies. Faced with a situation in which effective responses are unavailable, we behave in such a way as to make effective behaviors more likely to occur (Skinner, 1953). From the perspective of a functional analysis, such precurrent responses either modify the individual or the environment with which he or she is interacting so that other behavior can be reinforced. In thinking, much of the behavior is verbal and covert and is manipulated by the individual in an attempt to produce S_D's that will evoke a response more likely to be reinforced.

Practical Advantages of Problem Solving

There are several advantages that accrue to those individuals who are able to perform effective problem-solving behaviors. Individuals who are good problem solvers or decision makers are generally better able to analyze, diagnose, and identify the prevailing contingencies in their environment and behave more effectively with respect to those contingencies. These individuals are said to be able to "size up the situation quickly," "be alert to things that are happening in their group," "be sensitive to changes in their environment," "know when trouble is brewing," and "anticipate problems and plan for them in advance." Moreover, when placed in new environments, these individuals also are said to "adapt more quickly than others," "do things without having to be taught," or be able to "pick up on the job before others do". In short, effective problem solvers are better able to maximize net reinforcement, especially in the face of new and rapidly changing contingencies.

Individuals who have acquired effective problem-solving repertoires are also likely to behave in original or creative ways that may be functional to organizational survival and success. This may be of particular importance to organizational leaders. Not all contingencies encountered by organizational leaders are likely to be responded to effectively by them. This is particularly true in environments that are volatile or constantly changing. In such environments, precurrent problem-solving operants may result in the occurrence of relatively unique operants that contribute significantly to the organization's success.

Finally, effective decision makers and problem solvers are able to perform effective forms of self-management and self-control. This is no small point, for subordinates who are able to solve their own problems effectively require less time and effort on the part of managers and free them (the managers) to perform other important requisites of their jobs. This is not to say that managers should put subordinates into jobs and "leave them to their own devices." It is to acknowledge, however, that subordinates who are capable of sophisticated forms of self-control relieve the organizational leader to attend to other important matters.

CIRCUMSTANCES IN WHICH PROBLEM-SOLVING BEHAVIOR IS LIKELY TO BE EVOKED

Some problem situations are so novel or complex that the individual is faced with a setting in which there are no S_D's present that have played a prominent role in the individual's reinforcement history, nor are there any S_D's that, by stimulus induction, strengthen a particular operant. These situations are quite uncommon in human affairs, but if they are encountered, they will elicit a high level of arousal and other respondents, including species-typical withdrawal responses and not much else.

As in the case of other settings that produce high activation levels or arousal, the individual's initial responses to the problem situation described above are likely to be expressions of discomfort, anxiety, or fear. Individuals may, for example, say that they "feel uncomfortable" or are "nervous" or that they are "frightened."

Following these initial responses, habituation of the respondent activities may occur. As this respondent activity subsides, a wide variety of operants are likely to be emitted, one of which may eventually produce an S_D that evokes a response resulting in reinforcement. The "solution" response in this case may be nothing more than behavior on the part of the individual that permits him or her to escape from the setting. The individual, for example, may perform a response or a sequence of responses that allow him or her to "get as far away from the situation as possible."

When escape is impossible, however, or the individual is faced with the problematic situation for prolonged periods of time without being able to escape from it, respondent activity may continue at high levels and not habituate quickly or readily. As such, it may interfere with or preclude more effective operant responses. Under these circumstances, the individual may also develop feelings of chronic anxiety or depression or develop various forms of neuroses. And, in the extreme, these "psychosomatic" problems may also be accompanied by physical maladies such as ulcers and various types of digestive disorders.

The problem setting described above is, of course, relatively rare. More commonly, problems result from situations in which (1) stimulus events that have played a prominent role or are similar to those that have played a prominent role in the individual's conditioning history evoke an operant that proves not to satisfy the prevailing contingency, or (2) there are multiple S_D's in the environment, each of which has played a prominent role or is similar to S_D's that have played a prominent role in the person's conditioning history and that evoke incompatible operant responses.

In the former case, we may say the individual has been "misled," and this becomes evident when the behavior evoked leads to unanticipated consequences (usually aversive). These consequences may be rather immediate, or there may be a delay before it becomes evident that the response does not satisfy the prevailing contingencies. Whether the consequences are immediate or delayed, however, the individual is faced with the necessity of "reevaluating" the situation and behaving more appropriately in it.

In the latter case, where several S_D's evoke multiple but incompatible operants, the individual faces the traditional problem of "response conflict." Put simply, this situation exists because the responses evoked by the multiple stimuli interfere with or preclude the performance of each other. Leaders of organizations that interact with "turbulent" environments may frequently encounter these types of conflict situations. For this reason, such environments tend to evoke continuous monitoring behavior, as we shall note in Chapter 8.

The final type of problem situation is the most typical one. These are situations that do not include S_D's evoking a solution response, but they do include S_D's immediately evoking rudimentary forms of problem-solving operants. These problem-solving routines may be overt and sometime take the form of a systematic scan of the environment. The orientation of one's sensory receptors then produces an S_D immediately evoking the solution operant. The problem is solved. It is clear that in such settings, an S_D immediately evokes the problem-solving operant, which produces the S_D for the solution operant in a chain.

Because the behavior that occurs in these settings is relatively routine and repetitive, it is not often given the honorific title of problem solving, but it fits our definition of problem solving if it results in S_D's that evoke subsequent responses that satisfy the prevailing contingencies.

AN ANALYSIS OF PROBLEM-SOLVING OPERANTS

When an individual is initially faced with a situation in which he or she does not have any response of sufficient strength to be emitted, his or her first attempt to deal with the problem may result in nothing more than emitting *any* response that is strong at that time. The individual may, for example, turn and look at his or her surroundings or "take stock" of where he or she is. He or she may attend more closely to the objects around him or her or observe the behavior of those people who are in close proximity for S_D's on the appropriate types of behavior. Or such individuals may simply walk around or behave in a variety of different ways in the environment they find themselves in and note the consequences of their behavior. This behavior need not be very systematic and indeed may appear to occur in a relatively random fashion. For this reason, it is sometime referred to as simple "trial and error" behavior. Its primary effect is to produce S_D's that strengthen other operants in the setting.

A slight variation on this type of problem-solving behavior occurs when an individual emits verbal operants in mathematical form (adding, subtracting, etc.) or a simple rule of thumb or monitors and covertly tacts the behavior of another individual who behaves effectively under the prevailing contingencies. In using mathematical formulas or a rule of thumb, the individual takes advantage of S_D's previously constructed by himself or herself or by others that have proved helpful under similar circumstances in the past.

Not all problems are as easily solved, however, and the form of the precurrent behavior may not be as easily identified as in the examples above. In such cases, the individual's response may be to "reflect more deeply on the problem" or "think about it." As an initial step in this process, individuals may observe the environment in which they are present and tact their observations in some detail. For example, the individual may ask himself or herself to "describe the situation" or its more dominant features or simply to identify the "perceived" problem. Such behavior may serve as S_D's for other behavior, including other tacts and intraverbal responses that eventually evoke a "solution" response.

If a report of the circumstances doesn't have the intended effect, the individual may attempt to increase the likelihood of generating more effective solution operants by manipulating stimuli associated with the problem situation in a variety of different ways. He or she may, for example, try to redefine the circumstances as he or she sees them, or try to embellish them in greater detail. The individual may try to clarify the problem by seeking additional information about it from others or from written material. He or she may eliminate or discard some material that appears to be less relevant and amplify or magnify that information that appears important in order to get a better "fix" on the problem or make it more familiar. Again, the individual may reorganize, group, or regroup the information he or she has assembled in different ways in an attempt to "understand" it better or to get a different "perspective" on it. He or she may try to isolate various aspects of the problem or to break it into its component parts if it is very complex so as to augment or sharpen the salient characteristics of the problem. He or she may "try out" a potential solution by discussing it with himself or herself out loud or with another individual. Or the problem solver may ask himself or herself questions about the type of additional information that is needed to "solve the problem." These questions often take the form of various types of verbal prompts or probes about the problem situation. They may include queries such as "Where is the locus of the problem?" and "On whom does the problem impact?" and "Where can I get more information about the problem" and so on.

Finally, in an attempt to focus more clearly on the problem, a problem solver may lock himself or herself in the office and ask "not to be disturbed" so that he or she can "hear himself or herself think." Such behavior, or course, results in the elimination of distracting stimuli in the individual's environment.

The intended effect of modifying the problem situation in the manners described above is to produce stimuli that eventually strengthen a "solution" operant. In some cases, the S_D's resulting from the precurrent operants evoke behavior that satisfies the prevailing contingencies. In other less fortunate cases, the problem-solving operants generate several S_D's, each of which evokes its own solution operants. In this case, the individual may move from one situation where the "problem" exists because there are no behaviors of sufficient strength to be emitted to one in which several or many responses of approximately equal strength *compete* to be performed (are available to be emitted). Under such circumstances, we must necessarily also try to account for the behavior involved in determining which response is evoked as the solution operant.

One common strategy employed by problem solvers faced with a situation where several responses or "solutions" exist is to discuss the solutions and their possible consequences before behaving. Thus, the individual may "try the solution out" by analyzing, examining, or "reviewing the possibilities" of the potential solution operant and its likely outcomes and, if the solution seems plausible, perform the appropriate behavior. The individual may even "think out loud" about the potential outcomes of available responses, rejecting those that appear to produce less acceptable outcomes and elaborating on those that appear to have more acceptable outcomes.

The reasons for "accepting" one response as a solution to a problem and "rejecting" another are numerous but may be explained conceptually within the framework of the individual's prior reinforcement history. Potential solution operants associated with previous "failures," for example, are likely to be rejected as possibilities for obvious reasons. These responses are likely to be viewed by the problem solver as "dangerous," "impossible to accomplish," "doomed to failure," or "tried before without success." Likewise, responses that are similar to "solutions" that the problem solver has been punished for in the past are also likely to be rejected for similar reasons unless compelling new arguments for their use are provided. Responses generated as alternatives that have been related to reinforcement in the past or that are viewed as having significant potential, on the other hand, are likely to be retained as possible solutions.

This is not to say that the problem solver will make the correct "choice" of alternatives or, put more accurately, that the appropriate or "correct" solution operant will be strengthened. The problem solver may reject a possible solution operant that would be successful if emitted because its emission in the past has led to the removal of positive reinforcement or the administration of an aversive event. Or the problem solver may "hit" on a solution operant that is less than effective and reject others prematurely because the response or one similar to it has been reinforced in similar situations in the past.

Other reasons for defective problem solving also exist. The problem solver, for example, may not "have his or her facts straight," which is to say that the stimuli for such an individual's behavior are not the ones that control the appropriate solution responses. Or he or she may attempt a solution without "thinking through" the consequences. Such behavior is particularly likely to occur when an individual is tired, fatigued, or under extreme pressure to make a "quick" decision. In dealing with complex problems, the operant evoked may be strengthened adventitiously, or a component of the complex problem stimulus may reinforce behavior that is appropriate to the stimulus component but not to the whole problem. In complex situations, multiple and conflicting stimuli exist, any of which may eventually come to control the operant evoked as the "solution." In some cases, the operant evoked may be effective, but in others it may not be. Finally, it is worth noting that the special contingencies involved in the shaping of problem solving operants may be deficient or, in the case of some individuals, never have been applied. Problem-solving behavior is among the most complex forms of behavior, and, for that reason alone, the design of those contingencies necessary to produce it is not completely understood. Because of this, it is possible that individuals not exposed to the appropriate contingencies—or exposed to inappropriate ones—simply "do not know how to solve the problem."

REINFORCING CONSEQUENCES OF PROBLEM-SOLVING BEHAVIOR

Problem-solving behaviors, like other forms of operant behavior, are maintained primarily because they have certain reinforcing consequences. Among the most fundamental of these is the escape from indecision. Undoubtedly, the reader has experienced the uncomfortableness of situations in which he or she was unable to arrive at a decision as to "what to do" or "how to behave." Such situations are uncomfortable and are avoided, if possible, by most individuals because they frequently result in delays or a loss in reinforcement that otherwise may have have been forthcoming had the decision been made more quickly. As the individual vacillates in his or her response, increases in arousal and emotional responses also are likely to occur, particularly in those instances in which we are in the presence of others who are waiting for us to make the decision. Moreover, these emotional responses are likely to be magnified in the presence of others because indecision often is accompanied by severe social sanctions. We have, no doubt, all asked someone at some point in time, "What's wrong with you? Why can't you make up your mind?" or called an indecisive individual a "procrastinator." Under these conditions, virtually any behavior that produces or brings about a solution operant may be reinforced.

Being able to behave or respond more effectively in one's environment will likewise serve to reinforce an individual's problem-solving operants. Managers, subordinates, and other organizational participants who deliberate over their decisions are likely to find that they increase the probability of making the right choices. Such behavior will permit them to interact more effectively in their environment and maximize the amount and number of reinforcements they receive or reduce the magnitude of punishment.

This is not to say that all people make decisions readily or, for that matter, that "procrastinators" or people who avoid making decisions do not exist. As noted by Skinner (1953, p.244), escape from indecision or the net effects of deliberating before making a decision may not be particularly effective reinforcers because they are frequently delayed and their connections with the problem-solving operants that produce them may be difficult to identify, if not completely obscure. In addition, because our decision-making behavior is not always effective, some individuals probably feel that they are worse off when they make a decision than when they do not. Under these circumstances, it is not surprising to find that some people "put off" making decisions or wait long enough so that the decision is somehow made for them (which is to say that they wait long enough for contingencies to change). For these reasons, social support and reinforcement of problem-solving behavior is essential for its maintenance. In the case of children, such support may come in the form of telling them to "think before they act" or to "consider all the consequences of their behavior" and reinforcing them when we believe them to have behaved accordingly. Because much of problem solving and decision making occurs at the covert level, the parent may additionally ask the child to "explain his or her reasoning" before administering reinforcement. Managers, of course, may be somewhat hesitant to ask for similar explanations from their subordinates although they may request them to identify the alternatives they generated and why they chose the alternative they did, particularly when the subordinate is new or relatively inexperienced or when the decision is a complex or costly one. On many occasions, however, it may not be necessary for the manager actually to check on the behavior of the subordinate while he or she is making the decision, but only on the effectiveness of its outcome. In such cases, the effectiveness of the outcome may set the occasion for the manager to provide praise, commendation, or other forms of social approval to the subordinate. If such reinforcement is not received by the subordinate, at least intermittently, it is unlikely that such behavior will continue to be performed for very long.

SEVEN
THE BEHAVIOR OF INDIVIDUALS IN GROUPS

Organizations are typically comprised of several individuals whose presence and behavior are an important part of the controlling environment of each other. That the behavior of one member of the human species may serve as or produce stimuli that control the behavior of another became obvious in our discussion of verbal behavior. But it is necessary to provide a more detailed account of the behaviorial processes that will be observed when people behave in a common space and as members of groups.

As we shall note, a collection of individuals is not necessarily a group. However, we may find, on occasion, that the behavior of one or more individuals in a collection will facilitate or determine the behavior of another person in the collection. We, therefore, take up the behavioral processes of social facilitation, imitation, and competition first.

A collection of individuals may not remain a mere collection. A reinforcement contingency of considerable import is that in which the reinforcement contingent on the "cooperant" behavior of two or more individuals greatly exceeds the sum of the reinforcements each could achieve by behaving independently of others. When that condition prevails—and it often does—then the complex social system known as a group will evolve. Social facilitation, imitation, and competition, sometimes observed when individuals are simply behaving in a common space, can also be observed in groups, but additional behavioral processes also arise. Of the several that we shall describe, leadership is clearly the most significant. We shall, therefore, introduce the topic toward the end of this chapter and continue our analysis of organizational leadership in Chapter 8.

COLLECTIONS OF INDIVIDUALS

Human beings behave in a common space—the world at large—but some parts of the world are more reinforcing than others. As a consequence, several, often many, members of the human species can be found behaving in close proximity and for the *same reasons*. There is a more abundant supply of stimuli that have a common reinforcing effect, or there is a notable absence of events that are commonly aversive in the more circumscribed space. On the other hand, the world is quite complex, providing for multiple and independent reinforcement contingencies even in closely circumscribed parts of it. Therefore, it is altogether conceivable that many members of the human species will be found behaving in close proximity for *different* reasons. In either case, the stage is set for the occurrence of a wide variety of social interaction processes.

Social Facilitation

As we have noted, a collection of individuals may remain a mere collection, but even in that unusual case, important behavioral processes may be observed. One of the more fundamental of these is called *social facilitation*. The term refers to the "enhancing" effect of the presence of others on the ongoing behavior of a given individual. The behavior of both infrahuman and human organisms has been found to be more vigorous and persistent when other members of the same species are present (Zajonc, 1965). This facilitation effect is most pronounced when the others are behaving in a similar fashion ("coactors") and when the others have some control over the reinforcing consequences of the target performer (e.g., supervisors). On the other hand, the *mere presence* of others who are not coactors, competitors, or supervisors seems to produce little or no facilitation (Cottrell, 1968). Moreover, the presence and behavior of others have been shown to *impair* performance in those tasks for which effective operants are still in the process of being acquired or strengthened (Zajonc, 1965; Cottrell, 1968).

These seemingly mixed findings led Zajonc (1965) to propose that the most basic effect of the presence of others is an increase in arousal level. If we further assume, with Zajonc that an increase in arousal level will augment only *dominant* responses in that setting, the results of our several studies are satisfactorily explained. When the dominant responses are also those required for effective performance, social facilitation will be observed. If they are not, effective performance will be impaired or slower to develop.

Zajonc's hypothesis has some merit. As we noted in Chapter 4 novel stimulus events can be expected to elicit an increase in that respondent activity known as arousal level when first introduced. If the arousal level is low, as it might be in settings in which effective task operants were being routinely maintained, the increase in arousal level elicited by the introduction of others could be expected to enhance operant responding. If, however, the arousal level is already high, as it might be in learning and problematic settings, the increased arousal level is likely to interfere with the acquisition of effective operants and to intrude on dominant responses as well.

Both Zajonc (1965) and Cottrell (1968) have emphasized that the presence and behavior of others will typically have more complex effects than a change in arousal level. Given the fact that most human beings are not reared in social isolation, various features of the behavior of others will obviously have important functions as discriminative stimuli (S_D's). This complication does not necessarily render Zajonc's hypothesis invalid. As we have seen, an effective S_D, besides evoking operant behavior, will also elicit a change in arousal level by virtue of its being paired with reinforcing events. But we do have to qualify the simple proposition that a facilitation effect will always be the net effect. Rather commonly, the presence and behavior of others will combine with other S_D's in the setting to strengthen ongoing operants. Under these circumstances, there is no doubt that a pronounced social facilitation effect will be observed. In some instances, however, the behavior of others could serve to evoke operants incompatible with those occurring before the others came on the scene. If the behavior that was displaced was that required for effective performance, we could *not* say performance was facilitated though the behavior that displaced it might be if the resulting arousal level were not too high. Finally, it is possible that the behavior of others could serve to evoke and presumably facilitate more effective operants as in shaping and imitation.

Imitative Behavior

Imitative behavior is likely to be observed among a collection of individuals behaving in a common space for the same reasons. Two examples, one primitive and one modern, are illustrative. A collection of individuals may be found hunting on the same fertile plain because reinforcement in the form of food or game is plentiful there. In the modern case, a collection of individuals may aggregate on a college campus because it provides for the acquisition of behavior that is subsequently reinforced in other settings. We can be reasonably certain that the ongoing operants of each (hunting, studying, etc.) will be more vigorous and persistent than they would be if no others were present and behaving in a similar fashion. But as we know, the ongoing behavior of the young or inexperienced may not be the most effective in those settings. As a consequence, we are quite likely to find them closely attending to the behavior of some of the others in the collection. Eventually, if not immediately, their behavior will come to resemble the behavior of those who appear to be more effective in that setting.

We cannot be certain that their behavior is imitative simply because it resembles that of others in the collection. Because individuals behaving in the same setting may have been exposed to the same reinforcement contingencies, it is possible that the behavior of each has been independently shaped and maintained by those contingencies. But when it can be established that the operant behavior of one individual, whom we will call an Observer, is similar to, and under the stimulus control of, the behavior of another, whom we will call a Model, the behavior of the former is regarded as imitative.

Imitative behavior has attracted the attention of a number of scientists not only because it is widespread but also because it appears to have some unusual properties. For example, Observer operants, matching those of a Model, may occur though neither the Model's nor the Observer's behavior seems to be followed by reinforcing consequences. Secondly, a Model's behavior may evoke imitative operants that the Observer has apparently never displayed before. Finally, imitative operants may not occur until some time after the Model's behavior, and may even occur in the Model's absence.

As unusual as imitative behavior may seem, it is not so special that it calls for a different type of analysis. On the contrary, it has become increasingly clear that we can account for it just as we have accounted for other classes of operant behavior—without using any new term (such as "instinct") or presupposing any new principle (Skinner, 1957, p. 298; Church, 1968; Rosenbaum and Arenson, 1968; Gewirtz, 1971).

It may be recalled that, in shaping a child's verbal operants, parents often expedite the process by behaving so as to produce an auditory stimulus and then reinforcing the child's operants, which produce an ever-closer approximation of that sound. The shaping of a wide variety of nonverbal operants is often expedited in the same manner. In shaping the behavior of tying a shoe string, turning on a light, riding a bicycle, and many other operants, parents first "model" the behavior and then reinforce the child when it displays reasonable facsimiles. On numerous occasions, they will also interrupt a child who is, for the moment, ineffective, command the child to watch how they do it, and then proceed to emit the operant chain or step-by-step components of the chain.

Parents who apply these conditioning procedures, whether intuitively or by design, typically do not shape imitative behavior for its own sake. Rather, they are more reinforced whenever the child's behavior is effective and generally independent of the parent's behavior. Thus, they are likely to attempt to bring the child's imitative operants under the discriminative control of nonsocial stimuli and will often reinforce the child when its behavior comes to be evoked by stimuli other than the parent's behavior. We no longer refer to the child's behavior as imitative under these circumstances. But we should not forget its origins, nor should we be surprised when it appears similar in form to the parents' behavior.

Bandura (1965) has concluded that the shaping of an imitative repertoire is inevitable during human social development. We do not agree that the *deliberate* shaping of imitative behavior is inevitable, but shaping procedures incorporating versions of the "matching-to-sample" technique are, no doubt, widely practiced. Furthermore, once a few imitative operants have been shaped by parents, other imitative operants may develop more or less by accident. Parental behavior often occurs in the presence of the child, not because it is reinforced by the imitative behavior of the child, but because it has been, or is being, supported by other reinforcing consequences. When one also considers that a child who has been reinforced for imitating parents has also been reinforced for observing their behavior, it is predictable that the child will continue to observe the behavior of others and behave as they do in the absence of a deliberate influence attempt.

As a consequence of these conditioning experiences, both deliberate and incidental, the repertoires of most human organisms will include an extensive imitative component. Children and adults alike will, on occasion, attend to the behavior of "significant others" and behave as they do, especially in those settings that do not otherwise evoke effective operants.

As we have been suggesting, imitative behavior reflects a form of *antecedent stimulus control,* wherein the most significant S_D's are the operant responses of a Model. We can, therefore, expect that the process of stimulus induction will occur here as elsewhere. Imitative operants, shaped and strengthened in the presence of the behavior of a given Model, will also be evoked by the behavior of others who have never served as Models. But imitative operants also become discriminative. For that reason, the behavior of some Models, described in lay terms as vigorous, persistent, confident, and so on, is more likely to evoke observing and imitative acts than the behavior of others, described as hesitant, timid, or uncertain.

Imitative behavior also becomes discriminative in another sense. Neither the child nor the adult is always reinforced for imitating. In fact, children are sometimes punished for imitating their parents' behavior and that of others. Moreover, parents and other trainers often strive to transfer the control of the child's operants from their own behavior, which initially serves as discriminative stimuli, to appropriate nonsocial stimuli. For these reasons, imitative behavior is unlikely to occur in those settings in which effective operants are, or will be, evoked by stimuli other than the behavior of others. It is only when adults find themselves in novel settings that evoke little in the way of effective operants that the behavior of significant others becomes the dominant form of stimulus control.

Because imitative behavior is largely a matter of antecedent stimulus control, it is not surprising that it may be evoked though reinforcing events do not immediately follow either the Model's or the Observer's behavior. However, it has been found that the controlling effect of a Model's behavior is more pronounced when it is also followed by obvious reinforcing consequences. This is so because the reinforcing events serve as additional S_D's, further increasing the probability that imitative behavior will be evoked.

We will have to qualify the assertion that imitative behavior will continue to be evoked and sustained in the absence of reinforcing consequences. The reinforcing consequences need not be immediate or continuous. Nor are they always obvious. But we can be certain that they will be found if imitative operants are sustained, and we usually do not have to search very far for them.

One class of reinforcing events contingent on imitative operants are those that are also responsible for the Model's behavior. The imitative behavior of the young hunter and the college freshman may be maintained by the same consequences maintaining the behavior of those emulated—food and passing grades.

A second and quite subtle class of reinforcing events is found in the stimulus properties of the Model's behavior. When the Model's behavior, serving as a stimulus, sets the occasion for Observer operants, which are followed by reinforcing events, various features of the Model's behavior also take on reinforcing properties. Consequently, any behavior that reproduces various features of the Model's repertoire will be reinforced if it has reinstated the Model's behavior and if the Observer has learned to observe his or her own behavior. We should not conclude that imitative behavior is inherently reinforcing. The reinforcing potential of the stimulus features of imitated operants is obviously derived and short-lived if other reinforcing consequences do not follow the observer's behavior. However, reinforcing consequences will often follow the imitated behavior of Models who are effective in a given setting. Thus, it is not surprising that an Observer may come to talk like, dress like, and otherwise behave so as to reproduce large portions of a competent Model's repertoire. The effect has been called *identification*.

A third class of reinforcing events that are responsible for strengthening and sustaining imitative operants are those supplied by the Model, who may praise, recognize, or otherwise reinforce the Observer who successfully imitates. Such reinforcement does not occur in a mere collection of individuals and is not inevitable in groups. The person serving as a Model may not observe the Observer's behavior or, having observed it, may not be moved to reinforce it one way or the other. But when the imitative behavior of an Observer is reinforcing for a Model, as it may be in a group, the Model is quite likely to administer further reinforcement to the Observer.

Social learning theorists have insisted that a Model's behavior may evoke imitative operants that are unique in the Observer's history. In fact, the term *observational learning* implies that some classes of behavior can be acquired by observation alone. However, there has never been a convincing demonstration of that process, nor is there likely to be. On the other hand, it *is* possible that a Model's behavior may evoke imitative operants that have never appeared in precisely that form or sequence in the Observer's history. When we say that most human beings acquire an extensive imitative repertoire, we mean that a wide variety of operants have been shaped and brought under the control of the behaviors displayed by Models. If, therefore, a given Model's behavior occurs in a different or unusual sequence, we can expect that the Model's behavior serving as S_D's will evoke a chain of imitative operants that appears to be unique in the Observer's history. And indeed the particular pattern or sequence may be unique though the operants comprising the chain are not.

The "delayed" effect, in which the Observer's imitative acts occur sometime after the Model's behavior, is readily understood in the light of our analysis of problem solving. While attending to the behavior of a Model, the Observer may emit incipient or covert imitative responses and may even "rehearse" them covertly. The Observer who is an accomplished speaker may also describe, either overtly or covertly, the behavior of the Model as it occurs. Later, when the Observer is in the same or a similar setting, stimulus events in that setting will set the occasion for the imitative operants in overt form or for the verbal description of the Model's behavior and possibly some of the variables of which that behavior is a function. The Observer's verbal description need not be complete. In fact, an Observer may employ various kinds of coding devices. But whether complete or incomplete, the Observer's self-description serves to produce discriminative stimuli that evoke the imitative acts described.[1] The reinforcement for the pre-current behavior is the same as that which follows the imitative operants.

Interestingly enough, the delayed imitative behavior of Observers has occasionally been found to be more effective than the Model's behavior originally responsible for it. Bandura (1971) has suggested that the reinforcing consequences of the Model's behavior may elicit respondents that intrude on the effectiveness of his or her ongoing behavior. Moreover, according to Bandura, Models may be so absorbed in the task that they do not observe their own behavior or its controlling variables as may an Observer. Consequently, the Model may not discern the prevailing contingencies as quickly or as precisely as the Observer. What Bandura means, we believe, is that there is the possibility that the behavior evoked by a rule (in this case, the Observer's own verbal commentary on the Model's behavior and its controlling variables) may be simpler *and more effective* than behavior shaped and sustained by unanalyzed contingencies (Skinner, 1969, p. 167). Although contingency-shaped behavior may appear to be more "natural" than rule-governed behavior, contingency-shaped behavior may include components that are unnecessary but persisting because they have been adventitiously reinforced.

Competition

When the supply of available reinforcers in a given setting is limited (the game is scarce, or passing grades are granted only to the better students), a condition loosely described as *competition* prevails. It is a process that few of us take lightly. Karen Horney (1939), for example, deplored competition because, in her judgment, it is a major source of pathological conflict in human affairs. Others have maintained with equal fervor that competition is an essential component in human achievement, and the argument seems to continue unabated. We cannot hope to resolve the argument once and for all. However, a functional analysis of competitive behavior and of the conditions that give rise to it does provide some additional insights.

Multiple reinforcement contingencies typically prevail in competitive settings. But one of the most basic is that in which the reinforcing consequences

---

[1] We should not rule out "imaginal" responses here. Various features of the imitative setting may produce conditioned seeing (i.e., seeing again the behavior of the Model in the absence of his or her behavior). These imaginal responses may serve as S_D's facilitating the appearance of Observer operants similar in form to the Model's earlier behavior (Skinner, 1953, pp. 266–273).

are contingent on the behavior of each person *relative to that of others in the collection.* It need not be an all-or-none affair. The hunter who is more effective may simply catch more game, leaving less game for those who are relatively less effective. The more effective student may receive *A*'s whereas those who are relatively less effective may receive *B*'s or *C*'s but not *F*'s.

What are the behavioral effects of social settings in which the behavior of each individual may modify the reinforcing consequences accruing to another (or others)? More specifically, can we expect an enhancing effect above and beyond the usual social facilitation effect? Unfortunately, the answer to the latter question has to be somewhat equivocal. If the behavior of the respective individuals is reasonably similar in terms of its strength and effectiveness, the competitive reinforcement contingency will generally produce an enhancing effect. This may always be the case when the competitive allocation of the reinforcer results in differential reinforcement of the behavior that is the basis for the competition and when each individual continues to be intermittently reinforced. There are, however, several boundary conditions. If the performance of all individuals is enhanced in such a way that ever-increasing higher rates are required with no proportionate increase in reinforcer magnitude, a "ratio strain" is likely to result. That is, some, if not most, of the individuals in the collection will begin to receive less and less reinforcement for the same or higher rates of performance. We know, of course, that intermittent reinforcement can be effective in maintaining high rates of responding and that a ratio can be stretched. But there is an upper-bound limit to this process, and when it is reached, extinction sets in. A similar behavioral outcome is anticipated when, at the outset, there are large individual differences in the strength or effectiveness of the behavior required to meet the contingency. When these circumstances prevail, there will be a rapid separation of the winners from the losers. Competitive facilitation is not likely to be observed in either of our two conditions either because the winners are not pressed or because the behavior of several members of the collection undergoes extinction or both.

When no other reinforcement contingencies prevail, other more desirable forms of social behavior are not likely to be observed among those confronted with a purely competitive reinforcement contingency. Each person will be closely attending to the behavior of other competitors because it comes to serve as an important S_D for his or her own behavior and its reinforcing consequences. But the individuals will report that they like each other less (reduced interpersonal attraction),[2] and altruistic as well as various forms of cooperant behavior will also be diminished. Moreover, several classes of behavior, generally regarded as undesirable, may also occur. An individual may hunt under

---

[2]It has been said that we sometimes grow to love our competitors, which is, of course, just the opposite of *reduced* interpersonal attraction. We doubt that this happens often unless we occasionally win. However, we could grow to like our competitors, even when we lose, if they evoke from the most effective behavior of which we are capable and if other reinforcement, perhaps from an audience, is contingent on our behaving effectively. As has been noted, a social setting that includes a competitive reinforcement contingency typically includes other contingencies as well.

cover not so much to improve his or her chances of catching game as to avoid revealing his or her effective behavior to other competitors. And though competing students are not likely to study "under cover," they have been known to lie to classmates about how much time they spend in preparing for examinations.

As in other situations in which one member of the human species alters the reinforcement contingencies of others at the expense of the latter, various forms of countercontrolling operants may be evoked. Those individuals undergoing extinction (the losers) may, in addition to manifesting emotional responses elicited by the reduction in positive reinforcers, attempt to impede the behavior of the more effective by engaging them in conversation, stealing their lecture notes or spears, or inflicting bodily harm. If these and other forms of operant aggression are ineffective or are precluded by other prevailing reinforcement contingencies, the least effective individuals may, of course, withdraw from the setting. But aside from the temporary or permanent alliances between members of the opposite sex, a collection of individuals that is engaged in competition will typically remain a mere collection unless other reinforcement contingencies are introduced.

COOPERANT BEHAVIOR AND THE FORMATION OF GROUPS

A reinforcement contingency commonly found in social settings is that in which the behavior of two or more individuals is required for the effective reinforcement of each. More often than not, the reinforcing consequences produced by the "cooperant" behavior of several individuals will greatly exceed the sum of those consequences contingent on the independent behavior of each. When that is the case, a collection of individuals will no longer remain a mere collection. Rather, an interacting group will develop and will be maintained so long as that contingency prevails.

The possibilities are numerous. A single hunter, hunting independently, may catch little or no game, but several individuals hunting in concert may catch a large number of animals, greatly exceeding the sum of those that would be caught by the same individuals hunting alone. A group of students, by "reciting" and stimulating each other to recall propositions that have been cited in lectures and texts, may achieve examination grades that are better than those achieved by studying alone. And, of course, our formal organizations have evolved for the same reasons.

A collection of individuals may come to behave cooperantly as a result of the dysfunctional consequences of a competitive reinforcement contingency. For example, a collection of unsuccessful hunters may begin to hunt as a group in order to protect themselves against a powerful despoiler (an effective hunter who catches all the game or the individual who, because of his superior strength, simply takes the game captured by others for himself).

A cooperant reinforcement contingency may prevail in conjunction with a competitive reinforcement contingency. Cooperant hunting may prove effective in catching more game, but the more effective in the group may take or be accorded a larger portion of the kill than other group members. Better grades may be contingent on cooperant studying, but the more effective may receive better grades than the less effective when the instructor "grades on a curve." In our formal organizations, the reinforcing consequences contingent on the cooperant behavior of their members easily surpass the sum of the consequences that the individuals could produce if they were not members of a group. At the same time, however, a larger portion of the reinforcement is often allocated to the more effective or to those whose contributions are viewed as more important. It is, therefore, quite likely that the problem of equity (the manner in which the reinforcing consequences are distributed among the group members) will always be one with which an interacting group must contend. And unless the consequences are divided equally among group members, competitive reinforcement contingencies will be operating in conjunction with cooperant contingencies.

Simple Groups

Perhaps the simplest type of group that develops and is maintained by naturally occurring contingencies is that in which the cooperant behavior of each is similar in topography. Though each person in the group may be performing the same task, given differences in genetic and prior reinforcement histories, the behavior of the several members will rarely, if ever, occur simultaneously. Nor will it be perfectly identical in form when it does occur. The cooperant behavior of some members can be observed to be more vigorous and to occur, however slightly, before the behavior of others in the group. For the same reasons, one may also observe differences in topography that, though they may be slight, are typically in the direction of greater effectiveness. In fact, if we look carefully, we are quite likely to find that at least some of the cooperant behavior of one individual is under the control of features of the nonsocial environment whereas much of the cooperant behavior of the remainder is under the control of the behavior of that individual. We have come to designate that person as a *leader*. This relationship, though asymmetrical, is not a simple one-way affair. As the magnitude of the reinforcement contingent on the leader's behavior is also dependent on the cooperants of other group members, their behaviors serve as reinforcing events for the leader and as S_D's controlling certain features of the leader's behavior.

Complex Groups

In rare instances, the cooperants of the several members will appear similar in topography. In the more typical case, however, there will be notable differences in the cooperants exhibited by different group members. The behavior of the leader, as we have noted, is often readily distinguishable from the cooperants of other group members. However, other types of specialization may be shaped and maintained by the net improvements in reinforcing consequences. In the most complex group conceivable, the topography of each member's cooperants can be distinguished from those of all other members.

As specialization emerges and is reinforced, the leader's behavior becomes increasingly differentiated and considerably more complex. Initially, the individual who has acquired all or most of the operant chains effective in producing group reinforcement will also come to respond differentially to dysfunctional or incomplete forms displayed by other group members. If so, the individual, now a leader, will attempt to teach other individuals how to behave more effectively. But other more specialized forms of controlling operants may also be shaped and maintained. The leader, for example, may become fully occupied with the planning of the hunt or study session, analyzing and specifying the behavior of other group members. The leader may also initiate the behavior of other group members by signaling or verbal commands, control the sequencing of other members' cooperants, and sustain their behavior by applying intermediate reinforcers in the form of praise, encouragement, and so on.

A Functional Analysis of Group Leader Behavior

We have implied that leadership is behavior that serves to "influence" or determine the behavior of others. This conception of leadership is not exactly a novel one. Early in this century, both Allport (1924) and Bogardus (1928) came close to the view that leadership is behavior that affects the behavior of others, and Hemphill (1949) later defined it as "the behavior of an individual while he is directing group activities." However, their views did not jibe with the prevailing notion that true leaders did not seem to control behavior, and, as a consequence, the conception of leadership as behavior that determined the behavior of others was either ignored or rejected out of hand. But behavioral scientists kept returning to that original concept, and by the mid-1960s, Bowers and Seashore (1966) could report that the research emphasis had shifted from a search for personality traits that might differentiate leaders from nonleaders to a search for "behavior that makes a difference in the performance and satisfaction of followers." Subsequently, Scott (1977) suggested that attempts to identify and describe the structure of leader behavior were useful but that a comprehensive understanding of leadership would not be realized until we had analyzed more clearly the behavior of leaders *and* the variables of which it is a function. A similar position was voiced by Hollander and Julian (1968) and is reflected in the work of Fiedler (1967). But Scott went beyond leadership "styles" in asserting that leadership is operant behavior and began the task of describing those events that are likely to set the occasion for leader operants as well as those events that might serve to reinforce them. We wish now to continue that task.

In proceeding with a functional analysis, we do not mean to imply that some individuals in a group will always be leading whereas others will always be following. An interesting ramification of our conception of leadership is that individuals other than those formally appointed to lead will be controlling from time to time and that two or more individuals may be simultaneously leading, though possibly not the same followers if different and incompatible follower responses are reinforcing for the several leaders. In what is presumed to be the more typical case, the behavior of the leader, whether emergent or appointed, is under the control of certain variables in addition to the behavior of followers whereas the behavior of the followers is more exclusively under the control of the behavior of the leader or of variables that are the products of his or her behavior.

The classification of leadership as operant behavior leads us to the conclusion that though it may have a number of interesting and unique structural properties, it can be accounted for within the same framework found to be so useful in accounting for other classes of operants. In other words, it can be shaped and maintained, like any other operant class, by its consequences, and it also comes under the control of antecedent stimuli. Thus, in our analysis, we will examine some of the more important S_D's that set the occasion for leader operants as well as some of the more significant reinforcing consequences. We will also refer to certain broad classes of leader operants themselves, but a more detailed description of leader operants thought to be important in determining group effectiveness will be provided in Chapter 8.

Discriminative Stimuli for Leader Operants.   An analysis of stimuli that set the occasion for leader behavior reveals that they are numerous and, in some cases at least, quite complex. When, for example, leaders are appointed rather than emergent, several features of the formal designation may serve as S_D's for leader operants. The appointment may be accompanied by a job description, a policy manual, training materials, and other types of written or verbal instructions that imply or describe the manner in which the leader *and* group members are expected to behave, the circumstances under which they are to do so, and the consequences for behaving and not behaving as prescribed. If the instructions are specific with respect to the behavior of the appointed leader, then we have some basis for predicting his or her behavior. But in the typical case, the instructions that may serve, in part, as S_D's are somewhat vague and, in any case, incomplete. Therefore, the appointed leader is "left to his or her own devices," which is to say the leader then simply behaves as he or she has behaved in the past in similar circumstances, or he or she begins to manipulate or monitor the external environment in order to produce S_D's that might evoke appropriate behavior. The manipulation might be as simple as approaching a peer or a superior and requesting advice.

Many leader operants come under the control of S_D's in the form of the behavior of group members. Initially, the presence and behavior of group members will evoke leader operants conditioned in previous social settings or behavior described in instructions, policy statements, and personal advice from others. As interaction continues, however, the leader's behavior comes under the more precise control of the behavior of members comprising the immediate group. For example, unproductive or dysfunctional behavior on the part of a group member may evoke leader operants in the form of "corrective action." Group member behavior "above and beyond the call of duty" may serve as an S_D for leader operants in the form of praise, recognition, or the delivery of other reinforcing events.

A variety of nonbehavioral stimuli may also serve as S_D's for leader operants. The environmental effects of a group member's behavior rather than the behavior itself may come to control leader operants. A product that is flawed in some manner may evoke criticism or encouragement to do better whereas output that consistently meets specification might evoke leader expressions of appreciation and promise of other forms of reinforcement.

A number of important S_D's are found in what may be called the "external" environment of the group. The behavior of the game and the tracks they lay down are important S_D's for the leader of the hunt, just as the behavior of the instructor and his or her instructions are important S_D's for the leader of the study session. At the first level of supervision in the formal organization, the behavior and directions of other subgroups and their leaders constitute important features of the external environment. And in a consideration of the top level of leadership in a formal organization, the leader of leaders, the external environment becomes awesomely significant as well as very complex. The behavior of customers, suppliers, competitors, and government representatives are among the most important classes of S_D's governing leadership behavior at this level. The social reinforcement contingencies that these groups administer are multiple, complex, often conflicting, and sometimes changing. They may, therefore, evoke multiple but incompatible operants (response conflict); operants that fail to produce reinforcement ("Now what does one do?"); and respondent behavior sometimes described as anxiety, depression, frustration, or anger. Various features of this external environment as well as the respondent behavior may, therefore, come to serve as S_D's for a variety of monitoring operants and problem-solving operants in the form of consulting experts or staff members, reviewing alternatives, and other behaviors that we have described as thinking, problem solving, and decision making. This behavior, in turn, produces S_D's that serve to evoke leader behavior in a variety of forms that ultimately produce effects on the behavior of organizational members.

Leader Operants.   The leadership literature, including that concerned with traits, reveals most clearly that individuals must behave and behave overtly if they are to lead. Although trait names rarely provide clear descriptions of leader behavior, in his summary of traits and personal factors that have been found to differentiate leaders from nonleaders, Stogdill (1974, pp. 35–156) concludes that leaders have been found to be more "active," "lively," "persistent," "participative," "talkative," and "able to maintain a high rate of physical activity." In other words, leadership does not simply *imply* behavior. It *is* behavior.

Characterizations of the leader as "showing a long duration of verbal excitation," "verbally fluent," "vividly expressive," and "more intelligent than the other group members but not to the point of being unable to communicate with them" suggest that a large class of leader operants are comprised of verbal behaviors that serve as S_D's for the behavior of the followers. It is possible, as we have seen, to control the behavior of others simply by describing or clarifying the relationship between their behavior and its reinforcing consequences even though the "describer" does not control those consequences. If those descriptions are reasonably specific and accurate with respect to the behavior that will satisfy the prevailing contingencies, the follower behavior that the description may evoke will be followed by the occurrence of positive reinforcers or the absence of aversive events. Such descriptions are commonly referred to as advice, suggestions, proposals, or recommendations when the leader has no control over consequences; but when the leader is in control of powerful reinforcers, as may be the case when the leader is formally appointed or a property owner, his or her verbalizations are referred to as commands. They, like other verbal S_D's, serve to increase the probability of any behavior described or implied by the leader, but they tend to be rather more potent S_D's than advice. Discriminative stimuli serving to "direct" or evoke follower behavior are not limited to commands, advice, or other more-or-less complete descriptions of the contingencies. Gestures, nods, and changes in facial expressions are also included in this class of leader operants generally defined as *stimulus control operants.*

From the descriptions of leaders as "socially expansive," "sustaining interaction with a large portion of group members," "socially sensitive and insightful," and "tactfully considerate of others," we may infer that the leader's stimulus control practices are widely directed in the group. However, the controlling properties of an S_D are established and maintained by the reinforcing consequences of the behavior that follows or occurs in the presence of that S_D. For that reason, the efficacy of the leader's stimulus control operants depends on the nature and scheduling of reinforcing events contingent on the follower's behavior. Moreover, reinforcing consequences are essential in shaping follower behavior, in bringing it under the control of S_D's other than those provided by the leader, and in maintaining follower behavior over time. We come, then, to a second class of leader operants, namely, those that serve as or produce reinforcing events for followers. We may refer to them as *reinforcing operants.*

The reinforcing consequences of follower behavior are frequently delayed, in which case it becomes necessary for the leader to administer intermediate reinforcing events in order to maintain follower behavior. Social reinforcers in the form of praise, public recognition, expressions of appreciation, nods, smiles, and promises of future benefits may serve as reinforcers if the leader does not administer them on a continuous schedule. They must also be paired with other more powerful reinforcing events, including, of course, those responsible for the cooperant behavior in the first place—the "kill" in the case of the hunt, an acceptable grade in the case of the study sessions, and money and other forms of property in the case of the formal organization. The leader may or may not have unilateral control over these events, but the more effective leader typically has some voice in their allocation to group members. Thus, the leader's reinforcing operants may include not only the administration of personal or social "evaluative" reinforcers but also the administration of reinforcers supplied by the external environment of the group.

Some may wish to exclude the application and withdrawal of aversive events as examples of leader operants, but we do not. Effective leaders, whether emergent or appointed, will engage in the judicious use of punitive consequences from time to time. For example, in developing an appropriate sequence of follower operants and fine-tuning their skill properties, the effective leader will engage in differential reinforcement practices that include the withholding or withdrawal of positive reinforcers and their reinstatement as closer approximations to the skilled pattern are emitted. However, most differential reinforcement practices also include the simultaneous application of negative reinforcers (frowns, grimaces, verbalizations such as "That's wrong!") and their withdrawal as the closer approximation occurs. The combined procedures of applying a negative reinforcer while withdrawing a positive one and then withdrawing the negative reinforcer while reinstating the positive one are typically much more effective than either alone.

It should also be added that as neither the leader nor anyone else has perfect control over the environment of a group of human beings, it is to be expected that behavior dysfunctional to the group will appear on occasion and will have to be quickly eliminated. The leader will be required to apply an effective punishment procedure, one that will eliminate that behavior without producing undesirable side effects.

A third broad class of leader operants comprises those involved in *environmental scanning* or *monitoring*. It seems obvious that the immediate group setting is important to the leader in the sense that it includes S_D's vital in evoking effective leader operants. But we have also noted that some part of an effective leader's operant repertoire is under the control of features of the "external" environment in which the group is functioning, and such characterizations of effective leaders as "keenly alert to the surrounding environment" indicate that they learn which features to monitor and how often. The external environment may be characterized as simple-complex, suggesting that there are only a limited number of features or several that require monitoring and static-dynamic suggesting that some of or all the features change infrequently or, on the other hand, are in a constant state of flux. External environments that are both complex and dynamic obviously require continuous and reasonably sophisticated monitoring by the leader and quite probably a staff.

Monitoring operants do not inevitably produce S_D's evoking appropriate solution operants. Though certain features of the external environment may be observed by the leader to change, it is not immediately clear what those changes "mean" for the group. Moreover, characterizations of emerging or appointed leaders as "knowledgeable" and "able to diagnose situations" imply that complex forms of *problem-solving operants* will be required of leaders. Most of them will entail an analysis of the reinforcement contingencies with which the group is confronted as well as attempts to anticipate the nature of the contingencies with which they may be confronted in the future and, of course, the behavior that will be required to satisfy them. Operant behavior, sometimes described as "strategic planning," is, without doubt, an important feature of an effective leader's repertoire though it may not have an immediate effect on the behavior of the group.

Reinforcing Consequences of Leader Operants. Leader operant behavior is shaped and maintained by its consequences, the most fundamental of which are the responses of followers or the envionmental changes produced by the followers' behavior or both. Sustained high rates of follower operant responding or increases in those rates will serve as powerful reinforcers for the leader whose behavior is responsible for those rates. So, too, will the occurrence of effective problem-solving operants within the group and the occurrence of unspecified and possibly unusual forms of follower behavior that clearly appear to improve the probability that the group will continue to maximize their reinforcement. Conversely, low rates of responding as well as ineffective and dysfunctional follower responses will serve as negative reinforcers for the leader.

Follower behaviors would not serve as reinforcing events for leaders if they were not related in some way to the production of the reinforcing consequences responsible for group functioning in the first place. This fact brings us to the second class of events serving as reinforcers for leader behavior, namely, a share of the group's reinforcing consequences provided by the external environment. The leader's share is typically larger than that allocated to the other group members because the leader's contribution to group functioning is usually regarded as most crucial.

As in the case of follower behavior, the reinforcing consequences of effective leader operants may be long delayed or otherwise poorly scheduled. Therefore, intermediate reinforcers in the form of praise, encouragement, and reassurance from some group members and peers and others outside the group may be needed to sustain effective leader operants. Pay increases, bonuses, and similar kinds of social reinforcers are likely to be supplied by supervisors in the case of appointed organizational leaders. Intermediate reinforcers from all the above sources usually accompany changes in the behavior of followers produced by the leader's operants and other "signs" that the group is behaving effectively.

A fourth class of events serving to reinforce leader operants includes those group member responses other than "target" behaviors. Followers who have maximized their reinforcement or who have escaped or avoided aversive consequences by virtue of the controlling practices of an effective leader often provide a wide variety of social reinforcers in the form of recognition dinners, gifts, medals, certificates, and other expressions of appreciation in addition to a larger share of the group's reinforcing consequences. These also typically accompany, or come after, the effective behavior of followers that was produced by the leader, and only rarely during or before these changes.

Group Control

As a group continues to be effective, the cooperant behavior of each member is strengthened and maintained. But other important forms of interaction may also be observed. For example, the cooperants of each member become powerful secondary reinforcers for many, if not most, of the other group members. As a consequence, group members (in addition to the leader) may act in concert to control the behavior of a given individual. The relationship between the behavior of the young or inexperienced and the group's reinforcing outcomes may be obscure or otherwise ineffective in shaping and maintaining their cooperants. Their behavior will, therefore, be carefully monitored by other group members, who will also attempt to shape and maintain their cooperants by supplying intermediate positive reinforcers. Group members may not be very effective in this enterprise, for behavior that is maximally effective in shaping and sustaining the behavior of another individual is only rarely acquired by simple exposure to the complex contingencies prevailing in social interaction. When group members are not effective, they may turn to punishment. In other words, when the cooperants of a given member fail to occur or begin to extinguish after having occurred, that member is likely to "incur the collective wrath" of the rest of the group (criticism, ridicule, reduction in the individual's share of the group's positive reinforcing consequences, threats, or bodily harm). If those actions fail to produce behavior that is reinforcing to the group, the individual may leave the group or be ostracized.

Group Cohesion

Other classes of social behavior are likely to be strong and, therefore, frequently observed in a group whose cooperants are consistently effective in producing powerfully reinforcing consequences. For example, group members will behave so as to maintain personal contact with each other and will report that they like or are attracted to each other. They will also frequently interact with each other verbally. These exchanges may or may not be task relevant (and may at times, therefore, be incompatible with ongoing cooperants). Altruistic behavior[3] frequently occurs. For example, an individual dis-

---

[3]Altruistic behavior is often defined as behavior that produces reinforcement for another but that is not itself followed by reinforcing consequences. If it could be documented that altruistic behavior is never reinforced, then one would have to assume that such behavior is inherited or

playing signs of distress may serve as an S_D for approach, offers of assistance, solace, or any of a wide variety of helping operants, including the performance of the ailing member's task. The reinforcing consequences of altruistic operants are not difficult to find. They may be in the form of the appearance of more effective cooperants of the aided members, expressions of gratitude, and possibly other forms of behavior described as "returning a favor."

Groups manifesting the above behavioral patterns are often characterized as cohesive and as having high "morale" or a certain "esprit de corps." Such terms may come to refer to assumed causes of behavior, but, upon closer scrutiny, they are revealed to be descriptive terms referring, however vaguely, to certain aspects or features of the behavior shaped and maintained by the prevailing social reinforcement contingencies.

Group Development

Effective groups, providing reinforcing advantages for all their members, do evolve and manage to sustain their effectiveness over long periods of time. We have come to recognize, however, that serious difficulties may be encountered at any time in the history of the group.

Some of the most pressing problems may arise in the formative stages of interaction. If the setting in which the individuals are found is novel, having few, if any, properties in common with settings to which the individuals had been previously exposed, group members "may be at a loss as to what to do." There may be little operant behavior evoked that will satisfy the contingencies currently prevailing, and a wide variety of respondents may be elicited including a high level of arousal. (We often note that some members will tell jokes or otherwise behave so as to relieve "tension," "uncertainty," or "anxiety" and may become leaders at least for short periods of time.) It is more likely, however, that most of the individuals will have been exposed to prior reinforcement contingencies that were similar in some respects to the contingencies now prevailing. By stimulus induction, therefore, we can expect that operant behavior, shaped and maintained in previous settings, will be evoked. If only one individual manifests behavior that satisfies the contingencies or has stimulus properties (confident, behaving without hesitation, vigorous, etc.) typically associated with effective behavior, there may be no problem. But in the more typical case, two or more individuals will manifest operant behavior of different topographies or point up different contingencies to the group or both, and therein lies a potentially serious problem. As we have indicated, a group's reinforcing consequences are rarely evenly distrib-

---

that positive emotional responses manifested by others are inherently reinforcing whereas signs of distress are inherently aversive. We would then have the problem of accounting for the fact that we sometimes behave so as to produce stress responses in others. We do much better when we look for and find the reinforcement contingencies responsible for both altruistic and aggressive operants.

uted among its members with effective leaders typically receiving a larger share.[4] Thus, two or more group members with similar reinforcement histories with respect to leader cooperants may vie for leadership. The outcome of this "struggle," when it occurs, is not altogether predictable, though it is quite unlikely that the behavior of other group members will come under the control of the behavior of those who appear to be "self-seeking," "insincere," and not obviously "interested in their welfare."[5] But if the struggle is not resolved reasonably soon, the group may disband or splinter into subgroups or factions, each with its own leader.

Though the group may get over the first hurdle, other difficulties may be encountered. A continuous and often refractory problem is that of allocating the group's reinforcing consequences. An equal distribution is not usually satisfactory and rarely seen in complex groups where the cooperants of some members are more critical to the group's effectiveness than the cooperants of others. Workable solutions, based on notions of "merit," "relative worth," or "criticality," have evolved, but no solution that results in a differential allocation is completely free of problems. Furthermore, there is always the possibility that an effective group will exploit some of its members. The leader and other members whose behavior is more critical to group effectiveness may stretch the ratios of those whose behavior is less important. As we have seen, the degree of control achieved by schedules of intermittent reinforcement are quite powerful—so powerful, in fact, that an individual can be brought to perform at a high and stable rate with very little reinforcement. Such procedures, of course, leave a greater share of the reinforcing consequences for the more powerful group members. Therefore, the control exerted by some members of the group may work to their own advantage and at the expense of a given individual or individuals. But groups are as susceptible to social traps as individuals. The ratio may be stretched to the breaking point, at which time the individuals thus exploited may either leave the group or engage in aggres-

[4]As we have previously indicated, the reinforcing consequences contingent on effective leadership operants are several. They may include a larger share of the group's consequences and positive evaluations from group members (praise, admiration, a "willingness to serve the leader further") and from others outside the group. There is, furthermore, the possibilty that those who *effectively* control the behavior of others may produce increases in the group's reinforcing consequences over those produced by the group when another is in charge. Finally, the possibility of being exploited by others is reduced when we are in control. It is little wonder that many laymen and some behavioral scientists speak of a "need for dominance" or a need for "stature among one's associates." Control itself—or rather the immediate consequences in the form of changes in the behavior of others—becomes a powerful secondary reinforcer. Nor is it surprising that we often "resist" or "view with suspicion" another person's attempts to control our behavior even though it may be for our benefit.

[5]It is a difficult matter to specify the topographical details of such behavior though it needs to be done. Some claim that they can spot insincerity "a mile away," but, if so, they cannot articulate its details. For the same reasons, we cannot yet specify the topographical details of the "considerate" or "participative" leader although it may be that the person manifesting behavior with those properties will come to exercise more control over the other group members, at least early on. Perhaps it is because participative leaders widely evoke problem solving and other forms of self-control within the group, thereby reducing the probability of exploitation.

sive countercontrol. The resulting intragroup conflict will often reduce its effectiveness in producing reinforcing consequences. It must also be remembered that a differential allocation of reinforcing consequences may produce intragroup competition, reducing interaction and mutual helping behavior.

The reinforcement contingencies that have shaped and maintained the cooperant behavior of the group may change. This may be a serious problem for a group that has been effective for some time because the cooperants, having been powerfully reinforced, will be particularly resistant to extinction. Effective groups may, of course, develop means for "experimenting." The leader or other members comprising a problem-solving unit within the group or both may come to monitor their environment and to change their own behavior systematically while noting the consequences. If more effective cooperants are observed, the newer, more effective forms are then introduced. But experimentation is a complex form of behavior that may never appear. If it does not, the group is particularly vulnerable to the difficulties posed by a change in contingencies. Cooperant behavior, now ineffective, will continue. As extinction sets in, emotional respondents quite possibly interfering with effective changes in behavior will appear. Eventually the group may disband.

Contrived Groups

Despite the varied and potentially serious problems that an interacting group may encounter, the group often surmounts those hurdles and goes on to thrive and survive for long periods of time. In fact, the reinforcing advantages of cooperant behavior are typically so obvious that we human beings no longer wait for accidental or naturally occurring contingencies to shape and maintain it. With varying degrees of success, members of a culture often attempt to alter the environment so as to attract, select, and then evoke and sustain the behavior of those selected more or less according to predetermined specifications. That the consequences of this very complex operant behavior may be powerfully reinforcing is seen in the multitude of *formal organizations,* which are initiated almost daily in advanced cultures. That there are also risks may be seen in the large number that fail to survive for more than three years. However, formal organizations do not fail simply because they are contrived. As we have seen, groups that develop as a result of naturally occurring but unanalyzed reinforcement contingencies also fail to survive. We must, therefore, attempt to analyze as best we can those reinforcement contingencies responsible for continued group effectiveness. We now turn to this analysis, concentrating our attention on the behavior of the organizational leader.

EIGHT
ORGANIZATIONAL LEADERSHIP

The prominence of formal organizations in most cultures reflects the reinforcing advantages of cooperant behavior and our ability to design and implement systems that might yield those advantages. However, the fact that debilitating interpersonal conflicts and organizational failures are also observed suggests that much remains to be learned about cooperant behavior and the variables of which it is a function. In this, the concluding chapter, the focus is on the specialized cooperants of those we have come to designate as organizational leaders. The analysis is offered not simply as a reminder of the significance of leader behavior in determining the fate of an organization. There is the added hope that it may further our understanding of the conditions that evoke and sustain those forms of cooperant behavior that promote organizational effectiveness and survival.

The reader will recall that our analysis was initiated in Chapter 7 with the introduction of a functional analysis of leader behavior. There we described four broad classes of leader operants that are held to be essential to group effectiveness. It is clear, however, that our description of the behavior of effective leaders needs to be expanded. In what follows, we attempt to provide a more specific and comprehensive description of those leadership operants believed to be important, if not essential, to group effectiveness.

In our discussion it will be necessary to distinguish between the behavioral requirements of organizational leaders in general and the additional requirements of those we shall describe as the leaders of leaders. All leaders, at whatever level in the organization, will be required to perform certain basic functions that we offer as our prescriptions for effective leadership. We will then describe some of the additional behavioral requirements of the leaders of leaders, including the design and administration of reinforcement contingencies controlling the leaders subordinate to them, the monitoring of the organization's "external" environment, the determination of strategy, and the design and alteration of organizational structure.

SOME PRESCRIPTIONS FOR EFFECTIVE LEADERSHIP

The Specification of Group Member Operants

Analyses of leader positions have shown that organizational leaders must monitor various features of the task setting, including the behavior of subordinate group members, and behave as necessary to strengthen and sustain those cooperants most likely to maximize group effectiveness. The leader's reinforcing operants serve, in one sense, to specify those forms of subordinate cooperants that will be reinforced and those that will not. But there are advantages in being able to specify them in another sense, that of describing and possibly modeling them.

The specification of effective subordinate cooperants may be relatively straightforward in a simple group wherein the behavior of each member is the same or very similar. However, it becomes more complicated in the case of a complex group in which the behavior of each group member may be different from that of every other member. Leaders who have been appointed from the ranks may have a significant advantage if they have had the opportunity to acquire the different cooperants required of each member. However, the cooperants of the leader while serving in the various subordinate roles may not have been the most effective, and in any case human beings do not always scrutinize and tact their own behavior as a matter of course. Therefore, it usually remains for the leader to specify as clearly as possible those subordinate cooperants most likely to maximize group outcomes or to see to it that this function is carried out.

Job analysis has been developed as one method for specifying the cooperants required of each group member. By means of direct observation and interviewing procedures, a second party[1] determines the nature and variety of events that must be attended to (the S_D's), the cooperants required, and other task features such as job hazards, working conditions, and the incumbent's relationships with others. The results of the analysis are recorded in the form of a job description. The description or specification is typically rendered in narrative form, but in recent years inventories of "generalized work behaviors"[2] have been developed and provided for analysts who then simply check off those that are required in a given job. Whichever technique is used, the cooperants are typically specified in rather general terms. Nevertheless, the descriptions serve reasonably well as aids in the selection of new members,

---

[1]Although the incumbent himself or herself may be asked to serve as the analyst, this is not recommended for obvious reasons. The organizational leader may, of course, serve as the analyst, but the job of analyzing jobs is typically delegated to persons especially trained for that purpose.
[2]See McCormick and Ilgen (1980) for a review of one such inventory, the Position Analysis Questionnaire.

in training, and in the design and implementation of effective reinforcement contingencies.

The cooperant behavior of group members should not be defined too narrowly. Katz (1964), for example, has pointed out that members of effective groups will provide aid to each other when difficulties are encountered and may otherwise act to promote effective behavior among themselves. Such behavior is rarely specified in the job descriptions of subordinates and may not be recognized or otherwise reinforced by organizational leaders, but, as Katz noted, it may very well be the lifeblood of an effective group.

The task of determining and specifying the cooperant behavior of group members should be viewed as a continuing process. Once group member cooperants have been specified or strengthened or both by the leader's reinforcing practices, they become standard forms that are consistently displayed in the group setting. However, human adults come to that setting with different prior reinforcement histories, and, for that reason, the prevailing contingencies may produce variations in the standard forms that are strengthened when they prove to be more effective. As a matter of fact, the discovery and specification of ever more effective cooperants may themselves be regarded as a part of the roles of certain group members. Organizational leaders may and, in most cases, should encourage at least some members of the group to vary and observe their own behavior systematically while noting its effects and to otherwise study their work environment with the possibility of discovering and proposing alternative methods (behavior) that might prove more effective.

It should be acknowledged that all is not lost if the organizational leader can neither describe the cooperants of each group member nor otherwise discriminate between effective and ineffective forms. The leader may lead by specifying goals or objectives to be met and by reinforcing those who achieve those goals, and, in a modified version of that approach, both the leader and the subordinate may jointly specify goals to be met while leaving unspecified the manner in which those goals are to be achieved. In either case, the leader's reinforcing operants are necessarily under the control of "results" or the environmental changes produced by the cooperants of each group member. This may be the only approach available to organizational leaders who cannot, for one reason or another, model, describe, or otherwise respond differentially to effective and ineffective behavior. However, they are at a serious disadvantage when the goals are not realized unless they delegate the function of specifying and strengthening effective cooperants to another person, whether a specialist or a subordinate leader. There is nothing wrong with delegation so long as it is recognized that the delegator then becomes a leader of leaders and now must specify, direct, and maintain the behavior of the specialist or subordinate leader. Ultimately, therefore, the effective organizational leader cannot avoid the responsibility of analyzing, specifying, and otherwise responding differentially to the behavior of at least some members of the group.

Selection Decision Making

Whatever the origin of the group, its membership will almost certainly change over time. Some members will leave the group for higher level positions in other groups or to seek membership in other groups, some may suffer major illnesses or death, and some may retire. As a consequence, leaders are faced with the necessity of recruiting and selecting new group members periodically.

Should the leader be required to shape the role behavior of a new member from ground zero, replacement would be a problem of monumental proportions. Many—and perhaps most—roles require behavior that can only be shaped in a step-by-step fashion by conditioning procedures that would require months, if not years, to administer. Therefore, if the group is to survive, the only alternative is to seek out human beings whose reinforcement histories have been such that at least some of the operant behavior required for effective role performance has already been shaped and brought under the control of verbal stimuli. Then it is a matter of evoking and sequencing the operants in their approximate forms through instruction and improving their skill properties through appropriate reinforcement.

The selection of individuals with the appropriate reinforcement histories is a complicated and important process. It is by no means the case that all human beings are equally capable of acquiring the behavior that may be required in a given role. We have found that early conditioning treatments are important in determining the rate at which the nervous system develops after birth so that even if we could assume an intact physiology at the time of birth, the child might not fully benefit from the later exposure to parental and educational reinforcement contingencies. And, of course, the developing child might never be exposed to the contingencies responsible for shaping those operants. Human adults, therefore, show wide variations in those complex operant repertoires that are often called aptitudes or special abilities and that may be required for effective role performance. Whether these operants can be shaped at maturity is still an open question, but our research studies have indicated that they change very little over the lifetime of the human adult. And in any event, it is impossible for leaders to design and administer the extensive conditioning procedures that only *might* develop those operant repertoires.

The leader, therefore, is confronted with the problem of accurately discriminating between those applicants who are likely to behave effectively in given roles after reasonable exposure and those who will fail to do so. One apparent way to resolve this problem is simply to expose applicants to the prevailing contingencies and observe their behavior for some period of time. If effective behavior is evoked and sustained, the new member is granted permanent membership status. If not, he or she is rejected. Thus, we can see that in this case the behavior of discriminating is merely delayed, and though this procedure may be necessary on occasion, it is undesirable on many grounds when it becomes customary. Group effectiveness is always impaired during the trial period, and those who subsequently fail and are rejected may be devastated.

A much more desirable approach is to attempt to discriminate before the fact. The behavior involved in making these discriminations is complex and never perfectly accurate, but, in general, the leader or other group members or both gather extensive information about a prospect that serves as S_D's evoking a decision to invite the applicant to become a member or not.

Standard procedures facilitating this behavior have evolved and are reasonably useful when the information thus procured is relevant or valid. Application blanks that allow applicants to describe their prior behavioral (work) histories and educational treatments can be useful. Structured interviews in which the leader or staff specialist or both obtain and record descriptions of other facets of the applicant's prior reinforcement history have also been applied with some success. Psychological tests can be especially useful when it is ascertained that they are reliable measures of those special operant repertoires that are required for effective performance.

The organizational leader may delegate some responsibility for selection decision making to a specialized subgroup. In the larger formal organizations, for example, one is likely to find that a personnel staff has been appointed to develop and maintain contact with individuals who may be prospects for group membership. They also develop and administer procedures for selecting group members and study the validity or effectiveness of these procedures. Once again, however, the organizational leader has become a leader of leaders responsible for directing and sustaining the behavior of the staff specialists. Moreover, the effective leader may continue to play a role in the selection process because he or she may be as capable of making accurate discriminations as anyone else.

Training and Orientation

Most individuals bring a large number and variety of behaviors with them to the organization when they join it. If the selection decision-making procedures employed by the leader are reasonably valid, many of the behaviors required in the work setting will have been shaped and brought under the control of verbal instructions. But most functional operants will not be strong in the new setting, or if evoked by features of the group setting, they will not occur in the proper sequence or in the most effective forms. Organizational leaders will, therefore, be required to evoke approximations of the required operants through modeling and verbal instructions and to enhance the skill properties of such operants through the careful reinforcement of ever-closer approximations of the final form. This is typically accomplished by means of on-the-job training and, on occasion, by means of formalized classroom procedures.

Training is a process of establishing skilled behavior that is functional to the organization now or at a future time. When training is effective, its consequences produce many special advantages for the leader and other group members. Training can convert a newly hired individual into a useful, productive group member who contributes to the effectiveness of the group and the organization as a whole. Moreover, training prepares group members to perform more effectively on their tasks and, therefore, increases the probability that they will maximize their reinforcement through prolonged group membership. Finally, because training results not only in the evocation and strengthening of functional group member operants but also in the specification of the conditions under which these operants are appropriate, the leader is no longer required to monitor and direct the behavior of subordinate group members continuously.

The training procedures utilized in organizations have often been equated with the behavioral shaping process. In shaping, however, successive approximations of an operant with an initially low or zero probability are differentially reinforced until the desired response is evoked in its final form. In the training of new group members, on the other hand, it is assumed that many (if not most) of the operants that are functional or desirable have already been inserted into the individual's behavioral repertoire and that these operants can be brought under the control of stimuli in the task environment or properties of the task itself. Thus, the problem faced by leaders in training group members has less to do with shaping new responses than it does with evoking operants that may be of low probability and bringing them under the control of appropriate stimuli. In these situations, other methods of behavioral change, most of which require the leader to manipulate S_D's for group member behavior, are more likely to prove effective. A leader, for example, may provide instructions, written procedures, job descriptions, directions on how to perform a task, or other forms of verbal stimuli to bring about appropriate or desirable group member behavior.

Providing models for desired behavior is another way of evoking effective group member operants. In the case of adult human beings, a very extensive imitative repertoire has typically been previously shaped and is under the control of stimuli in the form of the behavior of others. Thus, in an organizational system, we might find some workers imitating the behavior of a peer who frequently receives reinforcement from the leader. Benefits will accrue to the group depending on whether the modeled behavior is productive. But a more direct application of this form of discriminative stimulus control can be utilized by a leader when training workers to perform a particular task simply by modeling the desired task behavior himself or herself. In this case, the leader's task behavior sets the occasion on which similar behavior by the worker is reinforced.

Whether the behavior evoked in training is imitative or results from verbal S_D's in the form of instructions, descriptions, advice, and so on, the leader should take care to monitor and reinforce functional operants when they are first emitted by new group members. Behavior that is characterized by its skill properties is often under the control of rather subtle environmental contingencies that may go unnoticed by new group members and may lead, therefore, to considerable delays in reinforcement. Because the operant behaviors evoked in training may only be approximations of the final form, it is quite important to monitor the behavior continually and provide reinforcement without delay. Delays may be particularly dysfunctional because relatively crude approximations of the requisite operants may be strengthened and interfere with later transitions to the more effective forms. Thus, the leader's attention to the details of the process is vitally important in the initial stages, and the leader is advised to observe group member behavior closely at this point and reinforce functional behaviors appropriately.

Employee training may be an ongoing process if the skill requirements of a particular job are complex or if an individual's job is altered or changed frequently. But training usually becomes less problematic the longer an individual works for the organization. New group members present particular problems to leaders because they are the least familiar with their jobs and the organization itself. For this reason, an integral part of the training process in many organizations is an orientation program designed to help the new subordinates get "settled into the job." Whether these programs are successful or not may have a substantial effect on the training program as a whole.

Individuals who are relatively new on the job seldom lack "motivation." In fact, rather than lack motivation, they may suffer from too much of it. Novel, new, or unfamiliar surroundings generally elicit a high level of arousal and other respondents, which may be incompatible with effective cooperant behavior. The effects of these novel stimuli are often compounded or made more acute because many organizations conduct intensive sessions for new group members in order to provide them with information not only about their job but also about the company, its history, the products it sells, and so on, long before the high level of respondent behavior elicited by novel features of the setting has subsided. To be sure, complete information regarding the group member's role is necessary, but organizational leaders are well advised to provide training in the primary role behaviors immediately and orientation training later.

It is only when the new member has adapted to the task environment that questions are raised about the meaning and significance of his or her particular role. Depending on the complexity or novelty of the task to be learned, this may not come until after a few months, a year, or even longer. Only when these questions are raised will the group member generally benefit from the usual orientation procedure. At this time a rather comprehensive discussion of how the group member's specific job fits into the total picture, the history of the company, the products it sells, and the markets sold to will prove useful.

Training new employees is time-consuming, and for this reason organizational leaders often delegate part of the orientation and training procedures to other subordinate leaders or to specialists or both. But whether these duties are delegated or performed by the leader, they should not be left to chance.

Evoking and Maintaining Subordinate Behavior

If the group is to remain successful, subordinate cooperants must be brought under the control of task stimuli and maintained at reasonable levels. An effective leader, therefore, is one who is able to identify stimulus events that will serve as positive reinforcers and who sees to it they follow on group member cooperants with some degree of consistency.

As noted in Chapter 3, stimulus events that have been found to serve as positive reinforcers for human beings can be conveniently grouped into two broad classes. The first to be considered are referred to as *intrinsic* reinforcers. It has been found that virtually any stimulus change will serve as a positive reinforcer when first introduced so long as it is not too novel or intense. Such reinforcers are called intrinsic reinforcers largely because they are inherent in the design of the task and include any sort of change in the task setting produced by task operants. Flipping a switch to turn on a motor or a light is reinforced by the hum of the motor or the appearance of the light. The operant behavior required for the manual assembly of a water pump is reinforced by the changes in the structure of the water pump as it nears completion just as the behavior of a carpenter or a typist is reinforced by the stimulus changes their behavior produces. Intrinsic reinforcers must be regarded as relatively weak unless they are paired with other reinforcing events because they show rapid habituation effects. That is to say, they will serve as positive reinforcers when they first appear but will lose that property rather quickly with repetition. On the other hand, they regain their reinforcing potential when they have been withdrawn or have not occurred for some time. The leader must, therefore, be aware that the nature of the subordinate's task is important in maintaining functional operants. Some tasks may be structured so that, over time, multiple operants, each producing different stimulus changes, are required. As these response-produced changes occur in some temporal sequence, they are likely to maintain the behavior that produces them. Other tasks, however, may require a limited number of operants that produce few changes in the environment. Those changes will quickly lose their reinforcing properties owing to habituation and will be relatively ineffective in maintaining the task operants that produce them.

Organizational leaders usually cannot do very much about the technology and hence about the task structure in the short run. On the other hand, jobs can be "enlarged" in a number of ways without significantly changing the technology. For example, because the manner in which a job is defined is arbitrary, subordinates can be assigned a greater variety of tasks, as in job rotation. The effective leader will look for ways to increase the intrinsic reinforcing properties of group member roles when they are lacking. If none can be found, he or she must necessarily turn to the more careful administration of *extrinsic* reinforcers.

Extrinsic reinforcers are those events that are mediated or delivered by a leader, and they include pay, smiles, nods, compliments, praise, and other types of acknowledgments of "good work." They may be regarded as powerful reinforcers for most human beings for two reasons. In the reinforcement histories of human beings, they are paired with a variety of other reinforcing events and continue to be paired with them in adulthood. Secondly, they are not often delivered on a continuous basis and for that reason do not suffer habituation effects. Monetary reinforcement in all its forms (wages and salaries, bonuses, periodic increases in pay, promotions, fringes, etc.) is a very important generalized reinforcer because it continues to be paired in incremental amounts with a host of other reinforcing events in adulthood, and it is never delivered on a continuous basis. It is something that most human beings never "have enough of."

It has occasionally been said that extrinsic reinforcers are not very effective. The implication is that they simply do not serve as reinforcers for some or all human beings. However, it is almost inevitably the case that when extrinsic reinforcers seem to be ineffective, it is because they are not administered properly by organizational leaders. The most common problem is that there is no clear-cut relation between functional subordinate behaviors and the occurrence of extrinsic reinforcers. Supervisors might supply extrinsic reinforcers on the basis of "perceived need" or to avoid respondent and operant aggression elicited or evoked by the absence of positive reinforcement or on the belief that rewarded group members will *subsequently* produce although they were not behaving effectively at the time the reinforcement was delivered. In all such cases, it is not that the events are not reinforcing, but rather that they are likely to be contingent on and therefore strengthen any behavior *but* functional subordinate operants.

A second problem is that the leader's administration of extrinsic reinforcers is often inconsistent. All of us are typically conditioned to reinforce another whenever they behave in a manner that is reinforcing to us, and leaders are no exception. When the leader reinforces a group member "without awareness," he or she may reinforce subordinate behavior that is pleasing but possibly not required for group effectiveness. This is merely another example of obscure or irrelevant contingencies discussed above. But leaders are inconsistent in their delivery of extrinsic reinforcers in other ways. Their administration takes time (a valuable resource) and, in the case of pay, the dispensing of a valuable resource that can be utilized for other purposes. As a consequence, reinforcers may be delivered after a long delay or too infrequently to sustain behavior. In this regard, organizational leaders must be careful not to "strain ratios." It is rather easy through the careful scheduling of a reinforcing event to get "more and more for less and less." Moreover, organizational leaders are often powerfuly reinforced for "conserving resources" such as money. It is, therefore, tempting to get as much work out of their group members at the lowest possible cost. There is inevitably an upper-bound limit, however, and human organisms exhibit a breaking point at which functional behavior ceases, emotional respondents set in, and operant aggression as well as other forms of counter control are likely to be observed. In these cases, the organizational leader has not only failed to maintain functional subordinate operants, but he or she has also evoked dysfunctional or disruptive behavior that may become commonplace.

A third problem arises from the amount of control exercised by organizational leaders over certain types of extrinsic reinforcers such as pay. A great deal is lost when wages are "negotiated" or when the wage specialist or the organizational leader unduly constrains a subordinate leader in the administration of those events. Under these circumstances, praise, recognition, and other positive acknowledgments provided by the leader will not, in fact, serve as effective reinforcers. On the other hand, when an organizational leader has unilateral control over monetary reinforcement, virtually any act on the part of that leader may serve as a powerful reinforcer. As a consequence, the leader may inadvertently reward or punish a group member, and, of course, reinforcing events that are "inadvertently" administered may not be delivered contingently.

One might conclude that the leader's behavior of maintaining functional subordinate behavior is impossible or at least hopelessly complex. But though it is a difficult chore, it can be done, and it must be if the leader is to be effective. As a matter of fact, a number of useful suggestions can be derived from our discussion of the problems that have been observed, but rather more specific prescriptions can be offered.

First, organizational leaders should take steps to determine how much control they may exercise over extrinsic reinforcers (pay increases, promotions, bonuses, and the like). When it is the case that they have little or no control, they should take steps to gain some measure of control. If they cannot, it would be unwise to accept a management position or to remain in the position for very long, for they would then have to rely on punishment (discharge or threats of discharge) and applications of the negative reinforcement principle in maintaining behavior. This may be effective in the short term, but it may spell disaster over the long term. Organizational leaders do no require unilateral control over such reinforcers, but it is necessary that they have some voice or "upward influence" in determining the magnitude and timing of extrinsic reinforcers. Otherwise, leaders cannot possibly effectively reinforce functional subordinate behavior by the contingent delivery and scheduling of pay, nor will it be possible to reinforce through praise, commendations, and other personal acts.

Secondly, organizational leaders are much more likely to maintain functional subordinate cooperants when they administer reinforcing events consistently. They are in a much better position to do this when they have specified the more effective forms of group member behavior and can respond differentially to effective and ineffective forms, as we have noted. But beyond this, they must identify those events serving as reinforcers and deliver them frequently and without too much delay. The leader is not required to monitor group member behavior continuously and "zap each member with a pay increase, praise, or a carrot" each time functional operants have occurred. On the contrary, supervisors may administer reinforcers contingent on the production of outcomes (quality and quantity indexes, reduction in waste, good housekeeping, no accidents or injuries, reports by one group member that another "helped him [or her] out" etc.) without monitoring group member behavior as such. Moreover, reinforcing events can be effectively delivered after some delay so long as the supervisor is also careful to supply S_D's that describe the behavior or accomplishment that needs to be strengthened and maintained. Examples include statements such as "I want you to know that I think you did an outstanding job in putting together the Davis contract last month" or "I want to thank you for your help in preparing the budget" or "I am recommending a——percent increase in your pay for the following reasons: (1) (2) . . . (N)."

It is not possible or necessary to administer reinforcing events continuously. Intermittent schedules of reinforcement have been shown to be far more effective in maintaining behavior than continuous schedules. But it is usually the case that organizational leaders do not reinforce frequently enough, especially in those instances when the given task structure is such that intrinsic reinforcers are ineffective in maintaining behavior. A rather crude but useful guideline is to look for instances of functional cooperants (or results) on each occasion the leader has other reasons for being present or for a total of at least one hour a day and to deliver social-evaluative reinforcers in those instances where functional behavior is occurring or has obviously occurred. A record of the administration of reinforcers proves especially instructive to the leader in at least three ways. Group members whose names are missing from this record will indicate that either they could benefit from further instruction or that the supervisor has simply not reinforced the individual enough. It will also provide a guide for changing the frequency of reinforcement (usually an increase) if the individual's functional behavior is not being effectively maintained. Finally, it provides a general guideline in the supervisor's determination of *equity*. It should be pointed out that equity or the determination of each member's *appropriate* share of the group's consequences is rarely achieved when each member receives an equal share. Equity is a condition that is met only when the magnitude of reinforcement is contingent on and proportionate to each member's contribution to the group's effectiveness. Questions of equity and the problems attendant with inequities do not often occur in the case of social-evaluative reinforcers because they are difficult to "count up." But they certainly arise in the case of monetary reinforcement where even slight variations can be observed. A very large increase in pay may not be possibly reinforcing when another group member receives the same increase but is "perceived to be contributing less."

The establishment of equity is never easy, but it can be reasonably achieved in complex groups through the use of job evaluation techniques that help determine the "criticality" of the role in the group's success and by means of adequate methods for observing, recording, and "appraising" the degree to which functional behavior within each role has occurred.

It is obvious that our prescription for effectively maintaining functional cooperants is time-consuming, if not complex. Effective leaders recognize, however, that it is one of the most important, if not the most important, behavioral requirements of a leader.

The Prevention and Elimination of Dysfunctional Behavior

Subordinates may behave in ways that are dysfunctional, unproductive, or unsafe to themselves or others. Ignoring or paying little attention to safety rules, interrupting the work of peers, playing practical jokes, using machinery in need of repair, and driving vehicles in a reckless or unsafe manner are examples of undesirable employee operants. If such unwanted behavior results in receiving aversive stimulation from the physical environment or social sanctions from one's peers, it may be eliminated or reduced without the intervention of the leader. But there is little reason to expect that all undesirable and dysfunctional behavior can be reduced or precluded in this fashion. It is inevitable, therefore, that organizational leaders will encounter situations in which the use of aversive events or punishment is appropriate.

Several social scientists have suggested that punishment is among the most widely employed procedures of behavioral control in organizational settings. One reason for this, as we have noted, is that managers who employ little control over traditional organizational rewards find it necessary to revert to punishment and coercive procedures in their attempts to eliminate dysfunctional behavior and to maintain more functional group member cooperants. Another reason is that the use of punishment is seductive. The effects of punishment are frequently much more dramatic than that of positive reinforcement. Aversive events almost immediately reduce the frequency of the behavior on which they are made contingent. For this reason, some leaders utilize the punishment and negative reinforcement principles almost exclusively in their attempts to influence group member operants.

Aversive control is not only frequently relied on, but it is also typically administered ineffectively. A common practice employed by many managers when they punish group members is called "bagging it." Supervisors who "bag it" avoid dealing with dysfunctional group member behavior directly when they observe it by depositing the incident into an imaginary bag that they carry on their back. As the incidents of undesirable behavior accumulate, the manager's "bag" becomes more and more difficult for him or her to carry. Then one day, usually without much warning or provocation, the manager "unloads the bag" on a group member. As one might expect, the result of this emotional display by the supervisior is seldom very functional. Initially, many group members respond to such an outburst by the supervisor with bewilderment and surprise. They find it difficult to understand why the manager has "overreacted" so much. But eventually the surprise may turn to anger, frustration, and other negative emotional feelings, as well as to a variety of countercontrolling practices on the part of subordinate group members.

Leaders, of course, cannot avoid the use of punishment. It may be necessary to use aversive events in some cases to eliminate unsafe or unproductive group member behavior. But punishment need not produce dysfunctional consequences. Although the effects of punishment are quite complex, there are several prescriptions derived from recent research on the administration of aversive events that, if followed, can improve the leader's ability to administer punishment more effectively. We now turn to those prescriptions.

Punishment should be delivered as quickly after the undesirable response as possible. Any delay between the occurrence of dysfunctional behavior and the administration of punishment increases the probability that other, more desirable forms of behavior will unintentionally be punished. Some managers make a point of reprimanding an individual's dysfunctional behavior only during formalized performance evaluation meetings, even when the behavior in question may have occurred days, weeks, or months earlier. The problems with this approach is that the behavior has continued and quite probably has been strengthened in the interim.

In order to be maximally effective, punishment should be administered at a reasonably high level of intensity from the very outset. Aversive events applied in a sequence of gradually increasing intensities permit habituation effects that may nullify the effectiveness of the punishment administered. Of course, in the case of adult human beings, not all aversive events have to be physically intense in order to be effective. Expressions of disapproval, reprimands, threats of the removal of privileges, and other forms of negative evaluative statements frequently serve as effective punishers if they have been paired over time with other aversive events. No doubt, very loud or shouted warnings or reprimands that may be characterized as physically intense may be used as aversive events. But verbal stimuli of moderate or low intensities may be more effective as long as the leader does not use them indiscriminately.

To the degree possible, those environmental events sustaining undesirable behavior should be eliminated. This may be accomplished by identifying and removing or withdrawing those reinforcing events maintaining the dysfunctional behavior. In general, the use of the extinction procedure in conjunction with the administration of punishment is more effective than the application of either procedure by itself.

Punishment should be directed at specific responses and should never be employed by the leader in order to "get even" with a group member. As noted earlier, many managers often overlook initial offenses by a group member in the hopes that the problem behavior will go away or in order to avoid the unpleasant feelings that often accompany having to tell someone he or she is making a mistake or performing poorly, only to become emotionally upset with the subordinate and "chew him [or her] out" or vow "to teach him [or her] a lesson he'll [or she'll] never forget" after repeated rule violations have occurred. Such emotional outbursts on the part of the supervisor are likely to be viewed as a personal attack by the individual who is punished, and he or she may respond in kind with an emotional onslaught of his or her own or by utilizing various countercontrol techniques in order to "pay the supervisor back." In order to avoid this problem, punishment should be administered in a consistent fashion and should focus on the behavior considered dysfunctional.

The reason for the punishment should be clearly explained to the individual being punished. For punishment to be effective, the group member whose behavior is being punished should be told why the punishment is occurring. As a part of this process, the leader should identify the dysfunctional behavior of the subordinate, explain why such behavior is aversive to the leader or why it impedes the progress of the group, and explain that the continuation of such behavior is likely to lead to more serious consequences. Once the aversive event has been administered, it is also generally an excellent opportunity for the leader to use S_D's to suggest more acceptable behavior and also to perform a useful diagnostic activity. It may, for example, be beneficial to ask the group member to examine his or her own behavior to determine why he or she responded dysfunctionally and how such responses can be avoided in the future. Such behavior by leaders may help them to understand better the causes of the behavior in question. It may also benefit the subordinate because it will provide S_D's for them to respond in a more appropriate manner.

Caution should be exercised so that punishment does not signal positive reinforcement. Aversive stimuli differentially associated with positive reinforcing events may acquire discriminative as well as secondary reinforcing properties. In such cases, the frequency of the punished response may actually increase rather than decrease. For the child whose father spanks him for swearing, but who is comforted immediately afterward by his mother because she feels sorry for him, the spanking received may acquire the properties of a conditioned reinforcer or a discriminative stimulus that signals that crying or looking sad will be followed by the mother's affection and attention. Increases, rather than decreases, in cursing or other undesirable behavior that are followed by a spanking may result. Similarly, the employee who gets chewed out by his or her supervisor for "goofing off" may increase this undesirable behavior because of the attention he or she gets from his or her peers when the boss gets mad at him or her. For this reason, a time-out or extinction procedure should always follow the presentation of an aversive event. Punishment in this instance becomes a signal that reinforcement will not be forthcoming for some period of time, and the elimination of the undesirable response should be more effective as a result.

In summary, then, an effective leader will apply a punishment procedure when necessary, but he or she will apply it only when necessary and only in conjunction with other behavioral control techniques. Certain limited classes of behavior may be regarded as so dysfunctional that both the behavior and the punishment are specified in a rule. The leader's behavior in these circumstances is unequivocal. He or she delivers the punishment, and it is usually harsh (typically dismissal). However, it is generally wise to suppress the tendency to write a rule describing every potential transgression and the punishment to be administered for it, for then the leader becomes a punitive agent and not much else.

When behavior distasteful or repugnant to the leader occurs, the first question to be asked is whether the behavior is replacing more effective behavior or is merely a personal reaction of the leader and of no consequence to group effectiveness. If it is the former, the leader should proceed without delay to describe the behavior to the subordinate and to seek out the reasons for its occurrence. (If operant behavior, however dysfunctional, is occurring, it is occurring for some reason. Either it is being effectively evoked and maintained by positive reinforcers, or it is avoidance behavior maintained by a reduction in, or the avoidance of, aversive reinforcers. In either case, both the leader and the subordinate involved might identify the supporting reinforcing events and work toward the elimination of both the behavior and its support.) The leader's investigation, however straightforward, will constitute a punishment procedure that, though it is a mild form of punishment, is likely to have a significant effect. In fact, the behavior may be eliminated at that point, never to appear again. However, the effective leader is guided by the general principle that the important thing to recall when individuals misbehave is *not what they are doing or have done,* but what they are *not* doing. A most important strategy to employ in conjunction with a punishment procedure is to evoke functional behavior incompatible with the transgression and to see that it is powerfully reinforced.

The Development of Subordinate Self-Control

It will be recognized that all our prescriptions for effective leadership are descriptions of behavioral control techniques. They describe or imply leader operants that, it is suggested, will either change or evoke and sustain group member behavior.

Individuals who have emerged as leaders in group settings or who have been effective as appointed leaders will have little difficulty with the notion of leaders as behavioral control agents. It is likely, however, that they will feel that something is missing, and indeed it is. The leader who unilaterally determines and prescribes the behavior of subordinates, who has near-complete control over potent reinforcing consequences, and who has learned how to manage the reinforcement contingencies of others can, in fact, produce behavior according to plan. There is the real danger, however, that group members will come to depend too much on the leader. They will behave according to the plan, doing nothing more or less than that which has been prescribed and reinforced by the leader. This condition, if effected, is problematical even when the leader's plan is the best that could be devised. Though by definition the group continues to be maximally effective, the leader under these circumstances tends to get most of the "credit" whereas other group members may get less and less. The net effect is that no deviations in prescribed behavior are reinforced (and are likely to be punished), but, in addition, *prescribed* group member behavior may be tentative or weak in the absence of the leader and his or her "blessing." Ultimately, therefore, the group may fail even though the plan is a good one.

A more serious problem is that the leader's plan is likely to be imperfect or, at least, incomplete. If it is imperfect, the group will fail to achieve the level of effectiveness it could otherwise have realized if a better plan, possibly developed with the assistance of other group members, had been implemented. When it is incomplete, behavior not prescribed by the powerful leader but necessary for group effectiveness simply does not occur.

The wise leader recognizes these dangers and attempts to preclude them by encouraging the development of subordinate self-control. Most group members and certainly most of those who have been on the scene for some time are capable of some degree of self-determination. When we speak of self-control or self-determination, we are not referring to an "inner will" or some other mysterious process. Rather, we are referring to operant behavior on the part of a group member that serves to evoke or sustain his or her own behavior. In other words, when the group member controls himself or herself, he or she is behaving just as the leader might behave.

There are many forms of self-control that a leader promotes simply by reinforcing the individual when these have occurred. For example, when effective group member behavior has already been identified (the subordinate "knows" what to do) but is not being maintained at a reasonable rate, at least some group members may strengthen this behavior by telling themselves to "get with it" or by establishing a quota for themselves, after which they promise themselves a "break." Self-controlling operants of this sort are automatically reinforced by the leader, if they occur, when he or she consistently reinforces a high and sustained rate of behavior though the leader may never observe the self-controlling behavior.

There are other, possibly more important forms of self-control that a leader can and should promote. Some, though probably not all, of the group members may be as capable as the leader of identifying and describing methods and behavior that would serve to make the group more effective. At the very least, they might be capable of identifying and describing alternative modes of behaving from which the leader might select those most likely to maximize the group's success. Effective leaders often promote or evoke and then reinforce participative decision-making behavior of this sort, and it has several advantages. When group members participate in the design of their own contingencies, they are likely to specify behavior that has been made a part of their repertoire, and, in some cases at least, it may prove to be more functional than behavior that the leader could identify. Secondly, group members who are encouraged to design their own reinforcement contingencies are typically more "committed," which is to say that the behavior specified is likely to be maintained at a high rate by the self-controlling operants of the members themselves. The reason they are committed in this sense is not that human beings naturally and inevitably prefer to exercise some control over their own destiny, but because they often receive a greater (or fair) share of the reinforcing consequences when they are successful. It is also the case that they, rather than the leader, will be punished when they are not successful. For this reason, some members, especially the new and inexperienced, will not benefit from this type of controlling practice and may reject it. The strategy for the effective leader is to promote this form of self-control among group members *gradually*.

As a final form of self-control, leaders may encourage "experimentation" by their subordinates. As noted earlier, contingencies that prevail in a particular environment may change over time and, as they do, it is possible that behaviors not specified by the leader may be effective. In such cases, leaders can encourage group members to experiment with the environment, that is, to observe and study the contingencies that prevail, try out new behaviors, and note the consequences of these behaviors. Of course, leaders can experiment with new contingencies themselves. But in a changing environment, other group members may perform functional behaviors not performed by the leader and, in such instances, may be more effective than the leader is. Under these circumstances, the leader may find it particularly useful to encourage these group members to participate in the experimentation process as well.

Whenever leaders undertake to develop and sustain subordinate self-control, they are not themselves denying or refusing control. They are merely engaging in behavior and controlling operants of a different sort or establishing an environment that will promote different operants that may be critical to the success of the group in the future. Leaders control the behavior of others and should promote the development of self-control. But in no case should the leader exercise control or seek control for its own sake. Leaders are only as strong as the group they lead, and they should keep in mind that behavior that strengthens the group also strengthens the leader in the sense of being able to behave effectively with respect to the prevailing contingencies and to those that arise in the future.

THE LEADER OF LEADERS

As a group continues to be effective, changes in its size and structure are almost inevitable. Success often breeds success, which is to say that under some circumstances, at least, the reinforcing consequences produced by the cooperant behavior of a small group can be increased many times simply by adding new members. However, the changes that may be observed are not limited to mere increases in the size. There are likely to be significant changes in group structure as well. We alluded to this possibility when we noted that an organizational leader might delegate the responsibility for specifying cooperants and other duties to others serving as staff specialists or subordinate leaders. In either case, it will be necessary to select *those* individuals and to design and administer the reinforcement contingencies that will promote and sustain their behavior. And it will be of crucial importance to design and implement the reinforcement contingencies governing the relationships between appointed leaders and other group members. Needless to say, there are other examples of the structural modifications that may occur with growth, but to make a long story short, we shall simply note that a complex organization typically evolves (or is deliberately formed) and is usually comprised of several identifiable subgroups, each with its own appointed leader and a number of staff specialists as well. Under these circumstances, the organizational leader becomes a leader of leaders with additional responsibilities.

We cannot here provide a comprehensive description of the additional classes of behavior required of the leaders of leaders. The behavior with which we are concerned is extraordinarily complex, and, for that reason, if no other, a thoroughgoing functional analysis has hardly been broached, much less completed. This is not to say that no progress has been made. Though the reader is likely to find that some culling and retranslation will be necessary, some prescriptions may be gleaned from the literatures of the currently separate but overlapping fields of organizational theory, organizational development, and policy.[3] Therefore, our analysis, though incomplete, should provide a useful framework for those who may wish to pursue the literature in these fields and to keep abreast of developments as the analysis proceeds.

By way of introduction, we can state with confidence that if an organization is to thrive and survive, it must be structured in such a way that the behavior of the members continues to satisfy the reinforcement contingencies prevailing in the external environment. However, the external contingencies are sometimes dynamic as well as complex. Therefore, some organizational members, including most certainly the leader of leaders, will be required to monitor the environment for "opportunities"[4] and "threats," to consider alternative modes of organizational adjustment, and to propose or implement such modifications in organizational structure as are required by the changes in the external environment or achieve a combination of these.

---

[3]We find it somewhat disconcerting that organizational behavior, organizational theory, and organizational development and policy or "strategic management" have evolved as compartmentalized fields of inquiry because the primary concern of all four is human behavior, its determinants, and its effects. Scientists in each field seem intent on developing their own paradigms (theories, principles, research strategies, etc.) when, in fact, an integrative and fruitful scientific paradigm is already at hand.

[4]It is possible that those who have learned to scan their environments for "opportunities" become the culture's entrepreneurs who are responsible for the origination of its organizations in the first place.

The Nature and Design of Organizational Structure

It is clear that leaders of leaders must be capable of analyzing, designing, and modifying organizational structure. What, then, can the literature of organizational theory tell us about the nature of organizational structure and the manner in which it is altered? Perhaps not as much as we would like, for though organizational theorists have been concerned with the task of identifying the essential properties of organizations, their metaphorical language has not been all that enlightening. For example, organizations are commonly viewed as behaving entities that (or who) "can take actions, utilize resources, enter into contracts, and own property" (Scott, 1981, p. 7). That the analogy has been extended is seen in the oft-noted parallel between biological and organizational evolution.

Skinner (1971, p. 132) feels that the parallel[5] is useful, if stated carefully, but we doubt it. To be sure, we can describe organizations by listing their structural features just as we described a species by listing its anatomical features, and different organizations may share structural features just as different members of a species may share anatomical features. Moreover, it seems clear that variations in organizational structure, possibly corresponding to genetic mutations, do occur, and those variations in structure that contribute to the adaptiveness of the organization appear to survive and are somehow "transmitted" to new generations of organizations.

We might agree that organizational structures show a certain inertia (Hannan and Freeman, 1977; Stinchcombe, 1965). We might also agree that contemporary organizations resemble each other and that newly formed organizations resemble old ones though significant "mutations" are often observed to occur. But, of course, organizations do not procreate, and changes in organizational structure can be "transmitted" to contemporary organizations and to those survivors of an earlier generation as well as to new ones. Thus, the notion that organizations are species or systems that behave and whose structures change by means of processes akin to biological evolution does not serve us well, even when stated carefully. In fact, history may reveal that the analogy led organizational theorists away from that task of examining the effects of variations (experimental or otherwise) in organizational structure and to ignore or de-emphasize the role of human participants in designing, altering, and "transmitting" it.[6]

---

[5]In fact, Skinner (1971, Chapter 10) discussed the parallel between the evolution of a *culture* and the evolution of a species. However, neither the substance nor the significance of his discussion is altered when we substitute the term "organization" for his term, "culture."

[6]It is not accurate to imply that all theorists have ignored the role of participants—and particularly the leaders—in the design and modification of organizational structure. Kmetz (1981), for example, has called for the integration of the study of leadership and the study of organizations and has noted some of the ways in which leaders may affect, and be affected by, changes in structure. Scott (1981) has also alluded to the significance of the "dominant coalition" in determining structure.

The analogy may have also slowed the task of isolating the fundamental properties of organizations. In any event, there is still widespread disagreement among theorists, and this state of disarray[7] is most clearly seen in the different uses of the term "structure." For some, organizational structure seems to refer, however obliquely, to *all* the essential properties of organizations, but, for most theorists, the structure of an organization appears to refer to only one of its several components. Leavitt (1965), for example, listed *social structure,* technology, participants, and goals as the basic elements of organizations, and his view is rather widely reflected in the literature. One may note, however, various interpretations of social structure even within that framework. For some, it appears to refer to those shared beliefs and feelings about the organization or the participants' perceptions of what the organization is like and what values and behaviors are acceptable, in which case, the terms "climate" or "culture" are often used.[8] For others, the essence of structure is to be found in the stable patterns of behaviors that can be observed in organizations, and for still others, structure refers to the formal rules or prescriptions for behaving in the several roles. Finally, organizational structure may refer to the formal prescriptions for behaving (rules, policies, job descriptions, and so on, which both prescribe and proscribe specific behaviors) *and* the behavior itself. Scott (1981, p. 14), for example, has pointed out that organizational structure includes a "normative structure" though it is not clear whether the latter refers to the behavior resulting from the formal prescriptions or to behavior in addition to that prescribed or to those "informal" rules for behaving not included in the organization's formal structure.

Given this rather confusing state of affairs, we might well rid ourselves of the term "organizational structure" and coin a new one. But we have chosen to retain the term and allow it to stand for something that can be readily abstracted from the several views of organizational theorists. That "something" is, of course, the set of social reinforcement contingencies that prevail in every organization and that "serve to shape and channel" the behavior of its participants. Organizational structure, thus defined, is certainly among the most important features of organizations, if not their very essence.

The structure of an organization, defined as the social reinforcement contingencies that prevail there, does not refer to the participants, important as they are, or to their shared beliefs, values, role expectations, or perceptions of what the organization is like, as important as these seem to be for some theorists. Nor does organizational structure refer to organizational charts, policy statements, rules, and other formal prescriptions for behaving. To be sure, charts,

---

[7]In describing the current state of the field of organizational theory, Pfeffer (1982, Chapter 8) noted that the literature has moved too far from the basic properties of organizations. He implies that there should be a return to the unfinished task of analyzing those basic properties that are shared by organizations.

[8]On the other hand—and to add to the confusion—organizational culture is sometimes viewed not as structure, but as something *in addition to structure* and that, like structure, serves as a determinant of participant behavior.

policies, and rules often describe or imply an important subset of those contingencies that prevail in organizations, but contingencies that are not described may also be observed, and, in any event, a rule like a command, a request, or a piece of advice is merely one aspect of a reinforcement contingency (the S_D). Individuals do not automatically follow rules or comply with them because they are "legitimate" or because of a "generalized acceptance of the rules of the game," but because they have been and will continue to be reinforced for following (behaving according to) the rules. Thus, if we are to comprehend fully the reinforcement contingencies that comprise an organization's structure, we must be certain to identify all that prevail *and* the major components of each. This will not be an easy task, but organizational leaders may now know what to look for and quite possibly how to look.

Leadership Reinforcement Contingencies. A most important set of reinforcement contingencies is that which controls the behavior of appointed leaders. It was Weber who first noted that a distinguishing feature of modern-day organizations is an "administrative structure" made of a series of positions arranged in a hierarchy and occupied by *appointees* who perform many of the functions originally performed by the owners of earlier patrimonial organizations. Those functions include planning, scheduling, accounting, selection, and, most important, the supervision or control of individuals in positions subordinate to the appointed leader. The major responsibilities (behaviors) of appointees to controlling positions are usually specified and ordered in such a way that an appointee to a given position reports to (is controlled by) those in higher positions and is, in turn, charged with the responsibility of directing and controlling the behavior of those appointed to lower positions in the hierarchy.

Weber was very much interested in understanding and describing the conditions under which *appointed* leaders may control the behaviors of other participants, and so, too, must organizational leaders when they become leaders of leaders. Apparently, we need not waste much time in explaining the fact that owners of property effectively control the behavior of serfs or employees, but how do we account for the fact that nonproperty owners control the behavior of other appointees in subordinate positions?[9] Weber's answer, was in part, rules and beliefs. Participants comply with the directions of those in higher positions because they *believe* that it is appropriate, just, or legitimate to do so. How do the controllees come to believe that such control is just or legitimate? Weber observed that organizations attempt to "legiti-

[9]Perhaps we should also attempt to explain the fact that owners of property are able to control the behavior of others. Not every culture, even in today's world, has incorporated within it a set of institutionalized contingencies that allow its members to acquire property and other goods and protect them from harm by others when they do. Those cultures that promote the acquisition of property usually have supplementary contingencies that allow property owners to reap the reinforcing consequences of "using their property" (wealth, capital, and so on) to control the behavior of others though the manner in which they may do so is often carefully circumscribed.

mate" or justify the control exercised by appointed leaders by carefully specifying controlling practices and by pointing up the potential benefits of this method of behavioral control.[10] These appeals to self-interest are assumed to strengthen the belief that the control exercised by appointed leaders is legitimate, which belief results in compliance.[11] This explanation is not very satisfactory if for no other reason than we now have to account for beliefs and the manner in which they cause their holders to comply with the directions of appointed leaders.

We do not deny that orders, directions, and other types of commands will be more effective in evoking behavior if supplemented by propositions describing the consequences of the behavior manded. But pointing out the consequences is not enough. Appointed leaders may have little control over the behavior of subordinates if they cannot or do not ensure that subordinate behavior in response to commands is reinforced, and they cannot if they have no control over consequences that are reinforcing for subordinates. Weber recognized this in discussing the dependence of subordinates on superiors for pay increases and career progress, and subsequent rational systems theorists have emphasized it in their insistence on "granting sanctioning powers commensurate with responsibilities" (Scott, 1981, p. 278).

To recapitulate, with increases in group size, the organizational leader (perhaps the owner-manager) is confronted with the additional responsibility of appointing individuals to perform some of the functions once performed by himself or herself. Those functions include a number of specialized staff activities and the all-important activity of directing and sustaining the behavior of participants subordinate to them. Thus, the leader of leaders should keep in mind that among the most important of the reinforcement contingencies that comprise organizational structure are those designed to govern the controlling practices of appointed leaders. These contingencies need not be formulated in rules, policy statements, and job descriptions. However, the more important ones are usually codified or formally specified in order to promote consistency in their administration and also to help ensure that the controlling practices of appointed leaders are both more consistent and, it is hoped, more effective. To promote further the effectiveness of the controlling practices of appointed leaders, the leader of leaders, serving as a designer, may

[10]Weber (1968) and others have also pointed out that control exercised by appointed leaders is more likely to be regarded as legitimate if those selected to fill those positions are *technically competent*. Presumably they mean that subordinates are more likely to believe that controlling practices are legitimate if the appointed leaders are steeped in the organization's technology and are in a better position than anyone else to identify and sustain cooperants that will maximize the net reinforcement for everyone.

[11]It is often further assumed that subordinates who hold these "normative beliefs" will supplement the controlling practices of appointed leaders by also reinforcing their peers or co-workers when they comply with the leader's directions and by punishing them when they do not. This is not a bad assumption if translated: Those who have been controlled and who have been powerfully reinforced, whether by the commander or because their behavior has produced reinforcement from other sources, will, as a group, reinforce individual members who comply and punish those that do not.

find it useful to provide supplementary policies that indicate the degree to which appointed leaders control such "sanctions" as pay increases, promotions, discharges, and demotions and the manner in which appointed leaders are to use this "reward and punishment power." Designers may also attempt to justify the controlling practices of appointed leaders by referring to the rights granted by the wider culture (and its government) to property owners to use their "wealth" to control the behavior of others *and* the constraints placed on them in doing so.[12] (These rights may, in turn, be justified by reference to the reinforcing advantages to members of the larger culture in creating and providing employment, etc.) The designers may take further steps to justify the organization's controlling practices by the provision of broad policy statements that point out the necessity for precluding or reducing certain "dysfunctional" behaviors as well as for promoting reasonable levels of productivity. Such statements may also include the assertion or implication that when these conditions prevail, *everyone* is more likely to maximize his or her reinforcement. Finally, designers may introduce contingencies (and rules generally describing them) that promote subordinate appeals to "higher authorities" if the controlling practices of a given appointed leader get out-of-hand. All these attempts to "legitimate" controlling practices may render them more effective in the sense that subordinate participants are not only more likely to comply with the directions of appointed leaders but also to support them by punishing members of the group who do not comply. However, neither wide-scale compliance nor support will continue if there are no reinforcing advantages accruing to those controlled.

Organizational charts, accompanying policy statements, and job descriptions developed by leaders of leaders may only describe the more obvious reinforcement contingencies governing the controlling practices of appointed leaders, and even these may be incomplete specifications. Rather than describing the topography of the controlling operants, they may merely state that appointees are responsible for directing and coordinating the activities of the groups to which they are assigned and will be reinforced for doing so effectively. Precisely how the appointed leaders are to behave in order to generate and sustain functional cooperants without engendering dysfunctional forms of countercontrol and high defection rates is often left unspecified. We might say that the specific manner in which appointees control subordinate behavior is left to their own devices if it is understood that we mean that their controlling operants are left to the control of other contingencies prevailing in the group setting. However, leaders of leaders, unwilling to leave the emergence of

[12]The designer's behavior, no less than the appointed leader's behavior, is also controlled. The designer's behavior in controlling control may be governed in part by contingencies established by the government of the larger culture in which the organization resides. Skinner (1974, p. 194) has pointed out that those who had great wealth used it without being subject to very much countercontrol until the nineteenth century, but one can hardly say that about our present culture. Today hundreds of contingencies, codified as laws and regulations, and less formalized contingencies having to do with "ethical practices" significantly limit the controlling practices of property owners.

effective controlling operants to the unanalyzed and perhaps faulty contingencies that may prevail, may take additional steps to control the behavior of appointees by selecting only "seasoned" persons (those who have had considerable exposure to the unspecified—and probably unanalyzed—contingencies and who seem to have emerged as effective leaders). They may also provide leadership training or on-the-job experience (exposure to the prevailing contingencies) or both by rotating trainees through a series of "assistant-to" positions before assigning them to major leadership positions. The further specification of controlling operants may evolve by negotiation. When controlling practices evoke subordinate appeals for relief, certain instances may come to be recognized as examples of a common but objectionable practice that is then codified as a general rule of conduct for appointed leaders and subordinates.

Subordinate Reinforcement Contingencies. Organizational structure also includes the contingencies governing the behavior of group members subordinate to the appointed leaders. In fact, it is difficult to speak about one set without reference to the other.

We have already discussed these contingencies, the possible benefits of describing some of the more significant ones, and the manner in which they control the cooperant behavior of individual group members. But they also serve, in part, to control the behavior of the appointed leaders. As we have seen, formulations of these contingencies (job descriptions) may "guide" the behavior of appointed leaders in selecting and training new group members and partially control their reinforcing operants. They may also *constrain* the controlling practices of organizational leaders (if the behavior is not specified in the job description, the leader cannot demand it, or so it is often implied). These are matters of some interest to leaders of leaders in their quest to develop optimal organizational structures.

Because reinforcement contingencies may be described with varying degrees of specificity ranging from no description at all to a reasonably comprehensive description of all those that prevail, the alternatives open to leaders of leaders are enormous. For example, the leader-designer may choose to supply only the most abstract of descriptions such as, "Organizational participants are to comply with the directives of their appointed leaders" (do what they are told), with the strong implication that they will be appropriately reinforced if they do and discharged if they do not. Under these circumstances, appointed leaders may command any pattern of cooperants that reinforces them at the time. But this contingency may also engender widely disparate and possibly ineffective reinforcing practices that, in turn, result in low performance, high defection rates, or dysfunctional countercontrolling practices on the part of subordinates. On the other hand, to design and specify in every detail all the subordinate contingencies that are to prevail are monumental, if not impossible, chores. A middle course is, therefore, recommended. As a pattern of basic cooperants emerges and stabilizes, that pattern, if regarded as optimal, should be formally specified with the clear understanding that it is not to be regarded as exhaustive and that it is, furthermore, subject to changes under circumstances that may also be specified. These descriptions are not unduly restrictive, though changes cannot be made whimsically, and they serve, in part, to control the controlling practices of appointed leaders as they direct, strengthen, or modify the behavior of their subordinates or effect a combination of these.

Formal Reward and Penalty Systems. Though we are prone to speak of formal reward and penalty systems or, more simply, "reward structures" as if they were one of several independent features of organizational structure, they are, in fact, integral components of the reinforcement contingencies comprising that structure. The leader of a small group or organization, in which there are no other leaders, reinforcers group members with pay increases, bonuses, and promotions with higher pay when they behave in ways that are considered to be important, if not essential, to organizational effectiveness and punishes them with modest or no increases in pay, disciplinary layoffs without pay, demotions, and discharge when they do not. The leader's reinforcing practices can, of course, be analyzed and described, though they usually are not, and he or she may "distribute rewards" and "punish" effectively in the absence of a formal system that controls his or her practices. When, however, the organization becomes large enough to require several appointed leaders, it is certain that problems will arise unless effective reinforcing practices are identified, formally specified, and systematically reinforced.

In the development of the contingencies that serve, in part, to control the reinforcing practices of appointed leaders and the cooperant behavior of their subordinates, the paramount objectives of the leader of leaders are to ensure that the delivery of monetary reinforcement is contingent on the occurrence of functional cooperants and that its magnitude is reasonably commensurate with each individual's contribution to organizational outcomes. The two objectives, that of maintaining a contingent relationship and that of bringing about a condition known as equity or distributive justice, are often treated separately, but they are, as we say, inextricably enmeshed. The "returns" of the cooperant enterprise could be distributed equally among its members. However, though that might satisfy someone's notion of equity, the underlying assumption that the cooperants of all individuals are of equal importance or criticality in determining organizational outcomes is one that never holds. Moreover, an equal distribution will not encourage the acquisition of ever more effective forms of operant behavior, a condition that surely cannot be allowed to prevail if the organization is to thrive and survive.

One alternative is to provide for the differential allocation of monetary reinforcement to individual members, the magnitude depending on the relative criticality of their cooperants, but an equal distribution of monetary reinforcement among members whose cooperants are at the same level of criticality. With the implementation of this contingency, however, the leader-designer assumes that individual variations in executing the same pattern of cooperants are insignificant, a very dangerous assumption indeed given the wide variations that are routinely observed. It, therefore, seems both necessary and just to develop contingencies that ensure that the delivery of monetary reinforcement is contingent on the relative criticality of the cooperant pattern and its skill properties *and* rate of occurrence.

Organizational participants at all levels usually come to regard differential reinforcement as both necessary and just when it becomes clear that the magnitude of their own reinforcement, indeed the very survival of the organization, is dependent on the efficacy of the behavior of others as well as their own. It is, therefore, incumbent on the leader of leaders to develop and administer contingencies that point up this reality. To do so, he or she will find it necessary to develop and implement measures of criticality or relative worth (job evaluation) that are reasonably accurate and straightforward and see to it that the skill properties and rate of occurrence of designated classes of cooperants are reliably observed and evaluated (performance appraisal).

The literature on job evaluation, performance appraisal, and other facets of "wage and salary policy" is too extensive to be covered here. Suffice it to say that there are a number of job evaluation systems available for ordering jobs (patterns of cooperants) along a relative worth continuum in a reasonably reliable and straightforward manner. Most of the better measures include such factors as general education requirements, specific job preparation requirements, and leadership requirements. A reasonable assumption underlying the inclusion of these factors is that the more complex cooperants, acquired over longer periods of time in educational and other specialized training programs, are more critical in determining organizational outcomes and survival. A second class of factors included in job evaluation systems are those having to do with physical demands and contextual factors (working conditions and job hazards). The contextual factors are included on the premise that, other things being equal, those required to work under stressful conditions should get a larger slice of the pie than those who behave under less stressful conditions. There is no assumption that the cooperants required under conditions of stress are necessarily more or less critical in determining organizational outcomes. However, the factors relevant to criticality are always weighted more heavily in job evaluation systems than are the contextual factors, reflecting contingencies that usually prevail in the wider culture.

Once jobs have been evaluated and ordered along the relative worth continuum, a wage curve and pay grades are constructed (see Fig. 8.1). There are all sorts of recommendations regarding the slope of the curve, the number of pay grades, and the rate range within pay grades. Decisions about the slope and location of the wage curve cannot be made in the absence of a consideration of pay rates prevailing in the "labor market," but we recommend a relatively steep curve, resulting in at least a 10 percent differential between the mean rates of adjacent pay grades, a limited number of pay grades (perhaps no more than 30 for the entire organization), and a 20 percent to 30 percent

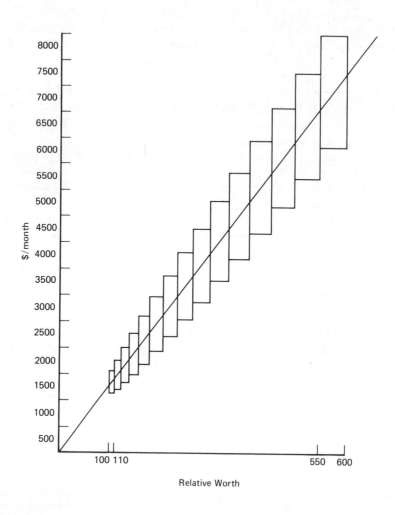

Figure 8.1 Hypothetical wage structure. A hypothetical wage structure, including the wage curve and pay grades. The wage curve has two important properties, slope and location. A steeper wage curve would result in a larger difference in pay rates between pay grades. If it were located at a higher or lower level, then pay rates would be higher or lower "across the board."

spread in the rate range within pay grades. The provision of rate ranges within pay grades indicates that a relationship between rate of effective responding and the magnitude of pay should prevail. However, the provision of a multirate structure may not, by itself, ensure that organizational leaders will administer the contingency in a consistent manner. Consequently, the leader-designer usually implements supplementary policies, including a performance appraisal system to ensure further that leaders will monitor and appropriately reinforce those whose cooperants are more effective or occur at a higher rate.

A wide variety of performance appraisal methods have been developed. None are without problems, and some appraisal programs have proved to be dysfunctional when appointed leaders are led to evaluate performance formally and provide feedback very infrequently (perhaps only once a year). However, the controlling practices of effective leaders must be under the control of variations in the cooperant behavior of their subordinates. Moreover, it seems clear that formal appraisal programs in which attempts are made to specify the major cooperants to be observed; that require periodic and frequent observation; and that include training in the observation, evaluation, and recording of subordinate cooperants are more likely to result in reasonably sensitive and accurate appraisals than those that are made in the absence of formalized practices. In any event, the contingencies designed to control the reinforcing practices of appointed leaders should ensure, as best one can, that organizational members at all levels are reinforced in proportion to the criticality of their cooperants and their effectiveness and rate of occurrence within levels of criticality. The reinforcing practices of leaders may be further controlled by wage policies in which progression from the starting rate to the maximum rate of pay grade is tied to performance, given a reasonable level of accuracy in appraising it.

Thus far, we have described some of the more basic properties of a "reward structure" that is nothing more nor less than a subset of the reinforcement contingencies of which organizational structure is comprised. These contingencies serve in part to control the reinforcing practices of appointed leaders and, in turn, the behavior of their subordinates. We have maintained that they should be comprehensive and powerful enough to ensure that organizational members at all levels are reinforced not only in proportion to the criticality of their cooperants but also in proportion to the skill properties and rate of occurrence of those cooperants if the organization is to thrive and survive. We have also outlined the features of wage structures designed to foster the effective administration of those contingencies. There is one ingredient, however, that remains to be discussed.

Though the density or magnitude of each member's reinforcement is ultimately dependent on the effectiveness of the organization in producing monetary returns, there is nothing inherent in the design of traditional reward structures that highlights that fact. Indeed, the slope and location of the wage curve—and hence the magnitude of pay for each individual—can be—and often has been—altered in the absence of positive changes in organizational effectiveness. Moreover, once a pay increase has been granted, it usually becomes a permanent part of the individual's total compensation whether cooperant effectiveness is maintained or not. In fact, it is rare that there are either "give-backs" or "take-backs" even when organizational decline is obvious. Leaders of leaders may, therefore, seek to design and implement additional contingencies in which some portion of the monetary reinforcement is more clearly dependent on each member's contribution to organizational effectiveness.

Much has been made of the efficacy of Japanese management practices, and though the manner in which they differ from those in other cultures as well as their presumed efficacy are debatable issues, one of their reported practices may well be worthy of consideration. Many observers have noted that one third to one half of the typical Japanese member's annual compensation is in the form of periodic (usually semiannual) bonuses, which are dependent on profits[13] or other indexes of organizational effectiveness or both. One of the most important features of such plans is that there is, in fact, a significant relation between each participant's contribution to organizational viability and the magnitude of his or her monetary reinforcement when the bonus payments are a percentage of base rate and the base rate is, in turn, dependent on the criticality and the effectiveness of the cooperants of each member. A second important property is that such a contingency and its administration serve as consistent reminders of the relation between organizational viability and the effectiveness of each of its members.

Organizational leaders may encounter some difficulties in adding this type of reinforcement contingency to traditional reward structures. However, they are quite likely to find that the returns are well worth the effort. An effectively designed "gain-sharing" contingency can be expected to promote a wide variety of important but usually unspecified cooperants such as assisting other group members with their work (the very antithesis of "jurisdictional disputes"), orienting new members, and identifying more effective work methods. Difficulties with material, equipment, or processes are much more likely to be quickly resolved or brought to the attention of appointed leaders for resolution. Because a wide variety of cooperants, including experimentation, are encouraged, job enrichment programs become less important and possibly unnecessary. Finally, changes in cooperant topography, which may be required to satisfy altered contingencies in the organization's external environment, are more readily induced.

Other Codified Contingencies. Leaders of leaders usually design and implement other contingencies for the purpose of controlling the behavior of appointed leaders and their subordinates. For example, they may find it necessary to formulate policies regarding the treatment of tardiness, absenteeism, theft, and other forms of dysfunctional behavior; and when they do, the punitive contingencies take their place alongside the positive reinforcement contingencies that comprise organizational structure.

Formulations of punitive contingencies are usually more specific with respect to dysfunctional behavior and the consequences than their positive

---

[13]It would be a mistake to tie bonus payments to annual profits and not simply because they are too volatile. Such a contingency usually produces behavior leading directly to organizational decline and disastrous long-term consequences.

counterparts. However, it is rare that formulations of either punitive or positive reinforcement contingencies are *complete* descriptions of those that have been deliberately arranged and assumed to prevail. One reason, we suppose, is that the complexity of the operants may put them beyond the reach of a useful description, but there are undoubtedly more important reasons. The leader-designer may deliberately refrain from specifying the cooperants on the assumption that the formulation would be unduly restrictive. If there is more than one effective way to assemble a water pump, to take care of a "disciplinary" problem, or, for that matter, to skin a cat, it may well be good strategy to leave the matter open, at least until the most effective cooperants have been identified. Finally, the leader of leaders may refrain altogether from describing certain contingencies that he or she may deliberately arrange and consistently administer on the assumption that codified reinforcement contingencies and the behavior they generate are more difficult to alter.

Given that the formulations of reinforcement contingencies as exemplified by job descriptions, policy statements, rules, and the like are seldom, if ever, comprehensive descriptions of the reinforcement contingencies that have been deliberately arranged, and given that some of the reinforcement contingencies, though more-or-less deliberately arranged and administered, are not described at all, it follows that the leader of leaders and others seeking to understand organizational behavior and to do something about it will be required to go beyond the formulations to analyze the contingencies themselves. When they do, they should also be prepared to discover something else.

"Informal" Reinforcement Contingencies. Thus far, we have discussed those reinforcement contingencies that, formulated or otherwise, are more-or-less deliberately arranged and administered by organizational leaders. But an examination of the contingencies that actually prevail will reveal that organizational structure is not limited to the "formal" contingencies. Individual participants and groups of participants at all levels may have or gain control over reinforcing events and then apply or withhold them contingent on the behavior of other participants. A particularly attractive male or female, for example, may attend to or ignore other members of the opposite sex when the latter behave in ways that are reinforcing or aversive to the would-be controller, and an assistant who controls access to the leader of leaders may provide that access only when the member seeking it behaves in particular ways. An appointed leader may "bend the rules," which is to say that he or she may refrain from administering the contingencies described in the rules when a subordinate behaves in ways that are especially reinforcing to the leader. An older member who "knows the ropes" by virtue of extensive contact with the prevailing contingencies may steer others away from (or into!) trouble when they behave in specific ways with respect to the adviser. In this case, the controller may not—and usually does not—control important reinforcing consequences. His or her "power" lies in his or her ability to tact accurately the reinforcement contingencies arranged and administered by others. However, it should be kept in mind that S_D's in the form of tacts of prevailing contingencies can also serve as reinforcing events, and when the adviser-controller provides or withdraws these tacts depending on the behavior of the advisee, there is a reinforcement contingency in effect, however subtle it may be.

Some of the informal reinforcement contingencies administered by one or several members of a group may *complement* those that are formulated and administered by organizational leaders whereas others may stand in opposition or *supplant* them. Co-workers may praise or otherwise "accept" a group member who has also been reinforced by the appointed leader for his or her good work, but co-workers may also threaten, scold, or ostracize a group member whose rate of performance exceeds "group norms" (rates of responding established by group members other than the appointed leader). An analysis may also reveal informal reinforcement contingencies that *supplement* those promulgated by the leader-designer, strengthening and sustaining cooperant behavior in addition to that required by the formal contingencies. The informal reinforcement contingencies are typically more subtle and difficult to spot, and they may change quickly with changes in group membership. They are "unauthorized" in the sense that they are not formulated in policies or rules or otherwise deliberately arranged and administered by leaders of leaders, and they may not be sanctioned by them. However, they can be quite powerful, and the behavior they generate, like the behavior strengthened by the more formal contingencies, may be functional or dysfunctional insofar as organizational viability is concerned. The leader of leaders will, therefore, be required to seek out and examine the effects of the organization's informal contingencies. Those that strengthen and sustain desirable forms of cooperants may be allowed to stand or may be further encouraged by reinforcing those who administer them. Those that are found to be dysfunctional will have to be eliminated or altered. They usually arise because certain of the organization's more formal contingencies are faulty. Thus, the discovery of informal contingencies that foster dysfunctional behavior becomes the occasion for reexamining those that have been deliberately designed and implemented.

Organizational Structure Summarized. Organizational structure is most fruitfully viewed as a *set* of reinforcement contingencies that includes those deliberately arranged and administered by organizational leaders and those informal contingencies that arise when human participants come together in a circumscribed space that is not completely structured. Though certain of the contingencies (in which covert operants are implicated) present problems for the scientist as well as the practitioner, all of them have natural properties. They can be observed, monitored, analyzed, designed, described, promulgated, administered, and, of course, altered. The leader of leaders will be critically involved in every one of those activities in organizations that survive and prosper.

Monitoring and Analyzing the External Environment

If it is imperative that leaders of leaders design, implement, and monitor the effects of organizational reinforcement contingencies, it is equally critical that they monitor, analyze, and attempt to forecast changes in the organization's external environment. Most organizational theorists hold that organizations are *open systems,* which is to say that they are in constant interaction with their external environment and will survive only if their participants manage to satisfy the reinforcement contingencies prevailing there.

It is not, however, the organization in the abstract that is in "constant commerce" with the external environment, but rather the leader of leaders and perhaps others serving in "boundary role" positions. The manner in which the external environment is monitored and analyzed cannot be detailed here, but certain of the features of the external environment that may require more-or-less continuous monitoring can be described.

Included in a master list of environmental components (Duncan, 1979) with which leaders of leaders are most likely to be concerned is that set of reinforcement contingencies administered by consumer groups. They place certain "demands" on the organization in the sense that they will purchase its products or services (reinforce organizational participants) only if those products or services meet specifications (if organizational members behave so as to produce a product or service that is relatively more reinforcing than other products or services of the same or different type).

Another component is the behavior of competing groups. When we recall that a competitive reinforcement contingency is one in which the magnitude of reinforcement is contingent on one's behavior (performance) *relative to that of another,* we can only conclude that it is necessary to monitor continuously either the behavior or the products of the behavior of competing groups. It is not that competitors arrange and administer the reinforcement contingencies relevant to the organization. They are simply behaving in the same contingency arena arranged and administered by consumer groups who show a propensity to reinforce those who offer the most reinforcing products and services at the lowest cost. Leaders of leaders will be required to monitor several classes of competing behavior or its products or both. Not only will it be necessary to monitor and evaluate the relative reinforcing properties and prices of a competitor's current products and services, it will also be important to monitor their developmental behavior that results in new, more reinforcing products or improvements in the reinforcing value of present products, advances in manufacturing technology (the development or adoption of more efficient equipment or of a less expensive but more durable material), and improvements in managerial practices (better selection procedures, the adoption of more effective reinforcement contingencies, and so on).

It may also be necessary to monitor the behavior of those who supply materials, equipment, and other technological requirements, noting what they forecast about supply relative to demand, depletions of supplies, anticipated technological developments, and so on.

Leaders of leaders may find it necessary to monitor and keep abreast of developments in relevant science and engineering fields, for advances in those fields may render current products and services obsolete or allow a new competitor to fabricate a product much more effectively.

It may become important to monitor the behavior and reinforcement contingencies administered by members of financial institutions when the need for capital extends beyond that which can be supplied by its members, and it may also be necessary to monitor trends in the economy at large or relevant subsections of it, noting changes and evaluating their possible impact on consumer behavior, the behavior of suppliers and technologists, and others who arrange and administer reinforcement contingencies relevant to the organization.

Finally, it seems clear that leaders of leaders of most organizations will be required to monitor and respond appropriately to the behavior and the reinforcement contingencies administered by various government representatives. The reinforcement contingencies administered by government representatives are more often constraining or punitive contingencies, ruling out or precluding certain forms of cooperant behavior rather than positive reinforcement contingencies, but the punitive consequences make compliance all the more important. It is also desirable, if not necessary, to monitor the behavior of government representatives as they consider new contingencies and enforcement methods.

It is not often that the leaders of leaders develop and utilize elaborate methods for monitoring and analyzing various features of their external environment. In fact, it is somewhat surprising to find so many leaders whose only contact with consumers and their responses to products and services is through informal discussions with the sales force. However, *effective* leaders usually come to discern those features that require consistent monitoring and either monitor those contingencies themselves or develop a coterie of specialists both within and outside the organization whose responsibilities are to observe and tact prevailing contingencies. The leader of leaders may, for example, attend trade association meetings where "mutual problems" and industrial trends are discussed with other leaders and experts in relevant fields. They may habitually peruse business periodicals or trade journals, where they find tacts of relevant contingencies currently prevailing or anticipated to prevail; changes in the supply of, uses, and prices of natural resources; technological developments; and other trends that may call for adjustments in organizational posture. Leaders of larger organizations often develop subgroups of experts who monitor and analyze "consumer attitudes," develop new products or new uses for old products, monitor technological development as well as develop new technologies, and maintain contact with government groups and advise the leader on the nature of the contingencies that the government agencies administer and those that may be imposed in the future.

Suffice it to say that the organization's external environment is replete with reinforcement contingencies, including those responsible for the development of the organization in the first place. Many of them are arranged and administered by the culture, and all are subject to changes over time. The leader of leaders will be required to identify those groups who administer the contingencies responsible for organizational survival and prosperity and to determine the nature of the contingencies they administer. They will also be required to monitor and forecast changes in those contingencies and other events relevant to organizational functioning. All these topics are of primary concern in the field of "business policy," and though the inquiring student should not expect a comprehensive account of effective monitoring and forecasting operants, some invaluable insights can be gained in studying the literature in that field.

We hasten to add, however, that more is involved than mere surveillance and forecasting. Our use of the term "analysis" implies that the leader and possibly other organizational members are required to determine the most effective means by which to satisfy those contingencies currently prevailing or forecast to prevail. This, too, is a topic of major concern in the field of business policy, discussed under the rubric of *strategy formulation*. Strategy is typically defined as a statement or description of those environmental contingencies relevant to the organization and its basic purposes as well as the courses of action to be taken in achieving those objectives. Its formulation is often portrayed as a rational-systematic process wherein the decision maker (our leader of leaders), after a lengthy study of the external environment and the organization's capabilities and limitations, determines those contingencies that the organization is most capable of satisfying and the means by which they are to be satisfied. As there are assumed to be many ways of satisfying a set of contingencies, the leader is presumed to engage in complex problem-solving activities in which the several alternatives are evoked and evaluated before a "course of action" is finally selected.

A number of management scientists have rejected this portrayal of the manager as a strategy formulator. Some have suggested that the human organism is not capable of maximizing net reinforcement given the complexity of the contingencies usually confronting an organization. Others have insisted that the decision makers simply do not engage in these more complex forms of behavior whether or not they are capable.

We, of course, take the position that the human organism is perfectly capable of analyzing complex contingencies and maximizing reinforcing consequences though we may overestimate our present capability of determining the "one best way." "Satisficing" may occur but is never deliberate. But we would also point out that the more extensive and elaborate forms of strategy formulation are not inevitably required. The external environments of many organizations are reasonably stable in the sense that the relevant contingencies may continue to prevail unaltered over long periods of time. Therefore, organizations are not usually required to undergo a *major* renewal or transformation process every few years. Leaders of leaders should remain ever watchful for environmental changes that might require dramatic changes in organizational behavior. Perhaps they should also develop a number of what-if scenarios in which strategies are formulated for each of a number of major changes in the external contingencies should they occur. However, it appears that though relevant external contingencies do change, it is not inevitable that major changes in cooperants will be required.

Finally, we should point out that strategy determination, however complex it may be, need not be formulated in elaborate plans and specific directions. In fact, the behavior of the leader and quite possibly the expression of a simple though abstract theme may be the only evidence that a strategy has been determined.

Strategy Implementation and Organizational Development

Although the external reinforcement contingencies *may* exhibit a certain stability over an extended period of time, eventually all of them can be expected to change. The reinforcement contingencies prevailing *within* the organization likewise show a tendency to drift with changes in group size and leadership. Such "mutations" may occur in the absence of changes in the external contingencies, and as they need not be adaptive, the behavior they generate may be just as ineffective in satisfying the external contingencies as the behavior that continues in the face of major changes in the external environment. In short, leaders of leaders must not only formulate strategy, but they must also *implement* it.

When we turn to the policy literature on the implementation of strategy, however, we find a "promiscuous use of the term strategy" (Bower, 1982), a confusion of means (strategy) with ends ("corporate purpose"), pleas to become more concerned with the vital "life and death issues" in formulating strategy, and not much that is useful in implementing it. We should not be surprised. Determining the means by which an organization is to survive and prosper in a turbulent environment is a complex process. Furthermore, the means for thriving and surviving may—and usually does—require more than adjustments in the behavior of organizational participants. (The organizational leader may find, for example, that he or she will have to procure added capital, set in motion an advertising campaign, sell off a marginal asset, or buy or merge with another organization.) Before we turn to other literature for advice on how to bring about changes in cooperant behavior, we should point out that the policy field is not completely devoid of wisdom in the area. It is recognized that organizational structure follows from, and is based on, strategy that suggests that when a strategy has been formulated, it is then implemented by altering organizational structure. This is a reasonable assumption when structure is viewed "as the means for defining and controlling organizational behavior" (Harrison, 1978).

The literature in the field of organizational development (OD) is more specific with respect to the prescriptions for altering behavior. However, some have expressed serious reservations about the efficacy of some of the methods that have evolved. Greiner (1972), for example, questioned the assumption that prepackaged *educational* treatments of the type typically utilized in OD efforts will produce significant changes in the behavior of appointed leaders or that the changes prescribed would be more effective if they were to occur. He also noted that attempts to shape a particular leadership "style" will almost certainly fail if the organization's structure (especially the "informal" contingencies) supports a different style. Greiner also cited evidence of notable failures resulting from some of the more conventional OD approaches—bottom-up team building, sensitivity training, the development of participative techniques, and so on. On the other hand, some OD treatments that begin with a diagnostic activity and include adjustments in organizational reinforcement contingencies have been found to result in improvements in organizational functioning.

The diagnostic activity typically includes the collection of information about the organizational members' "experience with the system" (Beer, 1980) by means of interviews and opinion or attitude questionnaires. Historically, the types of information gathered have been limited to information about attitudes or feelings about the supervisor, pay and benefits, co-workers, top management, and other organizational features. Feeling states and attitudes are, no doubt, important to organizational members, and they sometimes permit the consultant to make informed guesses about prevailing contingencies and what, if anything, is wrong with them. But one must ultimately get to the contingencies themselves for an accurate diagnosis, and that necessity may have led to other developments in the OD field. Organizational members may be capable of tacting prevailing reinforcement contingencies—or at least some of them—and various techniques for obtaining these tacts have been developed (see, for example, Johnson, 1970; Reitz, 1971; Podsakoff, Todor, Grover, and Huber, 1984). In addition, a great deal of information (about prevailing contingencies) can be obtained by "living in" the organization and observing the contingencies firsthand. Another recent development has been the collection of data about salient features of the organization's external environment. Such data can be of significant help in "broadening the horizons" of organizational participants, in providing the impetus for behavioral changes, and in providing a "unified sense of direction."

The diagnostic activity and resulting feedback of findings are also properly classified as interventions because information in the form of tacts of prevailing contingencies (both external and internal), along with data regarding the accuracy or inaccuracy of those "perceptions," can, like other S_D's, effect changes in behavior. However, the typical OD intervention provides for other change procedures, the most important of which are those that result in the direct alteration of faulty reinforcement contingencies and treatments (e.g., individual counseling) in which both faulty and beneficial reinforcement contingencies and their behavior ramifications are more accurately described for participants. (See French and Bell, 1978, or Beer, 1980, for a description of these and other OD interventions.)

Critics of conventional OD interventions have pointed out that there are other "informal change techniques" that are readily available and quite possibly more effective. Descriptions of these techniques seem rather fuzzy, but a translation will make it clear that all of them are nothing more nor less than behavior on the part of the leader of leaders that signifies what sorts of behavior will be reinforced and that results in the consistent reinforcement of those cooperants signified. We have had occasion to point out that, in the administration of organizational reinforcement contingencies, whether formal or informal, it is rare that the required cooperant topographies are precisely defined. Even those that are formulated in policies or rules are more likely to be tacts in the form of "You will be sufficiently reinforced when you follow the reasonable directives of your supervisor" rather than "You will be sufficiently reinforced when you consistently engage in Rx1, Rx2, Rx3 . . . Rxn in that order." There are considerable advantages in this lack of specificity when we realize that codified reinforcement contingencies may be more difficult to alter and that cooperants that are effective at the moment may become ineffective when there are significant changes in the contingencies prevailing in the external environment.

Some of the techniques for signifying the cooperants congruent with the organizational leader's strategy (whether formulated explicity or "in his [or her] head") have been described by Peters (1978). They include the leader's overt behavior such as flying off to visit an important customer, the manner in which he or she interacts with his or her immediate subordinates (the leadership "style"), the questions he or she might ask or the amount of time he or she devotes to reducing operating costs, and formal and informal meetings arranged to discuss strategic issues. Another rather subtle technique is the development of a "dominant theme" that describes in a simple, though somewhat ambiguous, way the strategy that the organizational leader wishes to implement or is pursuing. When it is said that a dominant theme such as "Everybody at Northrup is in Marketing" connotes a clear, directional emphasis but allows ample latitude for supporting initiatives (Peters, 1978), we take that to mean that the theme is an abstract tact signifying that all cooperants having some common property or properties are likely to be powerfully reinforced. It is coined by the leader of leaders to summarize the contingencies that have been introduced, and it is repeated whenever it is important to point out that a given cooperant has that property and to evoke and strengthen all cooperants meeting those requirements. The most direct of the "mundane tools" listed by Peters (1978) is the frequent, consistent, positive reinforcement of all cooperants congruent with the strategy being implemented. Peters' recommendation that leaders of leaders committed to change ought to be constantly on the lookout for opportunities to reinforce activities congruent with their strategy is one with which we heartily agree though we would not regard this technique as a "mundane tool." Though it may take time to wait for behavior congruent with strategy to occur before reinforcing it, his comment that consistent reinforcement "can substantially influence people's behavior over time, often several levels down in the organization" should come as no surprise to our readers.

MANAGEMENT IN THE TWENTY-FIRST CENTURY

At a Paris conference, jointly conducted by the American Assembly of Collegiate Schools of Business and the European Foundation for Management Development in 1980 (Walton, 1981), several hundred management practitioners and educators attempted to forecast cultural changes likely to occur in the next 30 years and also the implications of those changes for management practice and education. The participants managed to produce a number of clichés and a number of foolish statements about behavior and the manner in which it is shaped and sustained, but they also concluded with some pronouncements that may be worthy of our careful consideration. One conclusion was that though it is difficult, if not impossible, to forecast the path that societies will take, it seems virtually certain that the external environments of organizations are going to be much more turbulent and that the "onrushing changes" will place formidable demands on organizational leaders and those responsible for preparing them to assume those responsibilities. Not only will faculty (especially administrative and behavioral scientists) need to step up their research efforts and provide us with a better understanding of analytical, decision-making, and leadership behavior, but they will also need to develop more effective methods for shaping it.

A second conclusion was that we should dispense with the traditional view that organization leaders should have no voice in the design of reinforcement contingencies that comprise the culture at large. Organizational leaders, after all, are also members of the larger culture and have as much right *and* responsibility to "mold" a culture that will survive and prosper as anyone else. We would add that organizational leaders who have learned to analyze and forecast changes in reinforcement contingencies and who have learned how to design and administer organizational contingencies that prepare members to "meet the anticipated—and even the unexpected—as effectively as possible" are as well equipped as anyone to fashion and adjust a society that will endure and prosper.

It appears that the most critical requirement of management practitioners in the twenty-first century will be, as it is now, a comprehensive understanding of human behavior and the variables of which it is a function. Once sensitized to the latter by means of a management education program, aspiring practitioners may well be more effective leaders when exposed to the actual contingencies, but it may well be better strategy to expose aspiring practitioners to those contingencies first and then provide the educational treatment. In any case, management development will be a lifetime endeavor if only because there will continue to be experimentation and progress in the development of an effective behavioral technology in the culture that survives. We hope that this book will come to be regarded as a contribution toward those ends.

REFERENCES

Alderfer, C. P. *Existence, relatedness, and growth: Human needs in organizational setting.* New York: Free Press, 1972.

Allison, J. Contrast, induction, facilitation, suppression and conservation. *Journal of the Experimental Analysis of Behavior,* 1976, *25,* 185–199.

———, and W. Timberlake. Instrumental and contingent saccharin licking in rats: Reponse deprivation and reinforcement. *Learning and Motivation,* 1974, *5,* 231–247.

Allport, F. H. *Social psychology.* Boston: Houghton Mifflin, 1924.

Ayllon, T., and N. Azrin. *The token economy: A motivational system for therapy and rehabilitation.* Englewood Cliffs, N.J.: Prentice-Hall, 1968.

Baer, D. M., R. F. Peterson, and J. A. Sherman. The development of imitation by reinforcing behavioral similarity to a model. *Journal of the Experimental Analysis of Behavior,* 1968, *10,* 405–416.

Baird, L. S., and W. C. Hamner. Individual versus systems rewards: Who's dissatisfied, why, and what is their likely response? *Academy of Management Journal,* 1979, *22,* 783–792.

Baldamus, W. Incentives and work analysis. *University of Birmingham Studies in Economics and Sociology,* 1951. Monograph Al, 1–78.

Baldwin, A. L., and C. P. Baldwin. The study of mother-child interaction. *American Scientist,* 1973, *61,* 714–721.

Bandura, A. Vicarious processes: A case of no-trial learning. In L. Berkowitz (ed.), *Advances in experimental social psychology.* Vol. II. New York: Academic Press, 1965, 1–55.

———. *Principles of behavior modification.* New York: Holt, Rinehart and Winston, 1969.

———. Vicarious and self-reinforcement processes. In R. Glaser (ed.), *The nature of reinforcement.* New York: Academic Press, 1971.

———. *Social learning theory.* Englewood Cliffs, N.J.: Prentice-Hall, 1977.

Bauermeister, J. J., and R. W. Schaeffer. Reinforcement relation: Reversibility within daily experimental sessions. *Bulletin of the Psychonomic Society,* 1974, *3,* 206–208.

Beer, M. *Organization change and development: A systems view.* Santa Monica, Cal.: Goodyear, 1980.

Bem, D. J. *An experimental analysis of beliefs and attitudes.* Ph.D. dissertation, University of Michigan. Ann Arbor, Mich.: University Microfilms, 1964, No. 64-12, 588.

————. Self-perception: An alternative interpretation of cognitive dissonance phenomena. *Psychological Review,* 1967, *74,* 183–200.

————. Self-perception theory. In L. Berkowitz (ed.), *Advances in experimental social psychology.* Vol. 6. New York: Academic Press, 1972.

Bensberg, G. J. (ed.) *Teaching the mentally retarded: A handbook for ward personnel.* Atlanta: Southern Regional Education Board, 1965.

Bensberg, G. J., C. N. Colwell, and R. N. Cassel. Teaching the profoundly retarded self-help activities by behavior shaping techniques. *American Journal of Mental Deficiency,* 1965, *69,* 674–679.

Berkowitz, L., and B. I. Levy. Pride in group performance and group-task motivation. *Journal of Abnormal and Social Psychology,* 1956, *53,* 300–306.

Berlyne, D. E. *Conflict, arousal and curiosity.* New York: McGraw-Hill, 1960.

————. Curiosity and explanation. *Science,* 1966, *153,* 25–33.

————. Arousal and reinforcement. In D. Levine (ed.), *Nebraska Symposium on Motivation: 1967.* Lincoln, Nebr.: University Press, 1967.

Bernhaut, M., E. Gellhorn, and A. T. Rassmussen. Experimental contributions to the problem of consciousness. *Journal of Neurophysiology,* 1953, *16,* 21–36.

Bijou, S. W. *Child development: The basic stage of early childhood.* Englewood Cliffs, N.J.: Prentice-Hall, 1976.

Bills, A. G. Blocking: A new principle of mental fatigue. *American Journal of Psychology,* 1931, *43,* 230–245.

Blanchard, F. A., L. Adelman, and S. W. Cook. Effect of group success and failure upon interpersonal attraction in cooperating interracial groups. *Journal of Personality and Social Psychology,* 1975, *31,* 1020–1030.

Bogardus, E. S. World leadership styles. *Sociological and Social Research,* 1928, *12,* 573–599.

Bower, J. L. Business policy in the 1980's. *Academy of Management Review,* 1982, *7,* 630–638.

Bowers, D. G., and S. E. Seashore. Predicting organizational effectiveness with a four-factor theory of leadership. *Administrative Science Quarterly,* 1966, *11,* 238–263.

Brayfield, A. H., and W. Crockett. Employee attitudes and employee performance. *Psychological Bulletin,* 1955, *52,* 396–424.

Breland, K., and M. Breland. The misbehavior of organisms. *American Psychologist,* 1961, *16,* 681–684.

————. *Animal behavior.* London: Macmillan, 1966.

Brown, R. *A first language: The early stages.* Cambridge, Mass.: Harvard University Press, 1973.

Byrne, D. *The attraction paradigm.* New York: Academic Press, 1971.

Byrne, D., and G. L. Clore. A reinforcement model of evaluative responses. *Personality: An International Journal,* 1970, *1,* 103–128.

Byrne, D., and C. R. Ervin. Attraction toward a negro stranger as a function of prejudice, attitude similarity, and the stranger's evaluation of the subject. *Human Relations,* 1969, *22,* 397–404.

Byrne, D., and R. Rhamey. Magnitude of positive and negative reinforcements as a determinant of attraction. *Journal of Personality and Social Psychology,* 1965, *2,* 884–889.

Cartwright, D. The effect of interruption, completion, and failure upon the attractiveness of activities. *Journal of Experimental Psychology,* 1942, *31,* 1–16.

Casey, K. L. Pain: A current view of neural mechanisms. *American Scientist,* 1973, *61,* 194–200.

Cazden, C. B. Environmental assistance to the child's acquisition of grammar. Unpublished Ph.D. dissertation, Harvard University, 1965.

Cherrington, D. J., H. J. Reitz, and W. E. Scott, Jr. Effects of reward and contingent reinforcement on satisfaction and task performance. *Journal of Applied Psychology,* 1971, *55,* 531–537.

Chomsky, N. *Syntactic structures.* The Hague: Mouton, 1957.

——— *Verbal behavior* by B. F. Skinner. *Language,* 1959, *35,* 26–58.

Church, R. M. Applications of behavior theory to social psychology: Imitation and competition. in E. C. Simmel, R. A. Hoppe, and E. A. Milton (eds.), *Social facilitation and imitative behavior.* Boston: Allyn & Bacon, 1968.

Clark, E. V. What's in a word? On the child's acquisition of semantics in his first language. In T. E. Moore (ed.), *Cognitive development and the acquisition of language.* New York: Academic Press, 1973.

Cottrell, N. B. Performance in the presence of other human beings: Mere presence, audience, and affiliation effects. In E. C. Simmel, R. A. Hoppe, and G. A. Milton (eds.) *Social facilitation and imitative behavior.* Boston: Allyn & Bacon, 1968.

Cowles, J. T. Food tokens as an incentive for learning by chimpanzees. *Comparative Psychological Monographs,* 1937, *14,* No. 5.

Delgado, J. M. R., W. W. Roberts, and N. E. Miller. Learning motivated by electrical stimulation of the brain. *American Journal of Physiology,* 1954, *179,* 587.

DeVilliers, J. G., and P. A. DeVilliers. A cross sectional study of the development of grammatical morphemes in child speech. *Journal of Psycholinguistic Research,* 1973, *2,* 267–278.

Dewey, J. *How we think.* New York: Heath, 1933.

Dinsmoor, J. A. *Operant conditioning: An experimental analysis of behavior.* Dubuque, Iowa: Wm. C. Brown Company, 1970.

Duffy, E. *Activation and behavior.* New York: Wiley, 1962.

———. The psychological significance of the concept of "arousal" or "activation." *Psychological Review,* 1957, *64,* 265–275.

Duncan, R. What is right with organizational structure? Decision tree analysis provides the answer. *Organizational Dynamics,* Winter 1979, 59–80.

Eisenberger, R., N. M. Karpman, and J. Trattner. What is the necessary and sufficient condition for reinforcement in the contingency situation? *Journal of Experimental Psychology,* 1967, *74,* 342–350.

Farr, J. L. Incentive schedules, productivity, and satisfaction in work groups. *Organizational Behavior and Human Performance,* 1976, *17,* 159–170.

Ferster, C. B. Perspectives in psychology: XXV transition from animal laboratory to clinic. *The Psychological Record,* 1967, *17,* 145–150.

Fiedler, F. E. *A theory of leadership effectiveness.* New York: McGraw-Hill, 1967.

Fiske, D. W., and S. R. Maddi (eds.), *Functions of varied experience.* Homewood, Ill.: Dorsey Press, 1961.

Fowler, H. Implications of sensory reinforcement. In R. Glaser (ed.), *The nature of reinforcement.* New York: Academic Press, 1971.

French, J. D., F. K. Amerongen, and H. W. Magoun. An activating system in the brain-stem of monkeys. *Archives of Neurological Psychiatry* (Chicago), 1952, *68,* 577–590.

French, J. D., R. Hernandez-Peon, and R. B. Livingston. Projections from cortex to cephalic brain-stem in monkeys. *Journal of Neurophysiology,* 1955, *18,* 74–95.

French, J. D., and H. W. Magoun. Effects of chronic lesions in central cephalic brain-stem of monkeys. *Archives of Neurological Psychiatry* (Chicago), 1952, *68,* 591–604.

French, W. L., and C. H. Bell, Jr. *Organization development.* 2d ed. Englewood Cliffs, N.J.: Prentice-Hall, 1978.

Friedman, M. I., and E. M. Stricker. The physiological psychology of hunger: A physiological perspective. *Psychological Review,* 1976, *33,* 409–431.

Frye, R. L. The effect of orientation and feedback of success and effectiveness on the attractiveness and esteem of the group. *The Journal of Social Psychology,* 1966, *70,* 205–211.

Furman, W., and J. C. Masters. Affective consequences of social reinforcement, punishment, and neutral behavior. *Developmental Psychology,* 1980, *16,* 100–104.

Gardner, R. A., and B. T. Gardner. Teaching sign language to a chimpanzee. *Science,* 1969, *165,* 664–672.

Garza, R. T., and J. P. Lipton. Culture, personality, and reactions to praise and criticism. *Journal of Personality,* 1978, *46,* 743–761.

Gebhard, M. E. The effect of success and failure upon the attractiveness of activities as a function of experience, expectation and need. *Journal of Experimental Psychology,* 1948, *38,* 371–388.

————. Changes in the attractiveness of activities: The effect of expectation preceding performance. *Journal of Experimental Psychology,* 1949, *39,* 404–413.

Gewirtz, H. B. Generalization of children's preferences as a function of reinforcement and task similarity. *Journal of Abnormal and Social Psychology,* 1959, *58,* 111–118.

Gewirtz, J. L. The roles of overt responding and extrinsic reinforcement in "self- and vicarious-reinforcement" phenomena and in "observational learning" and imitation. In R. Glaser, (ed.), *The nature of reinforcement.* New York: Academic Press, 1971.

Glickman, S. E. and B. B. Schiff. A biological theory of reinforcement. *Psychological Review,* 1967, *74,* 81–109.

Gollub, L. Conditioned reinforcement: Schedule effects. In W. K. Honig and J. E. R. Staddon (eds.), *Handbook of operant behavior.* Englewood Cliffs, N.J.: Prentice-Hall, 1977.

Gray, B., and B. Ryan. *A language program for the non-language child.* Champaign, Ill.: Research Press, 1973.

Gray, J. A. Elements of a two-process theory of learning. New York: Academic Press, 1975.

Greene, C. N. The satisfaction-performance controversy. *Business Horizons,* 1972, *15,* 31–41.

————. Causal connections among managers' merit pay, job satisfaction, and performance. *Journal of Applied Psychology,* 1973, *58,* 95–100.

————. A longitudinal investigation of performance-reinforcing leader behavior and satisfaction and performance. *Midwest Academy of Management Proceedings,* 1976, 157–185.

Greene, C. N., and P. M. Podsakoff. Effects of the removal of a pay incentive: A field experiment. In Jeffrey C. Susbauer (ed.), *Academy of Management Proceedings,* 1978, 206–210.

Greiner, L. E. Red flags in organization development. *Business Horizons,* 1972, *15,* 17–24.

Griffitt, W. B. Attraction toward a stranger as a function of direct and associated reinforcement. *Psychonomic Science,* 1968, *11,* 147–148.

Griffitt, W., and P. Guay. 'Object' evaluation and conditioned affect. *Journal of Experimental Research in Personality,* 1969, *4,* 1–8.

Groves, P. M., and S. Lynch. Mechanisms of habituation in the brainstem. *Psychological Review,* 1972, *79,* 237–244.

Groves, P. M., and R. F. Thompson. Habituation: A dual-process theory. *Psychological Review,* 1970, *77,* 419–450.

Guttman, N., and H. I. Kalish. Discriminability and stimulus generalization. *Journal of Experimental Psychology,* 1956, *51,* 79–88.

Hannan, M. T., and J. H. Freeman. The population ecology of organizations. *American Journal of Sociology,* 1977, *82,* 929–964.

Harrison, E. F. *Management and organizations.* Boston: Houghton Mifflin, 1978.

Hemphill, J. K. The leader and his group. *Journal of Educational Research,* 1949, *28,* 225–229.

Hendry, D.P. (ed.), *Conditioned reinforcement.* Homewood, Ill.: The Dorsey Press, 1969.

Henton, W. H., and I. H. Iverson. *Classical conditioning and operant conditioning: A response pattern analysis.* New York: Spring-Verlag, 1978.

Hernandez-Peon, R., and K. E. Hagbarth. Interaction between afferent and cortically induced reticular responses. *Journal of Neurophysiology,* 1966, *18,* 44–55.

Herzberg, F. *Work and the nature of man.* Cleveland: World, 1966.

———. *The managerial choice: To be efficient or to be human.* Homewood, Ill.: Dow-Jones-Irwin, 1976.

Heth, C. D., and A. G. Warren. Response deprivation and response satiation as determinants of instrumental perfomance: Some data and theory. *Animal Learning and Behavior,* 1978, *6,* 294–300.

Hilgard, E. R., and G. H. Bower. *Theories of Learning.* New York: Appleton-Century-Crofts, 1966.

Hill, W. F. Sources of evaluative reinforcers. *Psychological Bulletin,* 1968, *69,* 132–146.

Hinde, R. A., and J. Stevenson-Hinde. *Constraints on learning: Limitations and predispositions.* New York: Academic Press, 1973.

Hingtgen, J. N., B. J. Sanders, and M. K. DeMeyer. Shaping cooperative responses in childhood schizophrenics. In L. Ullman and L. Krasner (eds.), *Case studies in behavior modification.* New York: Holt, Rinehart and Winston, 1965.

Hollander, E. P., and J. W. Julian. Leadership. In E. F. Borgatta and W. W. Lambert (eds.), *Handbook of personality theory and research.* Chicago: Rand McNally, 1968, 890–899.

Horney, K. *New ways in psychoanalysis.* New York: Morton, 1939.

Hunt, J. G., and R. S. Schuler. *Leader reward and sanctions behavior in a public utility: What difference does it make?* Southern Illinois University Working Paper, 1976.

Issacs, W., J. Thomas, and I. Goldiamond. Application of operant conditioning to reinstate verbal behavior in psychotics. *Journal of Speech and Hearing Disorders,* 1960, *25,* 8–12.

Jacobs, M., A. Jacobs, G. Feldman, and M. Cavior. Feedback II—The 'credibility gap': Delivery of positive and negative and emotional and behavioral feedback in groups. *Journal of Consulting and Clinical Psychology,* 1973, *41,* 215–223.

James, E., and A. J. Lott. Reward frequency and the formation of positive attitudes toward group members. *Journal of Social Psychology,* 1964, *62,* 111–115.

James, W. *Principles of psychology.* Vol. II. New York: Holt, 1890.

Johnson, R. D. *An investigation of the interaction effects of ability and motivational variables on task performance.* D.B.A. Dissertation, Indiana University, 1970.

Jorgenson, D. O., M. Dunnette, and R. D. Pritchard. Effects of the manipulation of a performance-reward contingency on behavior in a simulated work setting. *Journal of Applied Psychology,* 1973, *57,* 271–280.

Kahn, R. L. Productivity and job satisfaction. *Personnel Psychology,* 1960, *13,* 275.

Kantor, J. R. *The objective psychology of grammar.* Granville, Ohio: The Principia Press, 1936.

Kaplan, M. F., and P. V. Olczak. Attitude similarity and direct reinforcement as determinants of attraction. *Journal of Experimental Research in Personality,* 1970, *4,* 186–189.

Katz, D. Motivational basis of organizational behavior. *Behavioral Science,* 1964, *9,* 131–146.

Kazdin, A. E. *Behavior modification in applied settings.* Homewood, Ill.: Dorsey Press, 1975.

Keisler, E. R. Experimental development of 'like' and 'dislike' of others among adolescent girls. *Child Development,* 1961, *32,* 59–66.

Kelleher, R. T. Fixed-ratio schedules of conditioned reinforcement with chimpanzees. *Journal of the Experimental Analysis of Behavior,* 1958, *1,* 281–289.

———. Conditioned reinforcement in second-order schedules. *Journal of the Experimental Analysis of Behavior,* 1966, *9,* 474–485.

Kelleher, R. T., and L. R. Gollub. A review of positive conditioned reinforcement. *Journal of the Experimental Analysis of Behavior,* 1962, Supplement to Vol. *5,* 543–597.

Keller, R. T., and A. D. Szilagyi. Employee reactions to leader reward behavior. *Academy of Management Journal,* 1976, *19,* 619–627.

Kimble, G. A., and L. C. Perlmuter. The problem of volition. *Psychological Review,* 1970, *77,* 361–384.

King, G. F., S. G. Armitage, and J. R. Tilton. A therapeutic approach to schizophrenics of extreme pathology. *Journal of Abnormal and Social Psychology,* 1960, *61,* 276–286.

Kish, G. B. Learning when the onset of illumination is used as a reinforcing stimulus. *Journal of Comparative Physiological Psychology,* 1955, *48,* 261–264.

———. Studies in sensory reinforcement. In W. K. Honig (ed.), *Operant behavior: Areas of research and application.* Englewood Cliffs, N.J.: Prentice-Hall, 1966.

Kleiner, R. J. The effects of threat reduction on interpersonal attractiveness. *Journal of Personality,* 1960, *28,* 145–155.

Kmetz, J. L. Leadership and organization structure: A critique and an argument for synthesis. In G. W. England, A. R. Negandi, and B. Wilpert (eds.), *The functioning of complex organizations.* Cambridge Mass.: Oelgeschlager, Gunn & Hain, 1981, 145–172.

Kornhauser, A. and A. Sharp. Employee attitudes: Suggestions from a study in a factory. *Personnel Journal,* 1932, *10,* 393–404.

Kornilov, K. N. *Study of human reactions,* Moscow: Gosizdal, 1922.

Kuhn, T. S. *The structure of scientific revolutions.* Chicago: University of Chicago Press, 1970.

Landy, D. and E. Aronson. Liking for an evaluator as a function of his discernment. *Journal of Personality and Social Psychology,* 1968, *9,* 133–141.

Leavitt, H. J. Applied organizational change in industry: Structural, technological and humanistic approaches. In J. G. March (ed.), *Handbook of organizations*. Chicago: Rand McNally, 1965, 1144–1170.

Leventhal, G. S. Reward magnitude, task attractiveness, and liking for instrumental activity. *Journal of Abnormal and Social Psychology*, 1964, *68*, 460–463.

Leventhal, G. S., and J. W. Brehm. An experiment on volition of choice. In J. W. Brehm and A. R. Cohen (eds.), *Explorations in cognitive dissonance*. New York: Wiley, 1962.

Lindsley, D. B. Psychophysiology and motivation. In M. R. Jones (ed.), *Electrical stimulation of the brain*. Austin: University of Texas Press, 1957, 331–349.

————. The reticular activating system. In D. E. Sheer (ed.), *Electrical stimulation of the brain*. Austin: University of Texas Press, 1961.

Lindsley, D. B., J. Bowden, and H. W. Magoun. Effect upon the EEG of acute injury to the brain stem activating system. *Electroencephalography and Clinical Neurophysiology*, 1949, *1*, 475–486.

Lindsley, D. B., L. H. Schreiner, W. B. Knowles, and H. W. Magoun. Behavior and EEG changes following chronic brain stem lesions in the cat. *Electroencephalography and Clinical Neurophysiology*, 1950, *2*, 483–498.

Locke, E. A. The relationship of task success to task liking and satisfaction. *Journal of Applied Psychology*, 1965, *49*, 379–385.

————. The relationship of task success to task liking: A Replication. *Psychological Reports*, 1966, *18*, 552–554.

————. Relationship of success and expectation to affect on goalseeking tasks. *Journal of Personality and Social Psychology*, 1967, *7*, 125–134.

Lott, A. J., and B. E. Lott. A learning theory approach to interpersonal attitudes. In A. G. Greenwald, R. C. Brock, and T. M. Ostrom, (eds.), *Psychological foundations of attitudes*. New York: Academic Press, 1968.

Lott, A. J., B. E. Lott, and G. Matthews. Interpersonal attraction among children as a function of vicarious rewards. *Journal of Educational Psychology*, 1969, *60*, 274–282.

Lott, B. F., and A. J. Lott. The formation of positive attitudes toward group members. *Journal of Abnormal and Social Psychology*, 1960, *61*, 297–300.

Lovaas, O. Ivar. *The autistic child: Language development through behavior modification*. New York: Irvington Publishers, Inc., 1977.

MacCorquodale, K. On Chomsky's review of Skinner's *Verbal behavior*. *Journal of the Experimental Analysis of Behavior*, 1970, *13*, 83–99.

MacKintosh, N. J. *The psychology of animal learning*. New York: Academic Press, 1974.

Malmo, R. B. Activation: A neuropsychological dimension. *Psychological Review*, 1959, *66*, 367–386.

Maslow, A. H. A theory of human motivation. *Psychological Review*, 1943, *50*, 370–396.

————. *Motivation and personality*. New York: Harper & Row, 1954.

McCarthy, D. Language development in children. In L. Carmichael (ed.), *Manual of child psychology*. 2d ed. New York: Wiley, 1954.

McCormick, E. J., and D. R. Ilgen. *Industrial psychology*. 7th ed. Englewood Cliffs, N.J.: Prentice-Hall, 1980.

McDonald, R. D. The effect of reward-punishment and affiliation need on interpersonal attraction. Unpublished Ph.D. dissertation, University of Texas, 1962.

Miller, L. K. *Principles of everyday behavior analysis*. Monterrey, Cal.: Brooks/Cole Publishing Co., 1975.

Milner, P. M. *Physiological psychology*. New York: Holt, Rinehart and Winston, 1970.

Moruzzi, G., and H. W. Magoun. Brain stem reticular formation and the activation of the EEG. *Electroencephalography and Clinical Neurophysiology*, 1949, *1*, 455–473.

Moskowitz, B. A. The acquisition of language. *Scientific American*, November 1978, *239*, 92–108.

Myers, J. L. Secondary reinforcement: A review of recent experimentation. *Psychological Bulletin*, 1958, *55*, 285–301.

Nowlis, H. H. The influence of success and failure on the resumption of an interrupted task. *Journal of Experimental Psychology*, 1941, *28*, 304–325.

Olds, J. A preliminary mapping of electrical reinforcing effects in the rat brain. *Journal of Comparative and Physiological Psychology*, 1956, *49*, 281–285.

Olds, J. A., and P. Milner. Positive reinforcement produced by electrical stimulation of septal area and other regions of the rat's brain. *Journal of Comparative and Physiological Psychology*, 1954, *47*, 419–427.

Olds, M. E., and J. Olds. Approach-avoidance analysis of rat diencephalon. *Journal of Comparative Neurology*, 1963, *120*, 259–295.

Organ, D. W. A reappraisal and reinterpretation of the satisfaction-causes-performance hypothesis. *Academy of Management Review*, 1977, *2*, 46–53.

Osborn, A. F. *Applied imagination*. 3d ed. New York: Scribner's, 1963.

Pavlov, I. P. *Conditioned reflexes*. New York: Dover Publications, 1927.

———. Scientific study of so-called psychical processes in the higher animals. Excerpts of an address given by Pavlov in 1906 and published in full text in Chapter 4 of *Lectures on Conditioned Reflexes* (W. H. Gantt, trans.), New York: International Publishers, 1928.

Peters, T. J. Symbols, patterns, and settings: An optimistic case for getting things done. *Organizational Dynamics*, Autumn 1978, 2–23.

Pfeffer, J. *Organizations and organization theory*. Boston: Pitman, 1982.

Piaget, J. *The origins of intelligence in children*. New York: W. W. Norton, 1963.

Podsakoff, P. M. Effects of schedule changes on human performance: An empirical test of the contrasting predictions of the law of effect, the probability-differential model, and the response-deprivation approach. *Organiza-tional Behavior and Human Performance,* 1982, *29,* 322–351.

Podsakoff, P. M., W. D. Todor, R. A. Grover, and V. L. Huber. Situational moderators of leader reward and punishment behavior: Fact or Fiction? *Organizational Behavior and Human Performance,* 1984, *34,* 21–63.

Podsakoff, P. M., W. D. Todor, and R. Skov. Effects of leader contingent and non-contingent reward and punishment behaviors on subordinate perfor-mance and satisfaction. *Academy of Management Journal,* 1982, *25,* 810–821.

Premack, D. Toward empirical behavioral laws: 1. Positive reinforcement. *Psychological Review,* 1959, *66,* 219–233.

———. Reversibility of the reinforcement relation. *Science,* 1962, *136,* 255–257.

———. Reinforcement theory. In D. Levine (ed.), *Nebraska Symposium on Motivation.* Lincoln: University of Nebraska Press, 1965, 123–189.

———. A functional analysis of language. *Journal of the Experimental Analy-sis of Behavior,* 1970, *14,* 107–125.

———. Catching up with common sense or two sides of a generalization: Reinforcement and punishment. In R. Glaser (ed.), *Nebraska Symposium on Motivation.* New York: Academic Press, 1971.

———. *intelligence in apes and man.* Hillsdale, N.J.: Lawrence Erlbaum As-sociates, 1976.

Rabbie, J. M., and M. Horowitz. Arousal of in-group/out-group bias by a chance win or loss. *Journal of Personality and Social Psychology,* 1969, *13,* 269–277.

Rachlin, H., and B. Burkhard. The temporal triangle: Response substitution in instrumental conditioning. *Psychological Review,* 1978, *85,* 22–45.

Reitz, H. J. Managerial attitudes and perceived contingencies between per-formance and organizational response. In R. B. Higgens, P. V. Croke, and J. F. Varga (eds.), *Proceedings* of the National Academy of Management Meetings, 1971, 227–238.

Rescorla, R. A. Pavlovian second-order conditioning: Some implications for instrumental behavior. In H. Davis and H. M. B. Hurwitz, (eds.), *Operant-Pavlovian interactions.* Hillsdale, N.J.: Lawrence Erlbaum Associates, 1977.

Rescorla, R. A., and R. L. Solomon. Two-process learning theory. Relation-ships between Pavlovian and instrumental learning. *Psychological Bulletin,* 1967, *74,* 151–182.

Reynolds, G. S. *Primer of operant conditioning.* Glenview, III: Scott, Foresman, 1968.

Richter, C. P. Total self-regulatory functions in animals and human beings. Harvey Lectures, 1942–1943, *38,* 63–103.

Romanes, E. J. *Animal Intelligence.* 4th ed. London: Kegan Paul, 1886.

Rosenbaum, M. E., and S. J. Arenson. Observational learning: Some theory, some variables, some findings. In E. C. Simmel, R. A. Hoppe, and G. A. Milton (eds.), *Social facilitation and imitative behavior.* Boston: Allyn & Bacon, 1968.

Salancik, G. R., and J. Pfeffer. An examination of need-satisfaction models of job attitudes. *Administrative Science Quarterly,* 1977, *22,* 427–456.

Samuels, I. Reticular mechanisms and behavior. *Psychological Bulletin,* 1959, *56,* 1–25.

Schwab, D. P., and L. L. Cummings. Theories of performance and satisfaction: A review. *Industrial Relations,* 1970, *98,* 408–430.

Schwartz, B. *Psychology of learning and behavior.* New York: W. W. Morton, 1978.

Scott, W. E., Jr. Activation theory and task design. *Organizational Behavior and Human Performance,* 1966, *1,* 3–30.

―――. *A functional analysis of leadership.* In J. G. Hunt and L. L. Larson (eds.) *Leadership: The cutting edge.* Carbondale: Southern Illinois University Press, 1977.

Scott, W. E., Jr., and J. A. Erskine. The effects of variations in task design and monetary reinforcers on task behavior. *Organizational Behavior and Human Performance,* 1980, *25,* 311–335.

Scott, W. E., Jr., and P. M. Podsakoff. Leadership, supervision and behavioral control: Perspectives from an experiment analysis. In L. Frederickson (ed.), *Handbook of organizational behavior management.* New York: Wiley, 1982, 39–69.

Scott, W. R. *Organizations: Rational, natural, and open systems.* Englewood Cliffs, N.J.: Prentice-Hall, 1981.

Segal, E. F. Induction and the provenance of operants. In R. M. Gilbert and J. R. Millenson (eds.), *Reinforcement: Behavioral analysis.* New York: Academic Press, 1972.

―――. Psycholinguistics discovers the operant: A review of Roger Brown's *A first language: the early stages. Journal of the Experimental Analysis of Behavior,* 1975, *23,* 149–158.

―――. Toward a coherent psychology of language. In W. K. Honig and J. E. R. Staddon (eds.), *Handbook of operant behavior.* Englewood Cliffs, N.J.: Prentice-Hall, 1977.

Seligman, M. E. P., and J. L. Hager. *Biological boundaries of learning.* New York: Appleton-Century-Crofts, 1972.

Sharpless, S., and H. H. Jasper. Habituation of the arousal reaction. *Brain,* 1956, *79,* 655–680.

Sheffield, F. D., and T. B. Roby. Reward value of a non-nutritive sweet taste. *Journal of Comparative and Physiological Psychology,* 1950, *43,* 471–481.

Sheffield, F. D., T. B. Roby, and B. A. Campbell. Drive reduction versus consummatory behavior as determinants of reinforcement. *Journal of Comparative and Physiological Psychology,* 1954, *47,* 349–354.

Sidman, M. Operant techniques. In A. J. Bachrach (ed.), *Experimental Foundations of Clinical Psychology.* New York: Basic Books, 1962.

Sims, H. P. The leader as a manager of reinforcement contingencies: An empirical example and a model. In J. G. Hunt and L. L. Larson (eds.), *Leadership: The cutting edge*. Carbondale, Ill.: Southern Illinois University Press, 1977, 121–137.

Sims, H. P., and A. D. Szilagyi. Leader reward behavior and subordinate satisfaction and performance. *Organizational Behavior and Human Performance*, 1975, *14*, 426–438.

Skinner, B. F. *Science and human behavior*. New York: Free Press, 1953.

———. *Verbal Behavior*. New York: Appleton-Century-Crofts, 1957.

———. *Contingencies of reinforcement: A theoretical analysis*. New York: Appleton-Century-Crofts, 1969.

———. *Beyond freedom and dignity*. New York: Knopf, 1971.

———. *About behaviorism*. New York: Knopf, 1974.

Staddon, J. E. R. Operant behavior as adaptation to constraint. *Journal of Experimental Psychology: General*, 1979, *108*, 48–67.

Statts, A. W. *Social Behaviorism*. Homewood, Ill.: Dorsey Press, 1975.

Stinchcombe, A. L. Social structure and organizations. In J. G. March (ed.), *Handbook of organizations*. Chicago: Rand McNally, 1965, 142–193.

Stogdill, R. M. *Handbook of leadership*. New York: Free Press, 1974.

Stotland, E. Determinants of attraction to groups. *Journal of Social Psychology*, 1959, *49*, 71–80.

Teichner, W. H. Interaction of behavioral and physiological stress reactions. *Psychological Review*, 1968, *75*, 271–291.

Thorndike, E. L. Animal intelligence. *The Psychological Review*, June 1898, *2* (Whole No. 8).

———. *Animal intelligence: Experimental studies*. New York: Macmillan, 1911.

Timberlake, W. A. A molar equilibrium theory of learned performance. In G. H. Bower (ed.), *The psychology of learning and motivation*. New York: Academic Press, 1980, Vol.14.

Timberlake, W. A., and J. Allison. Response deprivation: An empirical approach to instrumental performance. *Psychological Review*, 1974, *81*, 146–164.

Timberlake, W., and M. Wozny. Reversibility of reinforcement by schedule changes: A comparison of hypothesis and models. *Animal Learning and Behavior*, 1979, *7*, 461–469.

Wallas, G. *The art of thought*. New York: Harcourt, Brace & World, 1926.

Walton, C. C. (ed.), *Managers for the XXI Century*. Hingham, Mass.: Kluwer Boston, 1981.

Watson, J. B. *Behaviorism*. Chicago: University of Chicago Press, 1930.

Watson, J. B., and J. J. B. Morgan. Emotional reactions and psychological experimentation. *The American Journal of Psychology*, 1917, *28*, 163–174.

Watson, J. B., and R. Rayner. Conditioned emotional reactions. *Journal of Experimental Psychology*, 1920, *3*, 1–14.

Weber, M. *Economy and society*. G. Roth and C. Wettich (eds.). Berkeley: University of California Press, 1968.

Weiskrantz, L. Emotion. In L. Weiskrantz (ed.), *Analysis of behavioral change.* New York: Harper & Row, 1968.

Wiest, W. A. Some recent criticisms of behaviorism and learning theory with special reference to Breger and McGaugh and to Chomsky. *Psychological Bulletin,* 1967, *67,* 214–225.

Wilkinson, R. Some factors influencing the effect of environmental stressors upon performance. *Psychological Bulletin,* 1969, *72,* 269–272.

Williams, J. L. *Operant learning: Procedures for changing behavior.* Monterrey, Cal.: Brooks/Cole, 1973.

Wimperis, B. R., and J. L. Farr. The effects of task content and reward contingency upon task performance and satisfaction. *Journal of Applied Social Psychology,* 1979, *9,* 229–249.

Wolfe, J. B. Effectiveness of token-rewards for chimpanzees. *Comparative Psychology Monographs,* 1936, *12*:60.

Worden, F. G., and R. B. Livingston. Brain stem reticular formation. In D. E. Sheer (ed.), *Electrical Stimulation of the Brain.* Austin: University of Texas Press, 1961, 262–276.

Zajonc, R. B. Social facilitation. *Science,* 1965, *149,* 269–274.

AUTHOR INDEX

SUBJECT INDEX